Further Praise for Back to the Futures

"As one of the most respected voices in agriculture, Dr. Scott Irwin has been studying, teaching, and participating in the world of commodity futures since growing up on his family farm in Iowa. There is no higher expert or more captivating storyteller to explain how these critical markets have developed over the decades while articulating the significant impact they have on the global economy, agribusiness, and everyday lives."

Terry Duffy, Chairman and Chief Executive Officer, CME Group

"As someone deeply involved in the legislative and regulatory history of the commodity futures industry, I was extremely impressed with this most interesting and behind-the-scenes background of the stories explaining the commodity futures markets. Fascinating and understandable reading for both the experts and novices in this important business. I learned a lot and really enjoyed it."

Dan Glickman, Former U.S. Congressman and Secretary of Agriculture

"Critics of futures markets blame speculators for both price increases and price declines. Somehow, the inherent contradiction of their knee-jerk scapegoating never seems to dawn on them. Scott Irwin, a renowned agricultural economist, has spent a good part of his career dispelling misconceptions and ignorance about markets with solid research and facts. *Back to the Futures* chronicles these experiences, as well as providing a tour of key historical events and perplexities in futures markets. *Back to the Futures* provides a breezy read filled with anecdotes related to market events and the author's accident-prone life."

Jack Schwager, Futures Market Analyst, Trader, and Best-Selling Author of *Market Wizards*

"...I'd recommend that anyone involved in agriculture, raising boys, or shopping at the grocery store should immediately stop whatever they are doing and read this book. Irwin tells the story of growing up in rural Iowa, which, if his life is any indication, is fraught with near-death experiences. The stories are laugh-out-loud funny, since we know he survived long enough to write this book.

Irwin makes the case for futures markets as essential to the ability of our economy to distribute risk to those who are best able to handle that risk. He makes his case in a manner that is accessible to the general reader, but still a sophisticated explanation of how futures transfer risk and smooth the workings of our mostly market economy. When commodity prices increase, we often hear criticism of speculation. Irwin has made a career of answering those criticisms with data, logic, and good cheer, and this book is a capstone to that remarkable career. I'm glad he wrote the book and would recommend it to everyone."

Blake Hurst, Farmer, Author, and Past President of Missouri Farm Bureau

"Scott Irwin's lifelong fascination with buying and selling grain invigorates this economic page-turner. It's a love letter to farm life in the Midwest, a confessional tale about fathers and sons making bad bets in the market, and a revealing, first-hand account of intellectual battles over whether those markets work for the common good. You'll never look at corn prices in quite the same way again."

Dan Charles, Science Journalist and Former National Public Radio Reporter

"Half memoir, half futures market primer, this delightful story of farm-kid turned world-renowned professor of commodity markets is as entertaining as it is educational."

Jayson Lusk, Distinguished Professor and Head of the Agricultural Economics Department, Purdue University

"Scott Irwin has written the book on risk and the commodity markets that I wish had been available when I was researching *Merchants of Grain* more than 40 years ago. In *Back to the Futures*, he breaks all the molds governing writing about agriculture and economics, beginning with violating the commandment that says, 'Thou shalt always be boring.'

In a brilliant stroke of imagination, he connects his heart-stopping youthful adventures on his family's farm to the risks accepted by modern commodity traders with billions of dollars at stake. The result is a page turner of a book that mixes erudite explanation, fascinating snippets from the bad old early days of the markets, and tales of a kid's country hell-raising. Admirers of Irwin's always essential economic research will never again think of him as a nerdy academic."

Dan Morgan, Best-Selling Author of *Merchants of Grain* and Former Agriculture Reporter for the *Washington Post*

"Scott Irwin has penned a marvelous intellectual autobiography—complete with dirt bikes, stock cars, trucks, and tractors. *Back to the Futures* mixes highly entertaining personal anecdotes (mainly involving near-tragic interactions with aforesaid machinery) with serious discussions of scholarship relating to a hardy perennial in debates over commodity markets—whether speculation on futures markets distorts commodity prices.

The personal anecdotes are more than interludes: they are really parables that illustrate findings Scott discusses in the scholarship-focused chapters and how he arrived at them. In presenting these findings to a wider audience in such an entertaining fashion, *Back to the*

Futures is an important contribution to matters that are not merely of academic interest."

Craig Pirrong, Professor of Finance and Director of the Global Energy Management Institute, University of Houston

"I love this book, especially how the author has weaved in his childhood memories of risk-taking. Scott explains the complex world of commodity trading in a way that is easy to understand and enjoyable to read. It is the perfect book for young people thinking of getting into the sector or for anyone looking to learn more about how food ends up on their table. Bravo, Scott, for taking this initiative and bringing it to completion."

Jonathan Kingsman, Author of *Commodity Conversations* and *The New Merchants of Grain*

"Irwin and Peterson take us on an entertaining and wild ride to explain futures markets in all their glory. Interspersed with the risk-taking stories from an adolescent childhood centered around the farms in Iowa, they intuitively (and entertainingly) explain all about futures contracts and markets—the most established, time-honored risk-management tools and venues in the world. Risk management at its finest! A fun read, an educational gem, and well worth taking the ride for learning about futures from stories reflected in the rearview mirror."

Jeff Harris, Gary D. Cohn Goldman Sachs Chair in Finance and former Chief Economist of the CFTC

"Academics can be a boring lot...but Irwin and Peterson break the mold with an entertaining and enlightening trip through the world of commodity futures markets. Peppered with good-humored parodies, puns, and wit, the prose easily engages the reader. The trading stories and interviews with industry giants—such as Leo Melamed—are just icing on the cake. Anyone with an interest in agriculture or futures markets will enjoy this read."

Dwight Sanders, Professor of Agribusiness Economics, Southern Illinois University Carbondale

"I've worked at the Chicago Board of Trade for over 20 years and even today my family will ask, 'Now what is it that you do?'...Through the eminently entertaining adventures of Scott, Jack, and Elvis, I may finally be able to answer that elusive question. If you enjoy an entertaining read and don't mind learning a bit about markets during the process, then this book is for you too."

Fred Seamon, Agricultural Markets Executive Director, CME Group

"Dr. Irwin, the inveterate Iowa farm boy, weaves a series of fascinating stories of youthful risk and survival into a compelling description of commodity trading and the critical role that the speculative risk-taker in futures markets plays in stabilizing the system. His scholarship, intimate knowledge of the market, its history and characters, adds a compelling level of authenticity to the perspectives that he offers. Above all, he has the courage to speak his convictions whether before a congressional committee or to a group of farmers. A real 'page-turner' indeed."

Bob Easter, President Emeritus, University of Illinois

"Scott Irwin is the preeminent scholar in the area of agricultural futures markets. So, when I saw this book, I expected it to be Introduction to Futures 101. Instead, it is a fascinating autobiography about growing up in Iowa, taking extreme risks, and making mistakes trading futures. Just as one can learn and remember a lot of history from historical fiction, one can read this book and learn about futures without ever thinking of it as work."

Dermot Hayes, Pioneer Chair in Agribusiness and the Charles F. Curtiss Distinguished Professor in Agriculture and Life Sciences, Iowa State University

"*Back to the Futures*…is a fun read that you'll find difficult to put down. It's a read that I highly recommend, for it will make a positive difference for your farm as well. Some might argue that today's commodity markets are impossible to understand, but Irwin's humorous stories break the commodity markets into basic, easy-to-understand principles that provide a new understanding to their value to the farm. It's a book you'll want on your coffee table to reference often."

Arlan Suderman, Chief Commodities Economist, StoneX

"Jumping from the farm to the 'trading pit'/boardroom and back, the book provides those with no prior understanding a fascinating look at the role and evolution of the futures markets. Irwin and Peterson bring to life the risks, energy, emotion, and characters that have shaped something which impacts our lives daily with the insight that only someone who has lived and studied the markets for a lifetime can provide. When you finish *Back to the Futures*, you will wonder how Scott Irwin is still alive, but you will also have new insights into the why, how, and where of these markets that play such a fundamental role in global commerce."

Jay Akridge, Trustee Chair in Teaching and Learning Excellence and Provost Emeritus, Purdue University

"*Back to the Futures* is a must read for anyone interested in commodity futures markets. Irwin and Peterson brilliantly weave together firsthand stories of rural life and risk-taking in explaining the important role of futures markets in our economy. As a university professor who teaches classes and conducts research in the area of futures and options markets, *Back to the Futures* will certainly be on the reading list for my students."

Mark Manfredo, Professor of Agribusiness and Dean's Council Distinguished Scholar, Arizona State University

"This book brings commodity markets to life. In his distinguished academic career, Scott Irwin has written at length about how commodity markets work, busting myths and bringing clarity. But academic publications reveal only a glimpse of his unbridled enthusiasm for the markets, which jumps out of these pages through stories of childhood shenanigans, college stunts, and mysterious gophers. Through these stories, Scott explains the inner workings of commodity markets and the things he has learned about them—things he has taught the world through his academic writing. I learned a lot from this page turner."

Aaron Smith, DeLoach Professor of Agricultural Economics, University of California-Davis

"Irwin is an economist and passionate defender of the futures market and speculation. This account of his life—and of his 'lifelong quest to understand the commodity futures markets,' as he puts it—blends first-person takes with interviews of industry leaders to highlight a business that he clearly loves."

Emily Lambert, author of *The Futures: The Rise of the Speculator and the Origins of the World's Biggest Markets*

Back to the Futures

Crashing Dirt Bikes, Chasing Cows, and Unraveling the Mystery of Commodity Futures Markets

Scott Irwin

Doug Peterson

Front and rear cover illustration by DogEared Design

Front cover picture courtesy of Shutterstock

Interior Design by Hannah Linder Designs

Index by Potomac Indexing

Published by Ceres Books, LLC

Mahomet, IL 61853

www.scotthirwin.com

ISBN 979-8-218-12193-8

For my wife, Kim

There are no words that truly do justice to the love and support you have blessed me with all these years. And never forget that you were the one who got me through business calculus.

Contents

Chapter 1
My Near-Death Experience

By the time I saw the Pepsi truck, it was too late. I remember turning my shoulder toward the truck's big radiator, feeling absolute terror seconds before it barreled into me, going at least 35 to 40 miles per hour. It hurled me 15 to 20 feet into the chilly, early-autumn air.[1]

My dad saw it all unfold in his combine's rearview mirror and was sure I had just been killed. Who wouldn't? It had to be one of the most horrifying moments of his life—and mine.

I was nine years old at the time, and I loved working with my dad on our farm near Bagley, Iowa. We grew corn and soybeans and raised hogs and occasionally cattle. On this Friday morning, October 20, 1967, I wasn't in school because all students in our small town had been given a holiday for the high school homecoming celebrations. I was a budding sports fanatic and could hardly contain my excitement about the upcoming night of small-town football. I was also anticipating attending the Iowa State vs. Missouri Big 8 football game with my family the next day in Ames, which would become an annual outing. I was a very loyal Cyclone football fan in those days despite their losing ways (and they would lose to Missouri on that Saturday, 23 to 7).

As it happened this Friday morning, something went wrong with the combine we used to harvest corn and soybeans, so my dad drove it into town for service. I tagged along as he drove the tiny (by today's standards) four-row combine harvester to the Allis-Chalmers dealership in Bagley. We had been farming for a little over a year, and it was one of my mom and dad's first major equipment purchases. I was the King of the Road during the drive between our farm and town along that stretch of blacktop, but once we reached the dealership and my dad started talking to the mechanics, I headed to the grain elevator next door.

A group of retired farmers, sitting in folding chairs, were lined up outside in front of the elevator on this crisp autumn morning. For small-town men like these, the elevator was the Cheers bar, where everyone knew their name. They came to drink coffee, swap stories, and complain about the weather and grain prices.

I was so enthralled by the goings-on of the elevator that I hadn't been paying attention to my dad. So, when he pulled the combine from the Allis-Chalmers dealership, I was sure he was leaving without me. As I learned later, he planned to drive the short distance to another part of the dealership. I assumed he had forgotten me, so I took off in a flash.

The road in front of the grain elevator, perpendicular to Main Street, was Highway 141. Without looking, I sprinted across the two-lane highway—directly into the path of the oncoming Pepsi delivery truck. The poor driver had no chance to stop. He must have aged decades in those few seconds as his big truck slammed full speed into my scrawny body, sending me flying like a football through the uprights.

The old farmers sitting in front of the elevator were witness to it all, sipping coffee one moment and slack-jawed the next as the truck smashed into the Irwin boy. Later, they told me I cartwheeled through the air, almost as high as the power lines.

I catapulted and skidded over one hundred feet. I'm well aware of the rough distance because when I came to my senses, I was shocked to be facing Chuck Leber's house. The approximate distance between the elevator and Leber's place was about half a block. My face ached and was severely scraped, a painful clue I didn't cover the entire distance through the air. After I saw the truck's radiator, I woke up moments later, disoriented and lying beside the curb, gazing at Leber's house.

My dad leaped out of his combine and sprinted toward me. Later in life, he confided he was certain he'd find me dead and was stunned to discover I was conscious once he reached my side.

The closest hospital was about twenty miles away in Jefferson, Iowa, but there was no ambulance service in Bagley in 1967. However, plenty of locals helped, including Fred Hunter, the father of my best friend, Jack. The Hunters ran a small grocery store a couple of blocks away on Main Street, and Fred had some first-aid training from his time in the Marines during World War II. He placed me on an ironing board—their makeshift stretcher—and loaded me into his 1960s wood-paneled station wagon (seriously, just like the one in the National Lampoon movie *Family Vacation*).

With my dad riding shotgun, Fred drove as fast as that station wagon would go—possibly pegging the speedometer at 120 miles per hour. I was lucid but in shock. I still remember looking out the window, thinking the telephone poles were flying by at light speed. While I never lost consciousness during the drive, I can't remember any pain. I recall, though, my dad trying to keep me calm while I chatted more than usual—a lifelong trait that served me well as it kept me conscious.

Our family physician, Dr. Thompson, was waiting when we reached the hospital. Getting inside was somewhat of a blur, but I remember laying on the cold X-ray table and the nurses cutting off my treasured green overalls. Those green overalls were my pride and joy— my official uniform on the farm. They showed I was part of a team, and I was proud of what they signified. So, I was devastated when the nurses sliced them apart.

While this was all happening, my mom and younger sister, Jan, were in the nearby town of Yale at the hair salon before the big trip to the Iowa State football game. My younger sister vividly remembers

Mom getting a call about my accident—a parent's worst nightmare. The ladies at the salon brought Mom a cup of coffee, trying to console her. Mom's hands were shaking so hard that the scalding liquid spilled all over her arm, but it didn't faze her. She was in such a state of shock that she couldn't react. I can only imagine what was going through her mind as they left for Jefferson to find out whether I was dead or alive.

It was a miracle I survived and an even bigger one that I was relatively unscathed. Well, almost. I broke my right leg in four places, had a slight tear in my liver, a mild concussion, and a minor cut on my chin requiring four stitches. That scar still taunts me today, reminding me how badly my body should have shattered.

How does a young boy get hit by a delivery truck going at least 35 to 40 miles per hour, get thrown over a hundred feet, and not sustain severe brain damage or paralysis? It was a one-in-a-million survival story, comparable to someone falling from a ten-story window and surviving.

I must have been spared by a guardian angel on direct assignment from God. There is no other explanation for how I escaped with minimal damage, not to mention how I later survived a string of other disasters on the farm. I kept my guardian angel extremely busy through college.

The first twenty-four hours after the accident, everyone was worried about me, but I was much better after vomiting a massive amount of fluids. This reaction was not unusual after the trauma I experienced and was even a good sign. As for the delivery truck driver, he was beside himself, as you might expect, and he visited me in the hospital. Those old farmers in front of the Bagley elevator told me I scared them half to death. One was a fellow named Em Whitecotton, and from that point on, whenever he'd see me, he'd shout, "Be careful crossing the road, sonny!"

Something like getting hit by a truck stays with you, and to this day, I have an unconscious twinge of fear whenever walking across a busy highway. Also, I have always wondered: How in the world did my black horn-rimmed glasses survive the accident, and who found them?

I still think of the surreal experience of getting a cast from my toes to my hip. I had to stay perfectly still as they wrapped my right leg with the plaster-soaked strips. Although I was brave in the aftermath of the accident, I became increasingly afraid of hurting my leg while it was in this cast. Once, while trying to get used to the crutches, I tripped and fell. After my mom dashed over and was about to help me to my feet, my dad shouted, "Stop!"

I'll never forget the expression on his face when he looked at me and said, "You've got to get up by yourself. You've got to do this, Scott."

Tears welled, and I started sniffling, but my dad wasn't going to give in. He was tough that way. So, although feeling sorry for myself, I struggled to a standing position, with my parents urging me on. My dad was firm—but he was also right. I wore that cast for six months, but I learned to deal with it and to rise when I fell.

Over the years, I've thought about the irony of almost dying near the grain elevator because it was one of the places where I felt most alive. My love for the agricultural markets began at the elevator. I breathed in the atmosphere—the farmers going on and on about the weather, prices, and the latest crop report from the U.S. Department of Agriculture (USDA).

Most of all, I loved the elevator's magical back room connected to an equally mystical place—Chicago. The beating heart of the room was the ticker machine—a box with a large roll of yellow paper, spitting out market prices and news stories to the rhythmic *clack clack clack*. I still use a picture of this kind of ticker machine in my lectures to college students explaining commodity markets. I also remember the grain elevator's chalkboard, which would display current market values for corn and soybeans. Those prices inevitably triggered many complaints from farmers, who threw around phrases laced with "words I wouldn't want in a book," as my dad used to say.

What I thought of as "the elevator" was a glorified scale house operated by a manager. Farmers would drive their trucks or their tractors and wagons, loaded with grain, onto the scale, get weighed, and receive scale tickets. Then they'd unload their grain at the dumping station and weigh the empty vehicles to determine the weight of the grain just delivered.

This circular journey was repeated over and over. Unlike me, not many kids my age were as fascinated with the grain elevator, but I found this world a breath of fresh air (literally!) compared to scooping manure or feeding pigs. I'd shoot the breeze with the old men for a few minutes, making me feel a lot taller. Of course, part of the fascination was due to my dad's influence. My father managed grain elevators in Oklahoma and another region of Iowa before farming in Bagley. Because of this, he paid more attention to the markets than most farmers, and I caught the bug from him. I was a market nerd from a young age.

Another magical and formative place for me was the dining room table at my Grandfather George and Grandmother Lurene Irwin's house on Sundays. We farmed with my dad's parents, and our farmhouse was only a few miles away from them.

My grandparents lived on what, to this day, we call the "home place." On Sundays after church, we gathered around their enormous table to share one big, raucous meal. We were a clamorous clan, with parents, grandparents, uncles, and aunts voicing opinions at high decibels. As my wife, Kim, likes to say, "The Irwins are an opinionated bunch that likes to argue." That's my family in a nutshell.

The Irwins were also an educated bunch. Everyone but my grandfather had college degrees, and several had master's and doctoral degrees, which was uncommon in rural Iowa at the time. We covered the political spectrum, with my Grandmother Lurene being a dyed-in-the-wool Roosevelt New Deal liberal. My dad and his father were free-market men—fairly traditional, middle-of-the-road, Main-Street Republicans—with one significant exception. They endorsed federal price and income supports for farmers.

My aunts and uncles generally backed my Grandmother Lurene in political arguments, and almost everyone joined. There was only one requirement: Argue as well and as loudly as you could manage. My two sisters weren't as attracted to the boisterous debating, but I was entranced. And when I became a high schooler, I dared to engage in the action, which was a bit like stepping off a high dive.

Even when I went to dirt-track sprint car races during hot summer nights with my gearhead father and his friends, the topic during the long car rides across Iowa was almost always the markets. Will corn prices go up this summer? Should I be selling soybeans now? Should I wait to sell? What's going to happen with the weather?

The constant topic of weather and markets was their psychological way of coping with the enormous uncertainty of farming. As I listened to my dad and his farming friends banter on those long car rides, I noticed they would sometimes veer into a darker world of conspiracy theories.

Iowa farmers often seemed to suspect someone was out to screw them over. And those "someones" generally fell into three categories —the big grain companies, the government (mainly in the form of the USDA), and the commodity futures market traders on the floors of the Chicago Board of Trade (CBOT) and the Chicago Mercantile Exchange (CME).

Of those three, this book will concentrate on futures traders, often given the much-abused label of "speculators." For nearly 150 years, speculators have been vilified as villains because they trade contracts for commodities that they have had no hand in producing, storing, transporting, or processing.

To the average person, they're just glorified gamblers, playing fast and loose with the product of other people's labor. As a result, they have been favorite targets for farmers, politicians, the press, and others who do not understand the speculator's crucial role in the futures market system. They may not produce anything physical that can be weighed, but their value can still be measured—and *has* been. I have spent nearly forty years as an agricultural economist at The Ohio State University and the University of Illinois at Urbana-Champaign studying precisely this question.[2]

Many in the media and political world tarnish speculators whenever commodity prices go high...and when prices go low. They're convinced the price variations must be due to sinister manipulations by traders rather than normal market vicissitudes. Attacks on the market happen with such regularity that I call it the Anti-Speculation Cycle. The critics do not understand that speculators make markets *less* volatile, not more, but I'll get to that in later chapters.

To understand the vital role speculators play, you first need to know how commodity futures markets work. For most people, futures markets remain a mystery. For many, the only thing they know is the outdated image of traders tightly packed in a pit, screaming numbers and waving pencils and pads of paper. It's much easier to understand the cash market, where you sell grain at the day's cash price. But how do futures markets work, in which you buy commodity contracts at a certain price for future delivery? And why are speculators so important to their smooth operation? These are questions I plan to answer.

Futures markets are not mere curiosities, for they sit at the very heart of our economy. They function as a critical nerve center for the market economy and are important to *everyone*. Futures markets set the prices for some of the most important commodities in our global economy: energy commodities such as crude oil, gasoline, and diesel; crops such as corn, soybeans, and wheat; metals such as copper, gold, silver, and platinum; and on and on. In 2021 alone, 62.6 billion futures contracts were traded, according to the Futures Industry Association. Of these, 2.7 billion were energy futures contracts, and 2.8 billion were agricultural contracts, with a total face value amounting to trillions of dollars in a single year.[3]

*Trillions of dollars in trading for markets such as crude oil and corn…*such staggering figures are the exclamation point on any argument about the importance of commodity futures markets.

My goal is to shed light on the market's mystery in a way that is understandable to the average person. By the end of this personal and professional journey, I will have lifted the veil on the origins of commodity futures markets; the process of setting prices for corn, soybeans, crude oil, and other commodities; the use of hedging to reduce risk; and the move from trading pits to electronic trading.

Most importantly, in *Back to the Futures*, I will defend the vital role that speculators play by taking you into the heart of the global controversy about speculation in futures markets that erupted in 2007-08—a controversy in which I became embroiled. I testified before Congress and in front of an international body based in Paris, during which I had running battles with everyone from the Bubble Boy to academic rivals. I was even targeted with a hit piece by *The New York Times*.

But I was prepared. I had been living and breathing the air of agriculture since I was a boy in Bagley, Iowa. I knew what it was like to get blindsided, both figuratively and literally, by my near-death experience at nine years of age.

In this book, I'll be doing plenty of time-traveling, *Back to the Future* style—although without the help of a DeLorean, plutonium, or a flux capacitor. Managing risk through hedging and speculation is a common thread through these chapters, so it's fitting that many of the experiences from my past have to do with risk—nearly being killed by a runaway steer, rotary hoe, tornado, and out-of-control snowmobiles and dirt bikes. These formative experiences on the farm connect directly to my life today as a researcher in commodities, futures trading, and biofuels.

To shed light on these mysterious markets, let's begin at ground zero with the commodity itself. What makes an item a commodity?

A commodity, such as corn, is mass-produced, but so are non-commodities, such as smartphones. What distinguishes the two is a million-dollar word—fungible. Fungibility means one unit of a commodity is roughly the same as another. A bushel of corn in Illinois is essentially the same as another in South Dakota or China. As long as they meet some basic grade characteristics, they are swappable. A smartphone is not fungible or swappable because one brand can vary dramatically from another, as any Apple aficionado will remind you (constantly). You cannot swap out a smartphone like you can with a bushel of grain.

Commodities also tend to be global in scope and typically are raw materials, such as crude oil, the world's biggest commodity market. The scale of the crude oil market is truly mind-boggling, as the world typically uses about 100 million barrels every day.[4] This amounts to a trillion gallons of crude oil per year. Corn is also a massive market, with a lot of it used around the world for animal feed, fuel, and as an industrial ingredient in all sorts of food products.

Because a bushel of corn in China is essentially the same as one in Illinois, the prices will be roughly the same worldwide—although the price is adjusted for the cost of moving it from one place to another. Athletic shoes, in contrast, are not commodities because they are not created equal, and different shoes draw different prices. Putting the Nike swoosh on a shoe will carry a very different price than one without it.

In other words, a commodity is not branded. Slap a Nike swoosh on the side of a bushel of grain, and you're not going to increase the price. (By the way, a bushel is a measure of dry volume equal to 32 quarts.)

Over the years, there have been many attempts to create branding among agricultural products to garner higher prices. We have Angus-certified beef, but it doesn't command much premium. You can choose between Tyson or Perdue-brand chicken, but they sell for nearly the same price. Chickens are commodities; cars are not. I wish I could swap out my Highlander for a Jaguar, but it's not going to happen. Cars are not fungible.

Because commodity markets are so large, they involve middle operators who transform the commodities in *space*, *time*, or *form* to be used by consumers. Transforming a commodity in space means moving it from one place to another. The farmer moves grain to the local elevator, which carries it to the larger terminal elevators along the Mississippi River. Then the terminal elevators move the grain to companies that use the commodity to make food, fuel, or other products.

Second, middle operators transform commodities in *form*. If I own a large hog farm in China, I want to purchase soybeans in the form of soybean meal, which I feed to my pigs. Therefore, the soybeans have to be crushed and processed into meal after they're shipped from the United States. Similarly, we don't want to fill our cars with crude oil at the pump; we want gasoline, so the crude oil is processed into gasoline. The commodity is changed in form.

But what about transforming commodities in time? This is the most complicated of the three concepts, and this is where futures contracts and speculators come in—something I'll be exploring in the next chapter.

As will soon become clear, speculators are the ultimate risk-takers, and it's fair to say I know about risk. Growing up, I was best friends with the wildest risk-taker west of the Mississippi.

His name was Jack Hunter, and it's a miracle either one of us is still alive.

Chapter 2
Daredevils

It was the dead of winter in 1973, a Sunday afternoon, when my best friend, Jack Hunter, showed up at our farm to help with chores. His family had recently purchased a snowmobile, which was all the rage back then, so he zipped on over, skimming across the snow-covered roads and ditches between his place in Bagley and our farm about two miles south of town. When he laid eyes on the snowy drifts south of the tree grove surrounding our farm, he knew how we would spend our afternoon after doing the hog chores.

We would use those drifts of snow to soar.

The trees surrounded our farmstead on the south, west, and north sides, creating a windbreak for the livestock lots and buildings within the rectangular grove. In the winter, drifts piled, forming miniature mountains at the foot of the trees, especially on the north and west sides, depending on the wind's direction during a snowstorm.

These hilly drifts could be up to seven or eight feet high after major blizzards. On this day, there was a massive drift at the southwestern corner of the grove—way too tempting for a crazy daredevil like Jack to pass up. I was fourteen years old and fairly crazy too, but not nearly as fearless as my friend. Jack loved risk and speed so much that he should've become a speculator or stuntman.

Like Jack, my dad and I were passionate about anything fast. Dad was a farmer with the spirit of a race-car driver who raced go-karts semi-professionally in his younger days. So, it was no surprise when he egged on Jack and me on this particular Sunday afternoon. My dad was always prodding us to do something daring on go-karts, minibikes, dirt bikes, or in this case, snowmobiles.

The snow's texture that day was flawless, with the drift's curvature perfect for jumping the wave-like mounds on our snowmobiles. There was also considerable snow blanketing the opposite side of the drift— ideal for a relatively soft landing. It didn't look like we would kill ourselves. Not today.

After completing the first part of our hog chores, Jack and I spent some time hitting the drift at a reasonably safe speed of about 20 miles per hour. Before reaching the snowbank, we would goose the accelerator and race up the six-foot-high, curved drift, flying a few feet above it and then hitting the ground running.

We did this over and over until I realized it was about time to bring in the sows. This was before hog confinement buildings were commonplace, so we would let the sows out of their farrowing stalls twice a day to feed and water in a concrete lot adjacent to their buildings. It was utter chaos because the sows were penned in with their baby pigs, and you had to keep the piglets in the crate while simultaneously letting out the sows. Then, when it was time to let the sows back in, we had to reverse the process. Crazy stuff.

After bringing in the sows, Jack and I returned to our snowmobiles for a few more jumps before my dad joined us to watch. He approached with a big grin, savoring the vicarious thrill from our stunts. There was a lot of razzing about who was the bravest and who could jump the highest.

It was then that we noticed the sun starting to set over the crystal-glazed snow. After I parked my snowmobile by the fence, I strolled toward my dad, who asked, "Where's Jack?"

I looked around and scratched my head, but there was no sign of him. He wouldn't have gone home without saying goodbye.

Then we heard the high-pitched whir of a snowmobile engine far in the distance. It was like a scene from a World War II movie, where the Americans hear the ominous sound of an approaching Japanese bomber before they see it. The sound kept getting louder and louder, and we were horrified when we suddenly realized what Jack was planning.

I stared at my dad. "He's not really going to do this, is he?"

"I think he is."

We both turned, watching and holding our breath. Jack Hunter had retreated to get as long a running start as possible because he intended to hit the snowdrift at full speed. When he finally breached the horizon, his snowmobile was wound to 40 to 50 miles per hour.

Reckless abandon—this is what made Jack Hunter Jack Hunter, and we stood helpless as he raced by the fence. I still remember him glancing over his shoulder with a sly smile. If you've ever seen the movie *Sandlot* (my all-time favorite movie, by the way), it was like the mischievous grin Michael "Squints" Palledorous flashes before he fakes his drowning to receive mouth-to-mouth from the gorgeous lifeguard, Wendy Peffercorn. Jack was just as scrawny as Squints—probably around 130 pounds dripping wet.

Jack hit that snowdrift wide-open, striking a virgin patch of snow and launching into orbit. This time, Jack soared a good ten or twelve feet into the air. And instead of flying a short distance beyond the snowdrift, he must've gone about fifty feet, riding that rocket until he was as high as the tree branches—and these were tall trees! Miraculously, he hung on to the machine, but he sailed so far that he landed on a frozen part of the field without much snow cover.

The snowmobile hit the icy ground with a WHOOMP! WHOOMP! WHOOMP!

Jack gripped the handlebars while his body dislodged and dragged behind the machine—like a cowboy flailing behind an out-of-control horse. Eventually, Jack could hold on no longer and released the snowmobile, which coasted riderless and finally ran out of steam. As we bolted to Jack's listless body from our perch near the fence, I glanced at my dad. This had to be déjà vu, reminding him of how he dashed to save me after the delivery truck accident.

We rushed to Jack's side, unsure of his condition. As we crouched in the dimming, late-afternoon light, Jack still wasn't moving. I was about to put my hand on his shoulder when he flipped onto his back with a grin, blurting, *"Beat that, Irwin!"*

Not only was Jack fine, but he didn't seem to care he'd wrecked his snowmobile, even though his dad would be furious, and he'd pay for snapping every thick suspension spring. The guy was fearless, which was part of his charm and why we got along. He was even crazier than I was.

During high school, my family moved from the farm into a house in Bagley, which meant Jack and I would live a few blocks from each other—a surefire formula for trouble. We attended Yale-Jamaica-Bagley (YJB) High School, almost ten miles away, in Jamaica, Iowa. And I did not make that up. There really is a Jamaica, Iowa.

The drive to high school was on Highway 141, the same one where I had almost met my Maker at nine years old. It was a long and straight trek, except at the "three-mile curve," where Highways 4 and 141 met with a gentle S-curve. While a sane person would take it at around 55 miles per hour, we knew nothing of the word. We treated the S-curve like it was our personal Daytona Super Speedway.

Jack drove an old white 1964 Mercury Monterey that we called the Merc-O-Matic. It was a large pontoon of a car with little or no shock absorbers left. Jack and I would push it to about 80 or 90 miles per hour as we hit the S-curve.

The Merc-O-Matic was so long that if we barely tapped on the brakes, the front right bumper would scrape the pavement, sending up a wave of flying sparks. Then we'd lean into the next curve, tapping the brakes, but this time the front left bumper would rake the road, shooting sparks.

Thankfully, we never flipped the car during that insane maneuver. My dad claimed to see us pull off this stunt while he worked in a nearby field. But he didn't scold me. He thought it was funny because he drove even faster than we did.

During her freshman year in high school, my younger sister, Jan, made the mistake of driving to school with us one morning. Jack maneuvered behind one of our high school's buses on Highway 141, just east of the S-curves. Unable to pass because of oncoming traffic, he finally ran out of patience and decided enough was enough. Without slowing or skipping a beat, he slid that old Mercury into the ditch on the right side, next to the bus, passed it, and then careened onto the highway as grass flew everywhere. Jack and I laughed our heads off, not even noticing that Jan was death-gripping the backseat, hanging on for dear life.

Somehow, the only person who got into trouble was Jan because the bus driver recognized her in the car. She vowed never to step into a car with us again. Who could blame her?

Jack's daredevil attitude in these misadventures is a fitting representation of the spirit of a speculator.

Speculators must approach the commodity market with Jack's same audacity when he raced headlong toward that massive snowdrift. Speculators require nerves of steel because one day, they might be soaring in the futures market, hitting dizzying heights, and the next day they crash, slamming to the ground with a WHOOMP!

Louis Winthorpe III, the character played by Dan Aykroyd in the movie *Trading Places*, described the insanity of the commodity trading pits this way: "Nothing you ever experienced can prepare you for the unbridled carnage you're about to witness. The Super Bowl. The World Series. They don't know what pressure is. In this building, it's either kill or be killed. You make no friends in the pits, and you take no prisoners. One minute you're up a half a million in soybeans. The next—BOOM—your kids don't go to college, and they've repossessed your Bentley. Are you with me?"[1]

Speculators take enormous risks, thereby reducing the risk on farmers and middle operators, such as those who run the storage elevators or process grain. But to understand exactly how this plays out, you need to know how the system works, which means digging into its history.

In the 1830s and 1840s, corn and wheat production in the United States began pushing out from its traditional base in Ohio, Pennsylvania, and the East Coast, spreading to Illinois, Iowa, Wisconsin, and

Minnesota. This was before railroads had pushed extensively into these new production areas, so the primary transportation method was either by horse and wagon or on slow-moving barges. Most farmers couldn't store their grain, so they had to keep it at the local elevator, which was probably a small, wooden structure at that time. But local elevators had limited space, so they had to ship the grain to the larger terminal elevators built in Chicago. Vestiges of these old elevators remain, such as the one that still operates at Burns Harbor.

Chicago, incorporated as a village in 1833, grew like wild because of its strategic location on the Great Lakes and in the Midwestern Corn Belt. Being centrally positioned, it became a major trans-shipment point for grain and meat, moving commodities from the Midwest to the growing population centers on the East Coast. From this, the middle operator was born. These large elevators in Chicago made money buying tons of grain in the fall, storing it throughout the year, and dispersing it as needed to companies (and consumers).

But how did they coordinate all the complicated communication among traders in the nineteenth century—the buying, selling, storage, and transportation of corn and other grains? There were no telephones and computer systems, of course, so there had to be a way to communicate.

Initially, trading took place on Chicago's street curbs, but this was haphazard and confusing. Traders needed a centralized exchange where they could buy and sell commodities, so the Chicago Board of Trade (CBOT) was born in 1848, boasting an initial 82 members. Its origin story was similar to that of Wall Street. According to legend, Wall Street began as an informal trading spot near a buttonwood tree, where people gathered to buy and sell securities.[2]

The CBOT started as a place where you could find a buyer or seller of corn, wheat, or rye in physical quantities. However, savvy elevator operators soon saw it could be risky to buy corn after harvest to store and sell later because the price might decrease, losing them money.

So, what to do?

Operators began using "forward contracts"—the precursor to the futures contract. After the fall harvest, elevator operators might approach a company that, let's say, buys grain to feed livestock on the East Coast. We'll call the East Coast company Vandelay Industries for our purposes.

The elevator operator, George, would contact Vandelay Industries by telegraph or letter and say, "I'm buying grain this October. Would you be willing to purchase grain from me now for delivery next May at so-and-so price?" This forward contract would take away the risk of falling prices, guaranteeing George's elevator will profit from the sale.

The first forward contract on record in Chicago, on March 13, 1851, called for 3,000 bushels of corn to be delivered three months later, in June, at 1 cent per bushel below the March 13th price.[3] These early forward contracts were especially important in dealing with weather-related woes. In the 1800s, winter weather froze rivers and canals and blocked roads, preventing grain from being delivered to Chicago. As a result, most grain deliveries had to wait until the spring thaw. But with all the deliveries arriving at once, supply far exceeded demand, and prices would plummet. By locking into a forward contract during the previous fall and winter, grain elevators were guaranteed a reasonable price for their spring deliveries.[4]

The CBOT became the model for trading exchanges that sprouted all over the world, from New York and New Orleans to Liverpool and London. But it was mandatory to become a member to trade at these exchanges. In Chicago, people had to purchase a seat at the Board of Trade, which did not come cheap.

But when forward contracts started in 1851, another problem soon arose. What if you wanted to get out of your side of the contract?

To understand why you might want to do that, let's go back to our grain elevator operator, George, and the company, Vandelay Industries. Let's say Vandelay agrees to buy corn from George at $1 per bushel for delivery in March. But in a few weeks, what if Vandelay Industries thinks it can buy corn for even less—75 cents per bushel?

Vandelay could do one of two things.

One: It could break the contract with George and probably get sued. Or, two: Vandelay Industries could find someone to take their side of the contract.

If another company, the Kramer Group, thinks prices will rise, not fall, they might be willing to take Vandelay's side of the contract. Buy low, sell high—basic trading rules.

Vandelay honchos think prices will go down, so they bail out, while the Kramer Group takes the contract because they believe prices will increase. Only time will tell who is right. The two parties do not deal with each other directly, operating through the exchange's clearinghouse, which acts as a go-between.

The genius of the futures market is that it allows everyone a way to manage price risk, also known as price exposure. There's always an escape hatch. If you want to get out of your contract, find somebody to take your side of the agreement.

But what if you can't find anyone who will take your side of the contract?

In the early days, this could happen because the markets were small. But today, the markets are so huge that you can always find somebody to take your side of the contract—and that "somebody" is often a speculator.

To make the trading of contracts easier, forward contracts had to be standardized. This is one of the features distinguishing a futures contract from a forward contract. A futures contract is standardized; a forward contract is not. In addition, the Commodity Futures Trading Commission (CFTC) regulates the trading of futures contracts in the United States, which must be done at licensed and supervised exchanges.

Up to this point, I've been talking only about people who deal directly with the physical commodity, such as growers, elevator operators, and companies that use the commodity in their products. But futures contracts aren't limited to these parties. You can be someone who never laid eyes on a bushel of corn or soybeans in your life, and you can trade futures contracts for those crops. In fact, there's a famous story about a guy who walked into the soybean trading pit one day and used a hammer to nail a plant to the wall.

"Hey, what do you think you're doing? What's that?" various people asked him.

"It's a soybean plant," he explained.[5]

These guys had been trading millions of dollars of soybean futures contracts, yet they couldn't recognize a soybean plant, but that's okay. They didn't need to know what the plant looked like to do their job and do it well. What they did need to know about were crop prices.

For example, a rich banker—let's call her Elaine—might think she knows something about corn prices, so she buys two futures contracts for corn at $1 per bushel. For corn, a standard contract is 5,000 bushels, so two contracts amount to 10,000 bushels at $1 per bushel. As the price rises, Elaine makes money, but as the price falls, she loses. She doesn't produce or store the physical grain, but she can still buy and sell futures contracts—buying low, selling high, and hopefully making a profit.

Elaine is a speculator.

Because speculators buy and sell contracts for products they don't own nor have a hand in producing, they have a reputation as rogues, trying to make a bundle at others' expense in the market. In the nineteenth century, critics said speculators traded "wind wheat" because they didn't actually grow or own the wheat. They were trading the wind. You can understand why speculators were seen as a bit shady. After all, how do you trade something you don't physically own? A speculator's purpose has confused people from the beginning.

Economist Thomas Sowell describes this perception problem as "the physical fallacy." According to Craig Pirrong, a University of Houston finance professor (who will play a significant role later in this book), "The physical fallacy is the belief that people who aren't engaged in the physical production of a commodity are somehow thieves. The anti-speculation movement is almost always the physical fallacy in action. People view speculators as not doing anything because they're not making anything. They're not the yeoman farmer growing the wheat, and they're not the roughneck in the oil field drilling the well.

"Futures traders are frequently very garish figures making a lot of money, spending four hours a day trading," Pirrong continued. "Most people can't understand what their economic function is. If they're making money, there must be something illicit. They must be doing something that seems suspicious."

So, what are speculators actually "doing" that has any benefit besides making money?

"Futures markets are all about the transfer of risk," Pirrong said. "That's something most people can't get their heads around. The important function of speculation is that it allows risk to be transferred to the people who are willing to bear it."

As Pirrong pointed out, those in the business of merchandising grain bear a tremendous risk because of the potentially dramatic shifts in the price of commodities such as corn, soybeans, or wheat. These merchants carry extensive grain inventories, which come with significant price risks.

"To absorb these price risks, they need a lot of capital. So speculators say, 'Hey, I'll take that risk from you. You focus on your business, which is getting grain from the farmer to the mill or from the mill to the ultimate consumer. I'll take care of the price risk,'" Pirrong said. "It's a classic economic function when different people specialize in different things. Speculators specialize in the bearing of risk. That means other people can specialize in what they're better at, whether it's merchandising or milling wheat, or trading oil. Speculation unbundles risk from the physical commodity."[6]

Understandably, many don't comprehend this. But when politicians fail to, they often unwittingly take actions that threaten the futures market stability—and the broader economy. It happens with unfortunate regularity.

When the price of commodities, from corn and wheat to soybeans and crude oil, rises or falls for seemingly inexplicable reasons, the political herd will panic. But more problematic, the herd will look for villains to blame. It's not politically expedient to blame the natural workings of the free market for dramatic price fluctuation; many believe they must find culprits with human faces. So, politicians turn to easy answers to explain a complicated phenomenon, and in most cases, they blame the speculators who trade contracts in the futures market. Then, they try to solve the problem with their go-to solution

—more regulations. With periodic predictability, they may try to ban futures trading entirely in certain commodities, as they did with onions in 1958 with less-than-desirable results.

The Anti-Speculation Cycle has been with us since futures contracts were first born in Chicago in October 1865. In her book, *The Futures*, Emily Lambert offers a sample of the invectives hurled at speculators in the nineteenth century. Speculators were called "bifurcated abominations in the sight of the Lord," "cannibal insects," "brotherhood banditti," and "members of a filching machine."[7] Politicians today are not as creative in their insults, but they are equally vitriolic. Some have even claimed that speculators have starved children by driving up grain prices.[8]

However, speculators are not only blamed when commodity prices skyrocket. They are also targeted when the commodity prices are unusually *low*. In fairness, speculators deserved some of their early reputations because, in the formative years of the futures market, they were sometimes able to corner the market for different commodities, creating an artificial shortage and driving up prices to exorbitant levels. Prominent examples include three major corners in the Chicago wheat futures market in 1888, 1898, and 1909.[9] But today, such spectacular examples of price manipulation are rare—although smaller episodes can still occur. What's more, these problems do not justify the blanket demonization of speculators, nor overregulation or outright bans.

I'm not alone in this assessment. Most U.S. economists believe the picture of the evil speculator creating havoc in the markets is far off the mark. Although some European economists are more apt to flagellate speculators for out-of-control commodity prices, most American economists on both ends of the political spectrum believe it is nonsense.

Every contract has two sides—a buyer and a seller—and if a company or middle operator wants to reduce risk and get out of a futures contract, it needs to find someone to take its side. Speculators serve that role. With so many speculators jockeying for trades, there is no longer the risk that a commercial company, such as Vandelay

Industries, cannot find someone to take their side of the contract. That's why I say speculators are the lubrication that makes the entire system work. They bring what we call liquidity to the market.

In trading lingo, selling a contract is "going short," and buying a contract is "going long." (To keep the terms straight, think of "s" for "sell" and "short.") The market is out of balance if you don't have enough people to take one side of a futures contract, such as the buying side. It creates a bottleneck, with insufficient people stepping in and taking the long side of futures contracts. Speculators prevent this from happening. As Tom Cruise famously said to Renée Zellweger in the movie *Jerry McGuire*, "You complete me." Speculators complete the market.

Another argument in favor of speculation is that they force market prices to be rational. Since speculators take significant risks, they're incentivized to gather the best possible information to be well-informed about the commodity they're trading. Otherwise, they might lose their shirt. Successful speculators must be experts at judging market fundamentals, such as supply and demand for corn, soybeans, milk, or pork bellies. The evidence shows that speculators, as a whole, excel at helping the market move prices to a rational, reasonable level.

Note that I say speculators "as a whole" do an excellent job. Individual speculators who don't know the market don't survive—and those who flame out far exceed those who succeed. Even with the shift to electronic trading, in which many traders rely heavily on pre-set computer algorithms, I don't think the ratio of people who succeed to those who blow out has changed that much.

Speculators still need to understand the market and be able to evaluate supply and demand. They need to be risk-takers and have good judgment since considerable capital is on the line.

This brings me back to Jack Hunter.

Jack was a risk-taker—a speculator at heart—but as a teenager, he didn't always have good judgment, nor did I. We were known for our reckless teenage behavior, including the day Jack showed up at my farm with his sister Pam's brand-new skibob.

It was Christmas day in 1974, and Jack's parents gave his little sister a skibob as her big present. Similar to a tricycle, a skibob has three skis instead of wheels, and every kid in the early 1970s wanted one.

Unknown to Pam, Jack had taken her skibob, and we came up with the idiotic idea to rope it to the back of my red Rupp snowmobile and pull it along at high speed. We did this even though I had totaled our previous snowmobile earlier that year (but that is a story for later in the book). We tied the rope to the front of the skibob, connecting it to the fork that turned the skibob right or left. From the start, it was clear we hadn't thought very hard about the physics of this stunt.

Jack, of course, insisted that he be the one being towed on the skibob because it was more thrilling and dangerous than driving. So, I hopped onto my snowmobile and jetted down the snow-covered soybean rows south of our farmhouse at about 20 miles per hour, with Jack holding tight and cruising like a water skier. When I glanced back, Jack twirled his fingers, which is the water-skier way of indicating more speed.

So, I upped it to 30 miles per hour.

I glanced back. Jack signaled, "faster."

Forty miles per hour.

I glanced back. Jack signaled, "faster."

By now, I was going all out, racing along the flat land and kicking up swaths of snow. But up ahead, I saw we were quickly running out of field and fast approaching a drainage ditch, so I decided I would make a wide, looping right-hand turn—exactly what you do when water skiing on a lake. A speedboat's centrifugal force carries the skier on a smooth, arcing turn.

But there's one thing we didn't calculate. The centrifugal force would also cause the skibob to accelerate dramatically. On water skis, this usually isn't a problem. But on the skibob, the speed of the centrifugal force was big trouble. Because we had tied the tow rope to the skibob's front steering fork, it kept trying to yank the skibob out from under Jack.

As I started the turn, I looked over my shoulder and saw Jack barely hanging on to the skibob for dear life. Then…PING! The snowmobile suddenly lurched forward. I had lost Jack.

I glanced back again, and to my horror, he flew from the vehicle at breakneck speed. I remember seeing him in his bright blue snowmobile suit cartwheeling around 40 miles per hour across the frozen, snow-covered field. Of course, he wasn't wearing a helmet. With God as my witness, I was sure I had killed my best friend. My stomach knotted, thinking we'd crossed the line of no return.

It took a while for Jack to stop somersaulting across the frozen field. Bringing the snowmobile around, I raced back to him, leaped off, and sprinted to his side. It was déjà vu all over again.

Jack lay on his back, the wind knocked out of him. Then slowly but surely, he sat up, dusted the powder off his clothes, and sent me that same colossal grin.

"Damn, Irwin, that was awesome!"

The guy was indestructible. The skibob? Not so much. It had become a twisted ball of metal.

Once again, Jack had to return home with another mangled piece of equipment, and I expected him to get into more than a little trouble for destroying his little sister's Christmas present. His dad was tough, so I was worried about my friend because you didn't mess with Jack's dad.

His dad was in one of the first waves of Marines to hit the shores of Iwo Jima and was wounded twice; yet somehow, Jack eluded a massive punishment and was left working off his tail to buy his sister a new skibob. Knowing Jack, I'm sure he thought it was all worth it.

Crazy? It was. Jack had the daredevil quality that every speculator needs, but as teenagers, he and I didn't always have the wisest decision-making abilities to go with it. In futures trading, even with wisdom, experience, and poise to make sound decisions, things can still go terribly wrong. All it takes is a bit of miscommunication, and disaster can strike.

As you will soon see, trading during the days when the pits flourished was not for the faint of heart.

Chapter 3
Pit Bulls

I stared at the vast floor of the Chicago Board of Trade (CBOT), high above in the visitors' gallery. It was spring 1978, and this was my first visit to the CBOT, the place I had heard about and imagined as a kid growing up in Iowa. I was in Chicago on a field trip—part of an introductory agricultural marketing course taught by Professor Paul Doak during my sophomore year at Iowa State University. The bus ride from Ames to downtown Chicago was the stuff of legends because the university (or at least Professor Doak) actually allowed us a keg of beer on the bus! Yes, that was the 1970s for you.

Traders packed the CBOT floor, standing on steps in the various hexagonal pits. There was a pit for every commodity—corn, soybeans, wheat, soybean oil, soybean meal, and many more. At each pit, traders were watching and waiting for the clock to strike 9:30 a.m., sounding the opening bell.

When it rang, it was like someone tossed gasoline on an open fire. There was an explosion of noise—a frenzy of shouting, gesturing, and jostling for position. During the pit's heyday, the Chicago trading floors were open until 1:30 p.m., but it was like a non-stop adrenaline rush for those four hours. If you wanted to buy or sell after the closing, you had to wait until the next day's trading, which is why that opening bell was so frenetic. Traders had stockpiled a large backlog of orders since the previous day's close and were eager to trade as quickly as possible. When the opening bell finally sounded, they released their pent-up energy in a split second.

The trading system was known as "open outcry" for good reason.

As I said before, the allure for me as a kid took place at the local grain elevator, and the most beguiling room was in the back, where the ticker machine spits out futures prices. On the other end of that ticker machine were the trading floors at the CBOT and Chicago Mercantile Exchange (CME)—ground zero for commodity futures trading. I was hooked when the opening bell sounded on that spring day in 1978. The place was electric. It was as if I had stepped into the inner sanctum, which is why the trading pits replaced the grain elevator as the place where the magic happened.

In his landmark book, *Economics of Futures Trading*, one of my professional mentors, Tom Hieronymus, described the futures market "pits" this way:

"There is a mystery about these markets that seems difficult to penetrate...One need only stand on the visitors' balcony, watching the trading and the expressions on the faces of the other visitors, to gain a sense of the mystery and confusion. The trading floor is two stories high and the size of a football field. On an ordinary day, some six hundred people are present, a few are sitting at telephones, but most are on their feet and in motion, some walking and some running. There are several dense concentrations of people standing on steps that form hexagonal pits. Here, the action is frantic, with as many as 300 men shouting, waving their arms, and signaling with their fingers simultaneously. In isolation, as on a television camera, one trader bellows at the man next to him with such vigor that his face turns red and waves both hands, a trading card and a pencil in his face. The other reciprocates; both write quickly on cards, and turn and repeat the whole process to other traders or to the pit in general."[1]

Hieronymus first released his book in the early 1970s, before electronic trading. If you go to the trading floor today, you'll still find a room enormous enough to contain a Boeing 747 airplane. But the pits are almost empty, and the noise is not very loud, except when the opening bell rings in the only options pit still operating. In 2021, the CME Group decided to permanently close them all, except for the one for Eurodollar options. It won't be long before all futures options go electronic, and the pits will become as quiet as the ghost towns of the Old West.

However, throughout my college and graduate school years, the pits were still where the action was. When I became a professional agricultural economist studying the futures markets, my trips to Chicago became routine, but the pits' allure never faded. Non-traders like myself weren't allowed on the floor without being accompanied by an exchange staff member. So, with a staff person in tow, I would camp out at the edge of one of the pits and marvel at the madness.

During the glory days, if you watched the action from the visitors' gallery, it was like staring down at an ant colony as hundreds of insects scurried in all directions. But, like an ant colony, there was a method to the madness. That same action in the pits—bartering over prices—has been going on for tens of thousands of years as face-to-face haggling. This basic form of negotiation is known as price discovery. Pit traders barter, trying to find a price suitable to both parties, doing it repeatedly with the same commodity, be it corn, soybeans, or crude oil contracts.

These mini-auctions take place at high decibel levels in the pits. Once again, speculators play a vital role in the price discovery process because, without them, there might not be enough people on one side of the market to balance out the other side during all the hashing out. Because this kind of face-to-face price discovery has been such an integral part of human commerce for so long, it's no surprise the idea of trading electronically initially met a formidable wall of skepticism. People wondered how you could haggle over price without reading facial expressions and judging tone of voice.

The price discovery process at futures exchanges is a *global* auction because buyers and sellers span the earth. The results of these competitive auctions are known to the entire world, allowing buyers and sellers to constantly update their estimates of the economic value of a commodity. As a result, price discovery unfolds in an open, transparent way—ideally.

For the major grain contracts, the global price benchmarks were long set at the CBOT. Each exchange had its own specialties, and the CBOT was known for grains. In contrast, the specialty of the crosstown CME was livestock contracts, such as pork bellies, live cattle futures, and hog futures. That all changed when the CBOT and CME merged in 2007, forming the CME Group. Today, the global price for grains is set at the CME Group, although it is beginning to face tougher competition from other countries. For instance, the international benchmark price for soft wheat is beginning to shift from Chicago to the Black Sea regions of Ukraine and Russia.[2]

When trading pits were at their peak, the seemingly chaotic process of price discovery began with orders flowing in from brokers around the country. My dad bought and sold futures contracts here and there, but if he wanted to sell one in 1978, he would call up his broker in Des Moines and tell him something like: "I would like to sell one December corn contract at $2.80 per bushel or higher." Each corn contract was 5,000 bushels, so at $2.80 per bushel, he was talking about selling $14,000 worth of his corn on the futures market.

"December corn" refers to a corn futures contract that must be settled by December by offsetting a long (buy) contract with a short (sell) contract or by taking delivery of the physical commodity in December. Every commodity has different delivery months, but for corn futures, there are five—March, May, July, September, and December.

Once my dad decided to sell a December corn contract, the broker in Des Moines would take down the order and call a CBOT clerk, who sat on the trading floor in a perimeter around the pits, with a bank of telephones close at hand. When clerks received an order, such as my father's, they would write it on a card, stamp it, and pass it to a runner, who would rush it to the pit, handing it to another clerk. Then that clerk would give it to a trader for execution.

It was natural for me to wonder over the years what it was like to get caught up in the maelstrom of trading in the pits. There were even a few times I toyed with becoming a trader. However, I ended up as an observer. So, to get a feel for what life on the trading floor was like, I sat down with Terry Duffy, who has spent decades at the CME, the CBOT's rival in the heart of the city.[3]

I had gotten to know Terry in recent years through my position on the CME's Agricultural Markets Advisory Council; we share a fascination with the futures markets, which, ironically enough, began for both of us with visits to the exchanges as college students.

Duffy's story began as a student at the University of Wisconsin-Whitewater when he was twenty-one and working weekends at Chuck's Bar on Lake Geneva in Wisconsin. Chuck's Bar was perched on Lake Geneva, so close to the water that "you could fall off of your barstool and go for a swim," Duffy said. The place was like a college bar for the rich, he added, and its patrons either worked at the CBOT or the CME. But Duffy was clueless about what went on at either of those exchanges. He didn't even know what an *exchange* was.

One day, a man strolled in who would change his life forever. The man was Vincent Schreiber, a Chicago trader in the futures markets. According to Duffy, Schreiber stood out in the crowd because he was the only one who tipped, even though the bar swarmed with the uber-rich.

Schreiber also stood out to Duffy because he retired in his thirties. Curious about how someone so young could accomplish that, Duffy asked about his career history, to which Schreiber replied, "I'm in the futures market."

Duffy gave him a blank stare. He also had no idea what a futures market was.

Schreiber invited Duffy to an after-party, where about thirty people would be in attendance. Duffy leaped at the chance, and before long, Schreiber was taking him up a long driveway leading to a stunning, Frank Lloyd Wright-style house on the lake. It was in one of the swankiest neighborhoods, nestled among big-money dwellings, such as the Wrigley estate—as in Wrigley gum, Wrigley Field, and the Chicago Cubs.

"Does the guy who owns this house know you're bringing thirty people here?" Duffy recalled asking as they approached the place.

"It's *my* house," Schreiber said.

Right. Duffy looked around in awe and thought, *If you want to pretend it's your house, I'm okay with that.*

Schreiber led them inside, where Duffy absorbed the extravagance as he scanned the tiger-milk white carpeting throughout the house. The home also had an indoor pool, not something he would've ever seen in his working-class Mount Greenwood neighborhood on the southwest side of Chicago.

"Are you sure the guy who owns this house won't be upset with you throwing a party here?" Duffy asked. "This carpeting will get ruined, and he's going to go ballistic!"

"I'm telling you, it's my house."

No way, Duffy thought.

Next, Schreiber ushered him into his home office, where Duffy scoured the many photographs around the room. He noticed a few that showed Schreiber posing with various influential people, including Ronald Reagan, the California governor running for president.

"You know Ronald Reagan?" Duffy asked, eyes wide, wondering if he had entered the Twilight Zone.

"We golf together." Schreiber shrugged.

Duffy was stunned speechless, a rarity for a Chicago Irishman.

"This really is your house, isn't it?"

"That's what I've been trying to tell you!"

Duffy took it all in, astounded that a guy in his thirties could own a place like this.

"All right, tell me more about this futures thing," he said.

Schreiber said Duffy had the makings of a good futures trader. Watching him tend bar, Schreiber noticed that this twenty-one-year-old never got overwhelmed with orders, no matter how hectic things were. Chuck's Bar bustled with business and never seemed to have slow stretches.

"I love the fact that you don't get flustered," Schreiber said. "You also seem to remember everything, and I'm impressed by your mathematical mind. I think you'd do good in the futures market."

"So, when are you going back to Chicago?" Duffy said.

"On Monday morning."

Duffy asked if he could go with him to find out what this futures business is all about, and Schreiber said, "Sure." So, come Monday, Duffy and Schreiber arrived at the CME at 444 Jackson Street—a location that has since changed.

When Duffy stepped into the trading room, it was like walking into a boxing arena, except instead of encountering a ring surrounded by screaming fans, he came face to face with several hexagonal pits, each packed with a mob of traders. The testosterone and energy, in anticipation of the opening bell, were every bit as intense as the expectation preceding the opening round of a prizefight.

"When the bell went off, I thought somebody dropped a nuke on us. I ducked and wondered what the heck was that," Duffy said, echoing my first experience at the pits as a college student. Suddenly, people on the trading floor were running around like madmen.

"What the hell are they doing?" Duffy shouted over the pandemonium.

Schreiber explained how the traders bought pork belly contracts in one corner, hog futures in another, cattle contracts at one end of the trading floor, and gold contracts at the opposite end.

"This is awesome!" Duffy exclaimed. "Can I get a job here?"

At the time, he majored in criminal justice at the University of Wisconsin-Whitewater. He had his eyes on becoming a policeman because most kids in his Chicago neighborhood either wound up as cops or firefighters. But after watching this mind-boggling spectacle, Duffy wanted a part of the action.

"I can get you a job as a runner, but it's the lowest form of humanity in the business," Schreiber said.

"Fine, I'll do it!"

"You'll be paid only $56."

"That's okay."

Schreiber, who seemed to wield great authority at the CME, strode up to one of the men on the trading floor. "I want you to hire my friend here."

So, the deal was done, although Duffy soon discovered that he wouldn't receive $56 *per day* as he thought. It was more like $56 *per week*. But that was still all right with him; he was off and running.

Schreiber started calling this Irish kid "Duffstein" because historically, the CME was known as a Jewish trading exchange, while the Irish controlled the CBOT. As Schreiber would routinely say to Duffy, or Duffstein, "How can an Irish kid end up in a Jewish exchange?"

Duffy left the University of Wisconsin to work at the CME as a runner, but Vince Schreiber kept encouraging him to finish his degree since he had only one year remaining.

"Yeah, yeah," Duffy would tell him. "I'll go back...next semester."

The next semester never came. He loved the CME too much.

Duffy still remembers his first day as a lowly runner, carrying orders from the clerks at the telephones to the clerks on the floor, who stood at the edge of the pits. To make sure they got to the right people at the right pit, newbies such as Duffy shadowed more experienced runners. On his first day, he shadowed a guy named Mike Moore, whose brother went on to become one of the biggest bond traders in the history of the CBOT.

"Mike and I were running all around the trading floor, delivering trade orders, and I thought, my God, this is crazy," Duffy said. He then told Mike, "You're pretty good at this. How long have you been working here?"

"I started yesterday," Mike said over his shoulder.

Duffy's jaw went slack. "You started yesterday?"

"Yeah, and I don't know what we're doing either."

In those early days, getting screamed at was part of the job. According to Duffy, if he and Moore carried a feeder cattle trade order to the pork belly pit by mistake, "those old traders would yell, 'Get the hell out of here, you dumb Irish kid!'"

Duffy learned quickly, however, and he moved up one rung of the ladder to become one of the clerks standing at the edge of the pits, conveying orders to the traders jockeying for position. As a clerk, he now made $100 a week but had his eyes on becoming a trader inside the pit.

So, Duffy approached his mom for a loan to either rent or buy a CME membership, enabling him to trade on the floor.

"I'm pretty good at this," he said. "I think I'd like to be a trader."

"Are you out of your mind?" She gave him a strange look.

Getting nowhere with his mom, Duffy tried the idea out on his dad. But his dad was old-school Irish and laid down the law from on high. "We don't have the money! You're not going to do this."

"But I think I'm capable."

"No."

Undeterred, it was back to Mom, who finally bent under the force of his persistence and asked how much he'd need. Duffy told her it would cost $50,000 to lease a CME membership and trade on the floor.

"Let's go to the bank," she said. Without his father's knowledge, Duffy and his mom went to the bank, where they met with a family friend to discuss a loan. When the banker asked what the money was for, Duffy said he wanted to become a trader at the Chicago Mercantile Exchange.

The banker burst out laughing. "Are you crazy? Does Jack know about this?" he asked, referring to Duffy's father.

"Jack doesn't know, so let's keep this between us." His mom offered a solemn look before suggesting they guarantee the loan with the title of their family house.

"But your house is only worth $26,000," the banker said.

"We'll take fifty grand," she said.

"But Barb, your bungalow is worth twenty-six grand tops."

"Okay, but we need fifty."

Evidently, Duffy's mom could be as persuasive as her son because the banker finally relented. So, with the $50,000 loan, Duffy started trading at the CME on September 19, 1981. As he put it, everything went "swimmingly" for a couple of months until sometime around Thanksgiving.

"Then we had a little problem," he said.

"Little problem" was an understatement. One of the clerks told Duffy to *buy* a certain number of contracts in the hog pit when he was supposed to *sell*. Although it was the clerk's error, Duffy was responsible as the trader. By purchasing when the price was high, instead of selling, he was suddenly looking at a several hundred-thousand-dollar loss.

Duffy turned to a friend, Mick Callahan, who would later become his trading partner. Mick was able to get him down to a loss of roughly $130,000, plus some ancillary costs. But still, add that to the $50,000 loan, and Duffy was in a deep hole.

"I had just lost my mom and dad's house," Duffy recalled. On top of that, his dad was still unaware his mom put the house up as collateral for the loan. Word quickly spread across the trading floor about the Irish kid who "blew up 130 grand."

As it happened, his friend Schreiber was there that day, and Duffy told him, "Vinnie, I'm done."

Duffy never forgot what Vince said in response.

"Duffstein, where are you going to make that money back in the real world?"

"I have no idea."

"I'll tell you what. Here's what I'm going to do."

For a moment, Duffy thought his friend was about to write a check to bail him out, and his hopes rose—then crashed.

"I'm not giving you any money," Schreiber said. "What I'm going to do is call the clearing firm and guarantee the loss. If you walk away from it, then I'll eat the loss. But you're *not* going to walk away from it. You're going to make twenty dollars today and thirty the next day. You're going to get a second job tending bar at Lake Geneva on the weekends, and you'll come back on Monday and trade."

Schreiber stared at him and paused, adding, "I'll call your dad and explain."

"Don't call my dad. Call my mom."

When Duffy's mom heard what had happened, she panicked. "What am I going to do? I've got three other kids in the house!"

But Schreiber assured her, "It'll be fine. I'm guaranteeing it."

Duffy described the experience of losing that much money when you don't have it as "teeth rattling." But with Schreiber's backing, he could continue trading, and slowly but surely, he paid off his losses after three years.

"It's unbelievable what Vince did for me," Duffy recalls today. "He didn't give me money, but he gave me something that was so much more valuable. He gave me his reputation."

According to Duffy, this kind of loyalty was not unusual among traders. There was a cut-throat side to the pits, but there was also a sense of solidarity, the type of camaraderie you find among soldiers in a war zone. I was never a trader like Terry Duffy, but even I noticed this shared sense of battlefield brotherhood whenever I visited the exchanges. Traders were like a band of brothers (with a few sisters in the mix), putting their financial lives on the line daily.

Duffy is now the CEO and chairman of the CME Group—a publicly traded company worth $74 billion as of July 2022. He works out of a spectacular office with dark wood floors, a large, polished desk, and gleaming bookshelves with photos of influential people, such as one with him and his presidential golfing buddy, George W. Bush, and Jeb Bush, former governor of Florida. On another shelf sits a framed picture of Duffy and his friend, actor Mark Wahlberg.

Duffy has been chairman since 2002 and CEO since 2016, a classic rags-to-riches story. One day, after Duffy was elevated to his position, Vince Schreiber entered the office. He plopped on Duffy's sofa in his black pair of Tommy Bahama slacks, a floral shirt, and loafers without socks—looking like a million bucks. He gave Duffy a long, satisfying stare and said, "Duffstein, we've come a long way."

During the pit's peak years, traders were known for being extremely rough, which was why men were more prevalent. While traders would crawl over others' backs to catch someone's attention, Duffy said he didn't consider the pits exceedingly physical, except right before the opening and closing bells. Many traders carry positions to the very last second of the day, when settlement prices are determined. At those times, it could get very active and intense, and if you look at old films, he said you can see waves of movement among the pit traders.

Some traders would intimidate using brute strength, but Duffy said he didn't believe in that strategy. "I always dressed nice, so I didn't want to get into fights. I was pretty much a peacemaker, but I saw some pretty good donnybrooks in my day—and I had to break up a few too." He recalled one incident in which a trader, a woman, in this case, stabbed someone with her pen.

"It was a Bic," Duffy said. "Those things hurt."

Traders became famous for their hand signals, and if you look at the pit scene in *Ferris Bueller's Day Off*, you'll see the truant high school students giving mock hand signals to each other.[4] However, Duffy said that when he started in the early 1980s, there were only two basic hand signals at the CME.

If you held up your hands with palms facing in, you wanted to buy —drawing the trade toward you. If you lifted your hands with palms out, it meant *sell*—pushing the trade away.

As time progressed, hand signals became more elaborate. Traders used their fingers to indicate how many contracts they were buying or selling and at what price, but these signals varied from exchange to exchange. For instance, to indicate that a contract is due in January at the CME, you would wrap your hand around your neck like a winter scarf. To indicate "March," you would wiggle your fingers horizontally —as if they were marching. And if you want to say "August," wipe your hand across your brow as if it were a hot summer day.[5]

Once a trader announced he wanted to sell a contract, he would make eye contact with someone who wanted to buy. If the guy you're trading with was fifteen feet away, Duffy said he would figure out a way to get in his face. This is when the potential for pushing and shoving came into play. To confirm the trade, you might say something like, "I'm checking two at sixty," which in hog futures trading would mean two contracts at $60 per hundredweight of hogs. Once confirmed, each trader records the deal, but mistakes happen with all the noise and confusion. That's why later in the day, smart traders will confirm the transaction details. Sometimes, it can go down like this:

"I sold you two at sixty."

"What the hell are you talking about?" the other trader might exclaim.

"You nodded your head when I confirmed the trade."

"No, I didn't! I was nodding to the guy next to you!"

These miscommunications were called unresolved trades, or "out trades," and they had to be settled at a special out-trade meeting before the next day's trading. All trades have to match up; for every short side (sell) of a contract, there has to be a long side (buy).

Another trademark of the pits was the colorful jackets. At the CBOT, those working for the same company wore the same color— very loud jackets, the kind someone could spot from Mars. They came in greens, reds, and yellows of the most vibrant shades, for the goal was to be noticed amid the chaos. At the CME, meanwhile, members were required to wear maroon, while clerks had to wear yellow jackets. Traders at both exchanges also had to wear ties.

Traders wore enormous badges displaying their identifier names or numbers. This was necessary because when they made a deal, the trader needed to jot down the person with whom they secured it, as well as the trade information.

For most of the history of futures markets, traders wrote this information on pads of paper before tearing off a slip and handing it to runners, who carried it back to the clerks. The pits would get so crowded that traders sometimes could only write by raising their paper and pencil above their heads.

When Duffy worked as a trader, he said he considered the process "the purest form of negotiation at a split second." Traders had to make whip-quick decisions to either buy or sell, and this high-tension-wire process helped to establish a price for various commodities.

At the start of each morning's trade, he said the trickiest part was establishing the opening prices through open bidding with all the traders functioning like many auctioneers shouting at once. But this was also the most "fascinating and fabulous" part of the experience for Duffy.

"I love that I can participate in the process to discover a price for a commodity. I like that about free markets, and I think it would be a shame if they ever went away—a shame for both our political and financial systems. Price discovery is critical to the fabric of this country."

Although virtually all pits have disappeared today, price discovery continues with electronic trading, which I will discuss later. But it is safe to say that the switch from open outcry to electronic trading was the most dramatic change to the futures market since its origin in the nineteenth century. Before electronic trading, if a trader from the 1880s had traveled in time to the 1980s, he would have been able to step right in and start trading. But no longer.

The change happened in stages. In the late 1980s, traders switched from scribbling orders on cards to using electronic pads. But the bigger revolution didn't come until the CME developed the electronic trading system, Globex, in 1992. Trading could now be done from an office.

While I am nostalgic for the color and excitement of the pits, as an economist, I am 150 percent behind the electronic markets. Electronic trading is a much more efficient way to match trades. Hands down. Although there are still issues that need to be ironed out, electronic trading is superior in almost every dimension. For starters, it's a faster and cheaper way to trade than open outcry. And ultimately, economic efficiency is what economists care about most.

Because some of us may be tempted to look back on the world of the pits with rose-colored glasses, it is important to recognize that this system had its share of problems. For example, in 1989, the FBI conducted stings at the CBOT and CME—Operation Sourmash at one and Operation Hedgeclipper at the other. These investigations resulted in forty-six floor trader indictments on 1,500 counts, including racketeering and fraud. Even so, the government was unsuccessful in convicting all of them.

A January 1989 *Chicago Tribune* article stated that "brokers rigged trades by themselves or in collusion with other traders in a variety of ways that prevented their customers from buying or selling the contracts at fair-market prices."[6]

Electronic trading has also done away with the physical intimidation that often took place on the floor. As one former trader said in a 2016 *Financial Times* article, he wasn't sorry to see the move to electronic trading because the trading floor was "middle school with money."[7]

In the same article, Duffy observed that someone with his 6-foot-1-inch height had a distinct advantage in the pit over someone shorter. In comparison, "The computer puts us all at the same height, the same weight, and everything else. It puts us all on a very level playing field."

Either way, working as a trader is "a hard business, a really hard business," Duffy told me. As he put it, "Everybody thinks they can do it, but it's not for everybody."

Many do not survive this battlefield, and if not for the generosity of Schreiber, Duffy might not have made it past his third month on the floor.

"I owe a lot to that man. May he rest in peace," said Duffy.

Schreiber passed away in 2004 at the young age of fifty-nine, and today his photo sits on Duffy's bookshelf, next to photographs of his mom and dad, who have also passed. However, the house Duffy almost lost while first trading in 1981 remains in the family. His father never discovered what happened until 1990, long after the crisis had passed. By then, Duffy was thriving and had even bought his dad a Cadillac.

"Dad, I've got to tell you what really happened back in '81," Duffy recalled saying as the two sat around, smoking and having a few drinks. "I blew up. I lost it all, including the house."

His dad just stared at him, surprised, before raising a brow. "I knew that," he finally said.

"No, you didn't! You would've killed me."

"You're right. I would've. But thanks for telling me."

Chapter 4
Elvis and Evel in Iowa

I 'm not sure which of us had the idea, but it was so much fun that it had to be Jack Hunter. He figured out that if we took turns getting a good running start on my motorcycle, we could race up a grassy bank and soar across a blacktop highway.

Our property was very unusual. The county blacktop highway stretched south out of Bagley and ran smack through our farmstead. Sadly, dogs did not survive long at our place. On the west side of the road sat the farmhouse, tree grove, and hog farrowing buildings. On the east side were a couple of barns, a corn crib, and several hog lots. We kept the place neatly trimmed and mowed, including the broad drainage ditches—or "road ditches" in our local Iowa vernacular—on either side of the blacktop. Ensuring they were trim was all part of the none-too-subtle expectations of keeping up appearances in our farming community. Well, Jack and I discovered that a neatly mowed road ditch made the perfect ramp for our motorcycle mischief. It had the perfect bowl shape for flying.

Jack and I would ride across the lawn behind the house, then roll down the bank of the ditch. When we reached the bottom, we would goose the engine and race up the opposite bank—just as we did on our snowmobiles when jumping huge snow drifts. With a burst of speed, we shot up the side and soared so high that we flew across the two-lane blacktop road, landing on the opposite side with a bone-rattling thud.

This trick required more skill than you might imagine. We had to slide the motorcycle to a sudden stop in the ditch on the opposite side of the road; otherwise, you would hit the wooden fence that ringed the hog lot along the far edge of that ditch. We envisioned ourselves as a young Evel Knievel launching across the road.

Of course, in our day, the real Evel Knievel was a famous folk hero and busy man, jumping much more than blacktop highways. In 1971, Knievel set a record by jumping nineteen cars on his Harley-Davidson XR. The prior year, when he tried to jump thirteen Pepsi trucks, he landed on his front wheel, was hurled from the bike, and skidded fifty feet along the ground. He busted his collarbone, fractured his right arm, and broke both legs.[1] (His run-in with Pepsi trucks was even worse than mine.)

Knievel kept trying to outdo himself, and in 1974 he attempted to soar across the Snake River Canyon in Idaho on his Sky-Cycle X-2, which was more rocket than motorcycle. I remember when he blasted from the edge of the cliff. Although it looked like Knievel would make it across the canyon, his parachute released prematurely. The wind caught the chute, carrying him backward, and he landed at the bottom of the canyon on the side where he had started. If he had landed in the Snake River, he probably would have drowned because of how snugly he was tied into the rocket.[2]

So, okay, Jack Hunter and I were not in the same category as Evel Knievel, the most famous stunt rider of all time. Still, for two young high school kids in the early 1970s, we imagined we were. We were skilled at what we did.

One hot July afternoon in 1973, Jack and I had time to kill while waiting for my dad to drive us to the Saturday night sprint car races in Knoxville, Iowa—our favorite thing to do in the summer. We lived to go to Knoxville to watch the sprint cars tear up the half-mile, oval dirt track. Of course, I wore my usual Saturday-night racing outfit: blue jeans, cowboy boots, and my favorite sprint car racing T-shirt from the

Weikert's Livestock Racing Team. The phrase, "When the green flag drops, the bull%$!@ stops," was emblazoned in large letters on the front.

While we waited for Dad, we hung around the farmhouse, deciding to while away the time with highway jumping. As usual, one of us would keep watch because cars and farm pickup trucks flew by at speeds of 50 to 70 mph, and we didn't want to jump the road with oncoming traffic. Maybe Evel would attempt that, but Jack and I were at least wise enough not to hurdle passing cars.

As Jack and I took turns leaping the blacktop highway, my dad finally appeared on the front porch, and he was a sight to behold. Remember, this was the early 1970s, and fashion was, well, different than today. It was the disco era.

My dad stepped onto the porch in a bright red polyester jumpsuit that you could see from miles away. Think of work coveralls, only made from stretchy red stuff instead of cotton. If the bottoms had flared, it would have resembled a jumpsuit Elvis wore in his later years—the "fat Elvis" years.

My dad struggled with his weight, so he looked, shall we say, plump in that red jumpsuit. (He also owned one in powder blue, but thankfully he left it in the closet that day.) Complementing his vibrant attire were his tennis shoes, so white that they could blind you if you stared at them too long.

It appeared my dad was in no hurry to leave for the races when he sat on the front porch with my mom, and they drank iced tea while watching our stunts. Soon, he started trash-talking, ribbing us about our jumps. He said they looked like child's play.

As he continued to razz us, Jack stopped short and sat on the motorcycle, staring at my dad, unwilling to let him get away with talking smack without a response. He shouted the words only Jack Hunter could get away with: "Show us how it's done, fat man!"

I was staggered by Jack's audacity. I was too scared to dare say any such thing. Ever. My dad had a bad temper and could be very intimidating, and he was a little sensitive about his weight, so I kept my mouth firmly shut.

But Jack and my dad were kindred spirits. In fact, Jack was like another son and was the only person I knew who could have taunted Dad like that. For such a scrawny kid, Jack had one big mouth. He was also fearless.

"Show us how it's done, fat man!"

So, my dad decided to do just that. He hopped onto my motorcycle, a bright yellow and silver Yamaha 125, technically classed as a dirt bike. He gave himself plenty of room for a long, running start. Then he took off, a brilliant blur of red fabric racing across our yard like a meteor wrapped in nylon.

He hit the road ditch just fine, but when he reached the bottom, he goosed the engine too much. The dirt bike took off like Evel Knievel's rocket, racing up the bank of the ditch with my dad barely attached. Then he flew into the air and was halfway across the asphalt highway when he lost his grasp.

The Yamaha 125 shot off, leaving him suspended in mid-air. I'm sure he was there for only a hairbreadth of a second, but in my mind's eye, I was watching a cartoon in which a character finds himself in mid-air for several seconds and tries to run, legs pumping like pinwheels.

When gravity finally took over, he plunged, landing squarely on his rear end in the middle of the asphalt highway. He had put the "ass" in asphalt.

Jack and I were rolling on the ground, laughing hysterically, but my dad didn't see the funny side of what had happened. He didn't understand why we thought that Elvis, losing control of his motorcycle and landing on his butt in a red jumpsuit, was so humorous.

Somehow the dirt bike ended up unscathed, but my dad hit the road so hard that he may have cracked his tailbone. Although he was in pain, we still went to the races that day, but he couldn't sit for long stretches. Either way, his pride hurt more than his tailbone. Jack gave him a hard time the entire day. While Dad never appreciated the teasing, he put up with it for the next several weeks because it was, after all, Jack Hunter.

"Show us how it's done, fat man!"

Outside of motorcycles, snowmobiles, and pretty much anything that went fast, the area in which my dad was most aggressive and competitive was in marketing his crops. He constantly tried to beat the market because he had the mindset of a speculator. The problem was that he attempted to speculate through his hedging, which brought him roughly the same result as when he tried to jump the blacktop highway running through our farm.

Up to this point, I've been primarily talking about speculators, but hedging is the flip side of the futures market. In fact, this is perhaps the most crucial function because hedging is a way for farmers and grain companies to contain risk. Think of it as insurance against the fickleness of the markets—a way to reduce your financial exposure.

As I mentioned before, anyone can be a speculator, and they're often people who have nothing to do with the commodity's production, storage, or use. But a hedger is involved with the physical commodity—a farmer, cattle producer, or grain elevator operator, for instance.

The classic textbook example of hedging is when a producer—let's say a corn farmer—decides to sell his crop on the futures market during the spring planting season to guarantee a specific price, no matter what the market does. To understand how this works, you need to know that there are two markets for many commodities—the cash market and the futures market. The futures price is the projected value of the commodity in the future, while the cash price is the true value of the commodity on any given day; it's what someone will pay to use the physical commodity. If you sell all your crop on the cash market, you are at the mercy of the ups and downs of the local cash price at the nearest grain elevator. Come harvest in the fall, when you want to sell your crop, you could be devastated if prices plunge too much.

Selling in the futures market is a way for farmers to ensure a certain return, even if prices in the cash market crash. But for hedging to work, the key is that the price in the futures market needs to move up and down parallel with price fluctuations in the cash market, which it generally does. When this happens, a hedge can be an effective way of reducing your price risk.

The best way to see this in action is with an example. Let's look at two farmers—Frank and Estelle. Frank does *not* hedge, but Estelle does. In both instances, let's also assume that in May, during the planting season, corn in the local cash market is $4.50 per bushel, while the price in the futures market is $5 per bushel—a fifty-cent difference.

FRANK

Frank decides to stay in the cash market all the way to harvest when he sells his corn in October. However, better-than-normal weather over the summer boosts corn yields and creates a surplus. Therefore, by October, the price in the cash market has dropped from $4.50 to $3.50 per bushel, a loss of a dollar. He sells 5,000 bushels of corn for a total of $17,500. (I'm using the small figure of 5,000 bushels for simplicity's sake.)

ESTELLE

Estelle decides to hedge. In May, she sells 5,000 bushels of corn in the *futures market* at $5 per bushel. A single futures contract for corn is 5,000 bushels. So, by selling 5,000 bushels at $5 per bushel, she controls a position worth $25,000.

But it doesn't end there. All farmers must eventually sell their crop in the local cash market. Therefore, in October, Estelle must buy back a contract for 5,000 bushels of corn in the futures market and then turn around and sell her grain in the cash market. If the futures market runs parallel to the cash market, as it often does, that means the futures market has also dropped one dollar to $4 per bushel. Again, this was due to good summer weather boosting corn yields and increasing supplies.

In October, she buys back 5,000 bushels of corn in the futures market at $4 per bushel, so her position at that time is worth

$20,000. But notice something important. She controlled a position worth $25,000 by selling in the futures market in May. That same position was worth $20,000 in October when she repurchased it. So, she had a net gain of $5,000 on the position between May and October because she was initially short (a seller) in the futures market.

Now, she must turn around and sell her 5,000 bushels in the cash market, which has also dropped one dollar to $3.50 per bushel. As a result, she makes $17,500 in the cash market. When you add the $5,000 she made in the futures market, her total is $22,500. Here's what this looks like:

> **May: Estelle sells 5,000 bushels of corn in the futures market at $5 per bushel—a position of $25,000. The cash price is $4.50 per bushel.**

> **Between May and October, the futures market drops $1, from $5 to $4 per bushel, while the cash market drops $1 from $4.50 to $3.50.**

> **October: Estelle buys back 5,000 bushels in the futures market at $4 per bushel—a total of $20,000. She makes $5,000 in the futures market.**

> **October: Estelle sells the 5,000 bushels of corn in the cash market at $3.50 per bushel. She receives $17,500 in the cash market.**

> **Estelle makes a total of $22,500—$5,000 in the futures market and $17,500 in the cash market.**

Estelle protected herself from the drop in cash prices, making $5,000 more than Frank. In fact, she made the same amount had the prices not dropped in the cash market and remained at $4.50 per bushel. Five thousand bushels sold at $4.50 per bushel is $22,500, which is the total she made by hedging in the futures market and then selling in the cash market.

Once again, the key to hedging is that the cash and futures markets must move together in tandem. Most of the time, the two markets move roughly in sync. When one goes up or down fifty cents, the other does about the same. If the two markets move in parallel, you can cover your losses in one market with gains in the other. It's like placing a side bet in one market to protect yourself from volatility in the other.

So, if hedging in the futures market effectively protects against catastrophic drops in the cash market, why aren't all farmers doing that?

The reason: Although hedging in the futures market protects against severe drops in the cash price, it can also prevent you from reaping healthy profits should the cash market go through the roof.

In my example, Estelle gained $1 per bushel in the futures market while losing the same amount in the cash market. The two offset each other, protecting her from loss. But what if the cash market *went up* by a dollar because a drought in China caused corn production to plummet there? In this case, the hedger would not share the benefits of the higher cash price. If the futures market runs parallel and goes up, Estelle would lose $1 per bushel in futures; she bought 5,000 bushels in the futures market in October at a higher price than she sold in May. This $1 loss in the futures market offsets the $1 per bushel gain in the cash market.

This is precisely why farmers hate hedging when cash prices increase. By protecting themselves against catastrophic price drops in the cash market through hedging, they miss out on the gains when prices skyrocket. If you want to win under all scenarios, you need to hedge when local cash prices at harvest will dip and *not* hedge when cash prices will rise.

In other words, in the spring or summer, farmers must be able to predict what prices will do come harvest in the fall. If they foresee cash prices going up, don't hedge; if they know cash prices will decrease, hedge.

This strategy is much easier said than done. Trying to hedge when you think cash prices will dip is like buying flood insurance only during years when you think torrential rains will flood the nearby river, spilling its banks and damaging your house. That's why hedging is better viewed as insurance or risk management than a money-making strategy.

In a textbook hedge, producers should sell all of their commodity using futures contracts or 100 percent of what they *expect* to produce. For instance, Fred Seamon, executive director in agricultural markets with the CME Group, told me about a Texas cattle producer who is always 100-percent hedged.

Every year, this Texan sells all of his cattle on the futures market as soon as they enter the feedlot. According to Seamon, this cattle producer says his returns are probably the same as a neighboring cattle producer who never hedges. But here's the big difference. The neighbor, who is at the mercy of fluctuating prices in the cash market, nearly went bankrupt two times. Seamon's cattle-producing friend never did. Hedging had taken away the price risk.[3]

Most farmers, cattle producers, or other commodity producers do not follow the textbook strategy. Only a small percentage will hedge 100 percent of their crop or livestock production. They prefer partial hedging, in which they hedge a portion of their commodity in the futures market. Then they take a risk in the cash market with the rest of the crop or livestock. They insure only a portion of their commodity.

In the past, many old-school agricultural economists (including some of my heroes) bristled whenever someone described hedging as purely a form of insurance.[4] Some argued that farmers could reduce risk by hedging during years when cash prices fall and make money by *not* hedging during years when cash prices rise. But there is evidence over the last fifty years showing these old-school agricultural economists overestimated the percentage of farmers who have the requisite skills to predict cash price movements and, therefore, make money hedging in the futures market. It can be done, but I believe only by a select small percentage of farmers.

My dad, unfortunately, thought he was one of them. So did many farmers in the 1970s because all kinds of farm advisory services told them it was possible, even likely. My dad would subscribe to these services, follow their advice faithfully, and try to sell his crop on the futures market only when the cash prices were expected to go down. But he lost more often than he won. If he sold in the futures market, as a way to protect from falling cash prices, he would try to get out of the futures market as soon as he had a hunch that the cash prices were going to go up. But in more cases than not, he predicted wrong and lost money.

Farmers like my dad get frustrated because they'd lose sight of the goal of hedging—that is, managing risk and avoiding going bankrupt if crop prices crash. If you look at it that way, you will feel much more secure—and less frustrated. When my dad tried to make money in the futures market, he was trying to be part hedger, part speculator. I invented a new term to describe how my dad approached the futures markets—he was a "hedgulator." My dad fought the market his whole life, but he discovered that outfoxing the market is like trying to beat the house in Las Vegas. A select few can do it, but most cannot.

My dad had a Type A personality, which is terrible for a trader. He was so emotionally invested in his production that it tainted his judgment. If his corn and soybean crops were burning up in July, he would project his situation on all farmers, believing everyone in the Midwest was going through the same turmoil.

Dad was prone to "looking out his backdoor," as the traders say. This would give him a distorted picture of what was happening in the entire corn and soybean market, which wasn't good when trying to trade wisely.

I became my dad's "market therapist" throughout my professional career because he constantly called and complained about prices. He would talk and talk, and while I would respond with what I knew about the market that year, I don't think I was much help.

Ironically, it would have been better if my dad had left the marketing up to my mom. After he passed in 2009, my mom and I took over the marketing on our family farms, and I discovered she was a natural.

Mom loves to play all sorts of card games, including bridge, and has a much cooler personality than my dad. Despite starting as a crop marketer in her seventies, she does not get easily flustered. She is cautious, yet when she sees a good price, she goes for it.

Unable to handle mistakes, my dad would beat himself up if he sold before the cash market rose. But my mom is always calm, moving forward to the next transaction. I'm dead serious when I say that if my dad had let my mom do the marketing for the thirty-five years they farmed together, my family could have owned half of the farmland in Guthrie County, Iowa. Like the pair highlighted in the previous hedging example, my mom was Estelle to my dad's Frank.

My dad had the "Ricky Bobby mindset." Ricky Bobby, the outlandish NASCAR driver played by Will Ferrell in *Talladega Nights*, famously said, "If you ain't first, you're last."[5]

My Dad thought that if he didn't beat the market, he was last. But the reality in car racing is you don't have to win every time, or even the majority of races, to come out the biggest money-maker at the end of the year. If you finish consistently near the top but never win, you'll do much better in the long run than the driver who wins a couple of races but crashes in most of the others. Likewise, hedging brings consistency, even if it means you don't beat the market.

To look at it another way, trying to make money through hedging would be like Evel Knievel thinking the parachute he built into his Skycycle could help carry him over Snake Canyon. That wasn't the parachute's purpose. Instead, like a good hedge, it was there to save his neck and prevent a crash landing.

My dad may not have been the wisest crop marketer, but I can't end this chapter on that note when he brought so many other great qualities to my life that his business shortcomings pale in comparison. He bequeathed me his passion for anything with an engine, but more importantly, he taught me to bounce back from setbacks. The best example of this involved the same motorcycle I rode during our road-ditch jumps—the Yamaha 125.

It was the summer of 1972, after my eighth-grade year, and dad had just purchased the dirt bike. Talk about excited! We had a neighbor, Chet Derry, a flying farmer, and my dad decided I should test the dirt bike on his land. Chet owned a plane and maintained a smooth grass airstrip on his property about a mile from our farm. It was an ideal place to ride.

After my dad gave me strict instructions to take it easy since it was my first ride on the new bike, he left me on the landing strip to practice while he, Chet, and Chet's wife, Bernice, had iced tea on their front porch. (It seemed as if my dad was always watching my antics while having tea on the porch.)

I hopped on my dirt bike and raced up and down that runway. The dirt bike was quick and could hit more than 60 miles per hour wide open, although I was not supposed to push it that hard since it was my first ride.

Of course, my teenage instinct was to do the opposite of anything my dad said, especially because I wanted to test how fast I could push my new bike. So, on my last pass for the day, I took off, tearing down the airstrip at a rate that shocked me. However, I didn't take into account that high speeds could affect depth perception.

At the end of the airstrip sat a cattle feed yard, surrounded by a thick fence made of two-by-six-inch boards to keep the cattle from escaping. But moving at high speed, I failed to properly judge the distance to the fence. It was too late when I realized I needed to brake. In a situation like this, the wisest choice is to lay your bike down, fall on your side, skid along the ground, and let the motorcycle absorb the impact instead of riding straight into a fence and possibly flying off headfirst. But I panicked, desperately trying to brake. I managed to skid some, which probably slowed down the motorcycle to maybe 25 to 30 miles per hour, but I couldn't stop, at least not until…BAM!

I hit that fence with a resounding crack.

I had been riding in cutoff jean shorts without a shirt or helmet. Safety was not such a big deal back in the "Easy Rider" days of the '70s. But I was extremely fortunate the bike struck between the fence-posts, or the crash would have been much worse. My angels were hard at work again.

Momentarily stunned, I looked around to find I was still sitting on the bike. I also noted that the cattle seemed to be staring at me with puzzled expressions. I hit the fence so hard that my front tire busted through the bottom fencing, my bare chest flush against the top board. I stared at my handlebars which hit the top board but managed to slide underneath, and blinked, wondering how I hadn't been broken to bits or thrown off.

Not surprisingly, Chet and my dad bounded from their chairs to check on me. My dad must've thought, *Not again.*

It was quite a sight, me on a bent-up dirt bike protruding halfway into Chet Derry's cattle yard. It was another miracle that I had only a few scratches and bruises, considering I was without a helmet or a shirt and hit those thick boards hard enough to knock a couple free.

The front wheel of my brand-new dirt bike, barely a few hours old, was completely mangled, and the handlebars were bent up as well. I'd pretty much trashed it and was in tears, already telling myself I didn't want to ever ride again because of how terrifying it was. My dad showed compassion and toughness. While he comforted me, he said, "Scotty, you're never going to ride this motorcycle again unless you get on it *right now*." His words took me back to when he made me stand on my own power after falling with my crutches following the Pepsi truck accident.

I tearfully protested, but he wouldn't take no for an answer. After dragging the bike from the fence, I held my breath. Although the motorcycle barely functioned, dad started the engine without a hitch. That little Yamaha 125 dirt bike could take a lot of punishment.

Dad made me climb onto that bike and ride it the entire way back to our house. Through my tears, I kept an eye on the wobbly front wheel, praying I'd make the long drive. I vividly remember the sun beating down on me as the wheel kept going *thump, thump, thump* all the way home. But I made it that one mile, even with a mangled bike and all my cuts and scrapes. What's more, I conquered my fear of getting back onto the motorcycle, riding it for years and years, and even jumping over highways.

I appreciate my dad for his tenacity and for teaching me perseverance. The markets may have driven him crazy, but he knew how to get up after a crash and taught me how to do the same. My dad was not Evel Knievel or even Elvis, but in so many ways, he was the King. He understood how to bounce back, which was an important lesson because, as you'll see, my motorcycle crash was not the last of my crack-ups. Not by a long shot.

Oh, and by the way, I had to go back the next day and repair Chet Derry's cattle fence. You break it. You fix it.

Chapter 5
My Spectacular Speculation Crackup

I idolized my Granddad Irwin growing up; he was an imposing John Wayne sort of man who sat tall in the saddle. He loved his animals and wanted to turn me into a horseman. But I was never a horse guy. These magnificent animals were a lot of work and finicky, and I'd already spent so much of my time scooping hog manure. Why would I want to clean out horse stalls as a hobby?

Until my later teen years, one of my jobs was to be a sort of "minder" to three older guys we farmed with—Granddad, his best friend Estle Templeton, and Harold Howick, all in their sixties. These guys had known each other most of their lives and had swearing down to an art form. Some of their more colorful phrases still echo in my mind: "It's colder than a well digger's ass in Montana in January" and "Scotty, it looks like it's going to rain like a cow peeing on a flat rock."

Those three constantly kidded around, making me the butt of their pranks, especially on vaccination day. When I was younger, we had to vaccinate our hogs for cholera, and I lived in fear of this dreaded annual event. We raised over 1,000 head of hogs a year and waited to vaccinate them until they were good-sized. As a grade-schooler ("young whippersnapper," by their description), I helped corral the pigs before we'd move them through a chute while the vet jabbed them one by one. But the worst experience was afterward when Granddad, Estle, and Harold would tackle me and pull down my pants, threatening to vaccinate *me* with an almost four-inch-long needle! My heart still pounds at the thought.

I think they drew blood more than once. Whenever my Grandmother Lurene witnessed this event, she would get furious as they tormented me, but it never dissuaded them from doing it again the next time.

That may sound like some extreme joking around at my expense, but I became close to them through my teen years, especially with Granddad and Estle. They taught me everything about livestock and crop farming because they assumed I would someday take over for my dad.

Granddad was also one of my biggest fans and never missed any of my sporting events. So, it was a terrible shock when he was suddenly killed in an accident right in front of his house during my sophomore year in high school. Train tracks ran in front of their farmstead, a crossing without warning signals, and Granddad must've driven across those railroad tracks thousands of times. But on a day I will never forget—January 14, 1974—he must not have been looking because his pickup truck was struck by a fast-moving locomotive, killing him instantly.

It rocked our entire family.

My parents and Grandmother Lurene tried to cope by escaping from everything. They took a trip to Mexico in February, hoping to soothe the grief and find a way to start the healing.

In those days, livestock farmers were notorious for rarely taking trips away from their animals, so I knew it was serious if my dad was willing to leave the farm to recuperate. But while they were gone, I was also nearly killed in a freak accident.

Despite being a sophomore, I was a starter on our YJB Raiders high school basketball team. Since I had some games left on the schedule, I remained in Iowa at my friend Marshall Hoyt's house while my family was gone.

One snowy mid-February night, Marshall and I talked his parents into letting us venture out on our snowmobiles. I had a girlfriend in Bagley ("town girl"), and Marshall had one out on a farm east of town ("farm girl"), so we left the Hoyt farm for our respective romantic trysts as the heavy snow fell. While it didn't quite qualify as a blizzard, it was coming down in bunches. Perfect for zooming around on our snowmobiles. My vehicle was a new yellow and black Ski-Doo.

After spending time with my girlfriend, I started for the Hoyt's house at about 10 p.m., with the dense snow still falling. As I blasted along the snow-covered country road on my snowmobile at a good clip, the night sky was nothing but a swirl of snow. It was difficult to distinguish where the road ended and where the ditches began. There was nothing but white for as far as the eye could see.

Suddenly, I noticed something odd about the terrain in front of me. In all of the whiteness, I realized I was fast approaching a vast, hulking mound of snow smack in the middle of the country road. I later learned that an older farmer had gotten his pickup truck stuck and abandoned it, leaving it sitting in the middle of the road. The snow had buried it so deep it was just a big, white mound, indistinguishable from the surroundings.

By the time I spotted the shape in the snowstorm, it was too late to stop. I struck the back bumper going at least 30 to 40 miles per hour. My snowmobile flew from under me, sliding beneath the snow-blanketed truck while I hurled forward. My helmet slammed against the pickup truck's tailgate and cracked down the center. Why the impact didn't break my neck, I don't know to this day. I was knocked out cold, exposed to deadly temperatures in the teens.

When I eventually came to, I was still straddling the back end of my snowmobile. The impact bent the handlebars like pretzels, and the engine was partly sheared and sitting in my lap. I was dazed, but not so much that I wasn't aware of the intense throbbing in my legs.

Somehow, through all the pain, I got off my snowmobile and limped a half mile to the closest house, which happened to be Doug and Sandy Becker's place. The couple had two daughters who were close friends of my sisters, and I'm sure I must have been quite a sight to them. It wasn't long before they made a quick phone call for Marshall's parents to get me.

Like my run-in with the Pepsi delivery truck and my dirt bike crash, I had been miraculously spared. Angels. It had to be angels because I had no broken bones or a concussion. The bruising, though, was horrific.

I'm not sure how to describe it other than I was more than just black and blue. I was black and blacker. The bruising eventually turned my skin completely dark from my knees up to my neck, including EVERYTHING in between. My sisters were convinced I would never be able to have children.

Of course, what came next was even more frightening. How could I tell my parents I had destroyed the snowmobile while almost killing myself? Since they were still in Mexico, I would have to wait until they got home to tell them I had destroyed the snowmobile and almost killed myself in the process. Back then, long-distance calls were expensive, so you did not make international calls.

I can still see that demolished yellow and black snowmobile sitting in front of the garage when they got home. My mom was just relieved that I was not seriously injured. Although my dad was happy I survived, he chewed me out pretty well, but we had too much work on the farm to dwell on it for long.

Since I was the leading rebounder on my high school team and among the top five in scoring in the conference, my basketball coach was furious I had gotten banged up right before the state playoffs. We had a home court advantage against Guthrie Center in the first round of the sectionals, but I could barely walk, so they taped me up to play. I tried my best but was too stiff and sore to do anything other than play miserably. And we lost—end of season.

Once again, Scott, the reluctant daredevil, not only cheated death but severe injury. Growing up in Iowa, my life was a string of mishaps and close calls. Still, these near-disastrous crackups were not limited to the world of snowmobiles and other vehicles. I also had a near-disastrous financial crackup the first time I tried my hand at speculation in graduate school at Purdue University. I found out first-hand just how risky and difficult speculating in the futures market can be—as dangerous as driving a snowmobile through blinding snow at breakneck speed. My speculation crackup nearly broke me financially, which would have forced me to leave graduate school.

Before I get to what happened in the futures market, let me say that my road to graduate school was not a straight line, beginning with a difficult decision to attend Iowa State University for my undergraduate years. My dad wanted me to be a superfarmer, who could outsmart everyone and everything, including the markets. So, for undergraduate studies, he pushed me in the direction of a classic ag school—Iowa State, where all the Irwins went. On the other hand, my mom came from a sports-obsessed family where basketball was a near religion. She wanted me to base my undergraduate decision on basketball, not farming.

I was a good player, at least for a small Iowa farm town. I was nearly six feet four in high school and owned the school scoring record of 44 points in a single game. In my senior year, I averaged nearly 25 points, but I was a big fish who played in a tiny pond.

Nevertheless, I got recruited by some small colleges and probably could have played at what would be Division II or Division III schools today. The only interest I got from a Division I school was from Army, coached at the time by Mike Krzyzewski. He would become one of the greatest college coaches of all time at Duke University. So, my only claim to hardwood fame was receiving a recruiting letter from the legendary Krzyzewski.

I was a compliant kid, a people-pleaser, but how was I going to please both my dad, who wanted me to go to Iowa State, and my mom, who wanted me to follow my hoop dreams? I overheard my parents having some rather heated discussions about where I should attend college. Finally, my father put his foot down and said, "Quit fooling around with these other things (like basketball)." He told me I was going to Iowa State. End of discussion.

I was upset, thinking he had squashed my basketball career, but looking back now, I think it was one of the smartest things anyone ever did for me. My mom still regrets that I didn't follow my basket-

ball passion, but I would've had to work extremely hard to be successful, even in Division III. I hustled and banged the boards, but I wasn't
athletic enough to keep pace with other college players. I was better
off at Iowa State, concentrating on agribusiness.

My mom didn't give up on her basketball dreams and wanted me
to try walking on with the team at Iowa State. But even though I was a
tall, lanky Iowa farm boy, I couldn't jump high enough and wasn't
quick enough. Even if I had succeeded in walking on, it wouldn't have
worked. I would've sat on the bench, and my time would have been
drained from academics and gone to waste on athletics.

As an ag business major at Iowa State, the plan for the first couple
of years was to return home and farm after receiving my bachelor's
degree. But I sensed my future might not be on the farm when I took
an introductory ag marketing course from Professor Paul Doak during
my sophomore year. This class offered my first in-depth exposure to
futures markets. He taught me a technical analysis system known as
"charting," using large swaths of graph paper to create charts of
commodity prices every day. I would tape these charts to my dorm
room wall, like some obsessed conspiracy theorist plastering his wall
with maps and photos.

In college, I finally discovered the world at the other end of the
ticker machine back at Bagley's grain elevator. As I mentioned earlier
(see Chapter 3), I traveled to Chicago for the first time as part of
Professor Doak's ag marketing course, and the pits entranced me at
the Chicago Board of Trade. I also got to talk with traders on the floor,
which was like going to your first professional baseball game and
getting to walk onto the field before heading into the locker room to
chat with players.

I may not have consciously known it at the time, but I think from
that moment on, my path was set. I would go into academics to study
commodity futures markets. However, I still didn't know where I
would wind up for graduate school, and it took my grandmother's
not-so-subtle nudge to help me decide.

When Granddad died, Grandmother Lurene lost her husband, and
I lost one of my biggest supporters. So, while I was in high school, my

grandmother filled that void, and we became extremely close. She was a remarkable woman—a true intellectual and savvy businesswoman who studied the markets closely. We discovered that we were kindred souls.

In fact, for my sixteenth birthday, she gave me a subscription to *Atlantic* magazine, insisting that I read it cover-to-cover every month—which I did, followed by intense discussions with her about the articles. That was Grandmother Lurene.

Later, when I was an agricultural economics professor at Ohio State, Grandmother Lurene sometimes would come to campus and knock on the various professors' doors. She'd then sit and interrogate them for an hour at a time. Afterward, my colleagues would come up to me to say what an "amazing woman" she was, adding that it seemed like they were being grilled for their PhD defense all over again.

In her later years, Grandmother Lurene spent her winters in Corpus Christie, Texas, with her daughter, Joyce, and Joyce's husband, a sociology professor. Her idea of fun was hanging out in the library, reading economics journals, and sitting in on classes. So, it's no surprise that Grandmother Lurene and I connected on an intellectual level. She visualized me as a professor before anyone else did and smoothed things over with my dad when I decided to choose academics over farming.

With her prodding, I applied to three graduate schools during my senior year—Oklahoma State, Texas A&M, and Purdue. She accompanied me over spring break to Oklahoma State and Texas A&M, and after those two visits, I settled on Texas A&M. The school had good weather and pretty southern girls. What else would I want from graduate school? I was so convinced Texas was my future that I wasn't even planning to visit Purdue. Still, Grandmother Lurene insisted I cover my bases. She was fond of saying, "If you have a plan, you have to stick with it."

One day after spring break, my mom showed up at my apartment in Ames unannounced, carrying an airplane ticket purchased by my grandmother. With it was a note, written in Grandmother's perfect, cursive handwriting, saying I would visit Purdue as planned, whether I liked it or not.

Off I went to Purdue, nonplussed about the trip. But not long after stepping off the airplane in West Lafayette, Indiana, I knew this was where I was supposed to be. During my visit to Purdue, I met several well-known names in agricultural economics, and when I became a graduate student there, some took me under their wing.

One was Professor J. William "Bill" Uhrig, a legend among Indiana farmers. At that time, I planned to return home to farm after getting my master's degree, but Bill pushed me to go on for my PhD. He also became my first professional mentor. So much of consequence in my life happened at Purdue. I changed my political views to become a Reagan Republican (much to my Grandmother Lurene's dismay), got married, had my first child, and decided to enter academics as a career.

I also nearly sabotaged all this when I tried my hand at speculation.

Professor Uhrig was quite the entrepreneur, and I kept hearing from other grad students how much money he had made in the futures market. If Bill—my advisor—could do it, I thought I could also succeed. But I needed capital to get started—money that a poorly paid graduate student like me did not have.

About this time, I received a tip from a graduate student who was also my basketball-playing buddy. I'll call this friend "Julius," after Dr. J, our favorite NBA player.

Julius had taken out a student loan, put all his money into the stock market, and had been making bank at the start of the great 1980s bull market in stocks. It's hard for students to imagine today, but if you were approved for a student loan back in the day, you'd receive the check at your home address. There was no real account-ability about whether you spent it on school expenses. I decided this was the perfect way to get my stake for trading in the futures market. I applied for the maximum amount of $3,000. With the help of a friend from my undergraduate days at Iowa State—a guy who had become a futures broker—I opened my first futures account.

I timed the opening of my futures trading account with the end of the spring semester of 1981. As soon as classes wrapped in May, I was up and running. I was supposed to be doing research for Professor Uhrig that summer, but I'm sure he knew I was trading. In fact, I don't think it bothered him at all that I spent most of my time analyzing the markets and trading. It turned out to be a *very* educational experience. By early August of 1981, I had made a couple of thousand dollars in the corn and soybean futures markets. A classic moment of maximum danger for a novice trader.

While I thought I was playing it smart and being careful, I learned a costly lesson. My specific mistake was the same thing that had plagued my dad and other farmers—"looking out your back door."

The spring of '81 had been extremely wet. When I returned home to Bagley, Iowa, in early August, I saw bare spots in many fields where ponds drowned out small corn and soybean plants earlier in the summer.

Many analysts were still expecting a good corn crop, but after studying the fields, I was convinced they were wrong. During the visit home, my dad and his farmer friends confirmed my hunch because they all kept moaning about the flooding and its impact on yields. They had looked out their back doors and proclaimed the corn crop less than stellar.

What I failed to consider was farmers' strong pessimistic bias in assessing their grain yields during the growing season. Farmers find it can be costly to be over-optimistic about yields, so they over-correct and are typically overly pessimistic. This has been well documented by research.[1]

I mistakenly took their pessimism as gospel, viewing the information about wet fields like someone who had a hot stock tip or a tip on a horse race. So, when I returned to Purdue, I closed out all of my existing positions in the grain futures market, ignoring the risk management rule I had followed all summer—"risk not thy whole wad." I put all my money toward going long (buying) several December 1981 corn futures contracts just before the important USDA August crop report was due to be released. I can't remember the exact number of contracts I bought, but it was around ten—definitely more than I had ever owned.

Because futures positions are purchased on margin, I was leveraged to the hilt. Purchasing "on margin" means you only put up a fraction of the face value of a contract to buy it. This is one of the secrets to making or losing a lot of money in the futures market. Although sentiment in the market was that the crop would be good, I expected a bad crop, pushing prices much higher. Buy low. Sell high. Make lots of money fast.

The USDA crop production report was released on Wednesday, August 12, 1981, a date seared into my memory forever. I can still picture myself standing on the seventh floor of the Krannert Building at Purdue, where part of the agricultural economics department was (and still is) located.

There was a ticker machine on the seventh floor, just like the one we had in the Bagley grain elevator. The device would spit out a continuous roll of yellow paper, and somebody would cut the paper and clip it to the wall every half hour or so. Anyone interested in the commodity markets would gather at this wall, studying the numbers. I was so confident and borderline cocky that I wondered whether I could make a career as a speculator and strike it rich. Maybe I didn't even need graduate school.

CLACK, CLACK, CLACK, CLACK. The paper spilled out of the machine as the USDA released the crop report at 3 p.m. EST sharp. I had this thing nailed. The report would show the crop was poor, prices would skyrocket, and I could sell high, making a bundle.

I was dead wrong.

The USDA reported that the crop would be huge, which meant prices would plummet, and I was screwed. I am sure my face dropped as a group assembled around the ticker machine. I was in shock.

Not only had I fallen for the "looking out your back door" mistake, but I also ignored another common piece of grain market wisdom— "Rain makes grain." Corn requires a lot of moisture. Even though heavy rains had created ponding, it wasn't enough to severely delay planting, and the crops growing on well-drained hills had more than made up for any dents in yield in the valleys.

Corn futures prices were going to crash, but there was a built-in circuit breaker in the grain futures market to prevent it from plunging too dramatically. The exchanges establish price limits for each market, which is the largest daily allowable move in prices. The limit for the corn futures market at that time was a price change up or down of 10 cents per bushel in one day. Trading can still occur when prices move to the limit, but in extreme situations, the markets can enter "lock limit" conditions. This scenario happens when news is so bullish or bearish that no one will trade at the limit price. The market is locked at the limit with no trading, and the market effectively shuts down.

I quickly calculated that a single lock-limit-down day would wipe out my account. For every 10-cent per bushel drop in the corn price, I would lose around $5,000. Therefore, the $3,000 that I had so carefully grown to roughly $5,000 over the summer would disappear in one day.

But it gets worse. There was talk of three straight lock-limit-down days—which means my losses could be catastrophic if I didn't get out of the market soon.

That Wednesday night was a bad dream, and my girlfriend (later wife) reminded me that I was an idiot, as if I needed to be told. I didn't get a wink of sleep. As a grad student, I lived month-to-month on my research assistantship check. I could pay off the original student loan of $3,000 over time, but I had no way to cover losses above that. If I had any hope of remaining a graduate student, I would have to beg my parents for money or get a job. I loved graduate school; they were some of the best days of my life, and the prospect of trading my way out of school was devastating. It was heart-wrenching.

If I got out of the market quickly, I could stem my losses, but unfortunately, when the market is locked at the price limit, there is no trading. Without trading, I had no way of maneuvering out of my situation. As predicted, when the corn futures market opened the next morning, the market was locked down at the daily allowable price limit of 10 cents, and it stayed that way the entire trading session.

It was over. I had flushed all my hard-earned trading profits and student loan money down the drain. Five grand vanished. Poof! If Wednesday night had been bad, Thursday night was even worse, and I was faced with the prospect of a similar loss when the markets reopened on Friday. If I failed to get out of the market before the price moved down another 10 cents to trigger a second lock-limit, I would lose another $5,000—big money for a poor graduate student in 1981.

The following morning, I prepared to accept my doom. But I had forgotten during all the stress that I had placed what is known as "sell stop orders" when I originally put on the December corn futures position. This option is a way to limit losses when you trade.

If you buy, as I did, you can also put in automatic orders to sell when the market hits a certain loss level. Shortly after the markets opened, and corn futures prices had resumed their downward spiral, I got a call from my broker friend telling me that I had gotten out of the market. I could scarcely believe what I was hearing!

In what I still regard as providential intervention, the December 1981 corn contract went up for a brief time—possibly as little as thirty seconds—shortly after the open. During those few seconds, prices actually rose by a penny and my stop orders were somehow filled. Even though my few orders were a drop of water in a tsunami of other sell orders, I managed to sell my contracts. I was free. It was yet another miracle, preventing a financially fatal crackup.[2]

After selling, I came out with a measly $50 or so left in my account, but it could have been much worse. I still had to pay off my $3,000 student loan that I had blown in one day, but I did it. After graduating, my wife and I took five years to pay off that loan. Every payment reminded me how close I had come to a financial disaster that would have irrevocably changed my life.

Although I learned an important lesson, it dawned on me that I had neglected to pay attention to the key factors determining a healthy crop. With corn and soybeans, you want to begin the season with adequate subsoil moisture; you don't want it to be bone dry when you start to plant—but you also don't want it to be so wet that it delays planting. The ideal planting time is from late April to early May.

From the time of planting through June, you want adequate moisture plus higher-than-average temperatures because that's the vegetative growth stage, when the green matter explodes. In other words, you want conditions to be a bit like a greenhouse—warm and humid.

A corn plant is a giant photosynthesis factory, converting sunlight into starches in the form of corn kernels. The bigger the leaves, the greater the photosynthesis production. Therefore, you want a plant that is as tall as possible with leaves as big as possible. July and August should be cooler than usual for ideal conditions. When the temps are cool during these months, the plant is not stressed during its reproductive phase, the green life of the corn is extended, and the plant continues to add weight to the ears.

These are all crucial, but precipitation in July is the most important factor in determining corn yields. The golden number is four inches. If fields receive at least four inches of rain in July, crops generally will prosper.[3]

I enjoy telling my students about my trading disaster. When I show them the precipitation charts for the three big Corn Belt states during 1981, they can see that rainfall in July was about as ideal as it comes. That month, Indiana received 4.94 inches of rain, Iowa saw 4.92 inches, and Illinois got a little bit more—6.46 inches.

No wonder it was a big crop.

Ironically, my disaster in '81 came only a few months before another college student, Terry Duffy, was in the process of losing even bigger in the futures market—$130,000. With Vince Schreiber's help, Terry Duffy survived and even thrived (see Chapter 3). But I realized I did not have the stomach to be a trader. I was just a small-time trader operating with a small amount of money—although it was a massive amount for a graduate student. Imagine the stress of operating with a large chunk of money, as Duffy was. Through this debacle, I received my first lesson on how risky speculating can be. I also learned the importance of good, solid information in the futures market because I had traded on the flimsiest of hunches.

Markets are powerful engines, and the fuel that powers them is information. Without good data, you're trading blind, like a snowmobiler racing through a snowstorm. While zipping down that country road, I never saw the snow-covered obstacle in my path. I crashed, was knocked out, and somehow managed to survive without a broken neck. It was the same with my first attempt at trading. I never saw the crop report coming, and it hit me like a two-ton truck. I came out of both crackups with significant bruising, but I survived. Somehow.

It took me almost thirty years to work up the courage to speculate again in the corn futures market. But this disaster sent me on an intellectual journey that I am still pursuing today. After that experience, I decided to better understand the markets and the role of information and began to question whether it was possible to beat the market in the long run. This quest also led me to the research of one of the three men who would become my academic heroes—Holbrook Working.

Chapter 6
The Engine of Efficiency

My dad was a gearhead farmer, a confirmed speed freak who preferred his engines large and loud. He raced go-karts semi-professionally in the 1950s and continued to dabble in it for a while when I was a toddler. One of my earliest memories, when I was around two, is of my dad lugging his go-kart into the back of his old pickup truck after a race. Given his love of speed, it seems poetic that this was an early memory.

Because Dad enjoyed his toys, we were always surrounded by go-karts, snowmobiles, and minibikes, which met our insatiable need for speed during any season. When I was in third grade, he even created a small dirt racetrack on a piece of land next to our farmstead—land that conveniently served as part of our "acreage set aside" under government price support programs in those days. My buddy Jack Hunter and I would spend hours racing around that track. We lived in go-kart heaven.

My dad let me use an old, beat-up go-kart, but of course, it had a fast engine. Jack's dad, who also raced semi-professionally in his younger days, let Jack use his old go-kart. Both karts were painted red and evenly matched in terms of speed. At eight or nine, Jack and I became two excellent little racers, drifting through the corners like professional drivers, battling for position inches apart. We didn't wear helmets, but I don't remember ever flipping our go-karts as we accelerated to 30 or 40 miles per hour.

My dad also had a tricked-up truck, which he bought in the mid-1970s. He started farming in 1966, but in the early days, there wasn't a lot of money to spend on big luxury items. Grain prices skyrocketing in the 1970s changed all of that.

One of the things my dad spent his newfound bounty on was a brand-new 1974 blue Chevy pickup truck fitted with a 454 cubic inch engine—a monster engine—and mag wheels, the ones with chrome spokes.

My dad's new toy also had chrome side pipes that snaked along the bottom near the floorboards, angling away near the back tires. What's more, he equipped the engine with a massive Holly four-barrel carburetor. The engine's high-compression heads made the WHOOOOOM sound you normally hear from tricked-out cars.

He did everything a street racer would do to create a hot muscle car. No wonder his nickname around town was "Diamond Jim."

However, it was still a farm truck. It carried a tank to fuel tractors and combines, was always covered in dirt, and hauled scoop shovels and other tools. But it was dangerously fast for a farm truck, and my dad would drive that thing 80 miles per hour down gravel roads. When it was dry, you could see a fast-moving dust cloud on the horizon. When Jack Hunter and I saw that dust storm appear, it was time to stop slacking off and hustle back to work.

My dad's buddies were as crazy as he was, including a somewhat mysterious farmer north of Bagley named Dean Perkins. My dad called him Perko. No one was quite sure where he got his money, but he always drove very nice cars. One was a Lincoln Mark III, a real 1970s cruiser. Perko also loved going to the sprint car races at Knoxville, often driving us all in his Lincoln. I would sit in the back seat and watch the speedometer, amazed it would rarely dip below 100.

Another of my dad's buddies was our veterinarian, Leo Klodt, from nearby Perry, Iowa. In those days, vets would visit hog farms with a pickup truck full of all their instruments and supplies. Leo had a white, four-wheel-drive pickup with an enormous V-8 engine under the hood that looked like it was straight off the drag strip. My dad and Leo would often drag race in their trucks south of Bagley, smoking the tires as they hit the gas.

My dad was not the only one who raced that '74 Chevy pickup truck. Jack and I also took it for spins. We would sneak out at night in high school and have great fun beating guys in polished and waxed muscle cars with our dirty farm truck.

I'm sure my dad probably turned a blind eye while hiding a grin. It was hard to sneak anywhere in a vehicle that made so much noise.

True to form, when Jack and I borrowed this truck, we couldn't resist a bit of mischief. We had learned (probably from my dad) that when rolling down the highway, you could create a spectacle to behold if you followed a specific series of steps in mid-motion:

1. Put the truck into neutral.
2. Shut off the engine.
3. Wait a few seconds.
4. Floor the accelerator.
5. Turn it back on.

This series of steps would flood the engine, and when that extra fuel hit the spark plugs…KABOOOOOOM!

Flames would shoot about four feet from the chrome side pipes, sounding like an explosion. At night, they would light up the area in all directions.

One warm spring night, Jack and I were cruising around while I was behind the wheel when we spotted one of our high school buses moving about 50 miles per hour down the highway. When we pulled close, with our windows rolled down, we noticed it carried a girl's athletic team. Probably the softball or track team.

Jack and I smiled knowingly, each thinking the same thing.

I put the truck in neutral, turned off the ignition, and waited a few seconds before flooring the accelerator and turning on the engine.

KABOOOOOOM!

A collective scream erupted from the bus as the girls watched our flames combust several feet from either side of my truck. The team probably thought the vehicle next to them had exploded. Jubilant, we took off, racing ahead of the bus before anyone could figure out who it was or what had happened.

Yes, we were almost as insane as Diamond Jim, Perko, and Leo, the vet.

Almost.

It goes without saying that I inherited my dad's race-mad, competitive streak. It's this spirit that convinced me I could beat the markets as a graduate student and make a fortune trading commodities. However, in the futures market, I found myself competing against an extremely powerful economic engine, and yet I still thought I was smart enough to beat it.

I came out of that bruising experience convinced that the market's economic engine was too efficient for *anyone* to beat in the long run. I converted to the Efficient Market Hypothesis, EMH, which maintains that the market works so perfectly that it's nearly impossible to beat consistently over time.

This revolutionary concept began to spread rapidly in the 1970s, thanks partly to Burton G. Malkiel's landmark book, *A Random Walk Down Wall Street*, published in 1973. The book points out that because it's challenging to beat the stock market consistently, a better investment strategy is to "buy and hold." With this approach, people invest in "index" funds that mimic the overall behavior of the stock market. The idea is to hold on to them through the market's ups and downs, watching them grow over the long run. Investors are advised not to obsess over short-term price movements because they're in it for the long haul.[1]

Before this revolution in thought, most believed a sound investment strategy was built on the efforts of an active manager, keeping an eye on short-term price movements, and buying and selling constantly, trying to stay a step ahead of the market. People tried to beat the stock market's average returns, which you get by buying and holding an index fund. But with this kind of drag race, the market's engine is just too big and efficient.

Investors looking for short-term gains will inevitably lose because the market, as a whole, is always faster in reacting to new information than any individual investor. This principle applies to both the commodity futures markets and the stock market. When investor John Bogle learned of the idea of an efficient market in the early 1970s, he established the first index fund. His goal was not to try to beat the market; instead, he aimed to keep pace with the stock market. He started Vanguard, now the world's largest mutual fund operator.[2]

Proponents of the EMH believe the market is so competitive that when a piece of valuable information appears, people will trade on it instantly, and the price will reflect it. For instance, when the USDA crop report came out in August 1981, prices plummeted immediately when the futures market opened. Back then, I couldn't move fast enough to get out of the market. As a result, I lost virtually everything.

I discovered Malkiel's book soon after my trading debacle in graduate school, and the strategy that he touted more or less became conventional wisdom. Around the same time, I also discovered the research of Holbrook Working, who laid the foundation for the Efficient Market Hypothesis and would become one of my intellectual heroes. Working and his brother, Elmer, were farm boys like myself, and they wrote some of the most famous early papers on what today we call econometrics—statistical analysis applied to economic data.

Somewhere along the way, after moving from the University of Minnesota to the Food Research Institute at Stanford in 1925, Working became fascinated with agricultural futures markets. But he didn't lock himself away in an ivory tower. Instead, he did research on the ground, in the thick of the trading. At least once a year, he took a train from Palo Alto, California, to Chicago, where he watched traders at work. He talked with speculators and hedgers on the floor of the Chicago Board of Trade (CBOT) and interviewed people in businesses that operated in the grain futures markets.

Then, in 1934, Working published a landmark article in the *Journal of the American Statistical Association*—the top statistics journal in the United States. This article pointed out a strange similarity between what he called "random difference charts" and the charts showing price movements in the grain futures market.

Working created his random difference charts by arbitrarily selecting numbers from special tables. This process was the equivalent of choosing numbers based on flipping a coin—purely random. When he showed these random difference charts to futures traders at the CBOT, people were amazed at their remarkable similarity to charts that track changes in grain prices. It was the first clue that the price movements in the futures market were random—or unpredictable.[3]

I ask my students to recreate what Working did, giving each of them a penny and a piece of graph paper, saying we're going to simulate a grain futures market for soybeans or corn by flipping coins. If the coin is heads, their chart should go up one box on the graph paper —with each box representing a price change. If tails, their chart should go down one box. After thirty coin flips, I ask them to analyze any patterns.

"Tell me how this pattern shows you how to predict price changes," I say.

My students make intriguing arguments about how their patterns predict future price changes. But one bright student will inevitably speak up and say, "Hey, this doesn't make sense! Our charts can't predict *anything* because we created them by flipping a coin. No matter what the patterns show, that doesn't change the fact that every coin flip is 50-50."

Bingo! Because the price changes on their charts are purely random, they are unpredictable.

Working was the first to discover that price changes in the futures market are remarkably close to random, which means it is challenging to predict price movements with any consistent level of accuracy. This discovery was the precursor to the Efficient Market Hypothesis, which has to rank as one of the top revelations in economic science of the past century. The tragedy is that even though Working made these findings as early as the 1930s, his peers largely ignored him, giving him next to no credit.

Much later, in the 1960s, financial economists also began to see that changes in stock market prices were very close to random. But even then, people overlooked Working's research. For instance, in 1964, an MIT economist named Paul Cootner edited a famous book called *The Random Character of Stock Market Prices*. This publication was a collection of the most important papers up to that point on what is called the Random Walk Model—the idea that market prices follow a random pattern. When Working discovered that the soon-to-be-published book would not include any of his papers, he protested. Eventually, the book included a relatively obscure paper by Working, but none of his pioneering work.[4]

The theory behind the randomness of price changes is called the Random Walk Model because researchers thought that the erratic, up-and-down price movements resembled a drunk weaving his way home from a pub. One of the leading financial economists working in this area was Eugene Fama of the University of Chicago, who started studying random price changes in the stock market as part of his PhD dissertation in the 1960s. As his career unfolded, Fama continued to explore the subject, and he coined the term Efficient Market Hypothesis in a famous 1970 article. He also received a Nobel Prize in 2013 for his work on the EMH.[5]

Fama is well deserving of the honor, which he shared with Robert J. Shiller and Lars Peter Hansen. There's no question about that. However, I argue that, once again, Working was overlooked. His work was so foundational and essential that it deserved a Nobel Prize while he was alive. (He died in 1985.)

From the 1930s through the 1950s, Working labored on the same research as Fama and others in later years—only he was working in commodity futures, not the stock market. He also didn't use the same terminology as the financial economists in the 1960s.

For instance, Working talked about a "perfect market," but it was basically identical to today's famous concept of an "efficient market." People back in the '30s would look at his research, shake their heads, and say, "I don't know what in the world this guy is talking about." He was that far ahead of his time.

It's tempting to think people ignored Working because he toiled in the relatively obscure commodity futures markets. Futures markets were only for agricultural commodities back then. It wasn't until the 1970s that futures markets dramatically expanded to include currencies and non-ag commodities such as crude oil. However, that doesn't explain why Working was ignored. After all, many of his papers appeared in the *American Economic Review*, the top economics journal in the world, so how could other researchers overlook them?

Ironically, some well-deserved but late recognition has gone to the French mathematician Louis Bachelier. In work completed in 1900, Bachelier applied the random walk statistical method to the movement of stock prices. Still, his research went unrecognized because it appeared in his unpublished dissertation and was in French. His work went undiscovered until the late 1950s and early '60s, and now he has been given overdue recognition for his pioneering research.[6]

But not Working. In all fairness, the EMH should be called the Bachelier-Fama-Working Efficient Market Hypothesis. But life isn't fair.

Working was also known for exploring another crucial question facing commodity futures markets: How does the market ensure that we have enough grain to carry over from year-to-year? In a way, he was exploring the modern equivalent of the Biblical story of Joseph in Egypt.

As the right-hand man to Pharaoh, Joseph ensured grain was set aside during the years of plenty so food would be available during a famine. While Joseph made this happen in ancient Egypt, how does a modern market make it happen? Working discovered how a commodity market sends a signal so grain will be set aside during the years of plenty and stored for the lean years—what is now called the Supply of Storage Theory.[7]

Working's development of the Supply of Storage Theory and his work on the Efficient Market Hypothesis represent truly pioneering intellectual contributions to economics over the last century. He was far ahead of his time, and when the rest of the economics world finally caught up with him, he was a forgotten man. From what I understand, sadly, he was embittered by the lack of credit he so richly deserved.

As I said, in my later years in graduate school, my study of the Efficient Market Hypothesis led me to believe that you just can't beat the market in futures trading. But my dad never bought into this theory. As part of his perpetual effort to beat the market, he subscribed to a prominent market advisory newsletter, *Pro Farmer*.

Every Saturday morning, he'd go to the post office and pick up his copy, and we all read it, including Grandma Lurene and me. He also dialed up a daily update—a service that provided advice about when farmers should sell their corn, soybeans, or hogs. My dad spent thousands of dollars each year for advice like this, but did it pay off? At the time, no one knew if the services were worth it.

After my conversion to the Gospel of the Efficient Market Hypothesis, I decided this was fertile ground for research and wanted to dig deeper into these advisory companies. So, when I joined the Ohio State University faculty in 1985, I pitched the idea of tracking farm market advisory services. But I didn't progress very far until I did my sabbatical at the University of Illinois during the 1993-1994 academic year. That's when I met Darrel Good, a professor in the office next to mine during my sabbatical year. Talk about a lucky break!

Darrel and I immediately clicked and decided we would track the best-known commodity market advisory services, around 25 in total. We would become paying customers with each of the services, installing a satellite dish and printing out all of their market advice in real-time every day.

When I returned to Ohio State, Darrel continued our joint project between both universities. And when the University of Illinois lured me away from Ohio State in 1997, the project came with me. Darrel and I were like a two-person *Consumer Reports*. Only we were looking at the viability of farm market advisory services rather than appliances and gadgets. We didn't invest real money; everything we did was hypothetical, seeing what would have happened if we had followed the various advisory services' advice for marketing corn, soybeans, and wheat.

Our project blossomed throughout the late 1990s and early 2000s. We eventually hired a full-time person to run what became known as the Agricultural Market Advisory Service Project or AgMAS. With total funding of over a million dollars in grants, AgMAS collected around 30,000 daily observations over the project's life.

Every day, we would hypothetically follow the advice of these top market advisory services—kind of like playing fantasy football, except this project was fantasy farming. We compared these corn, soybean, and wheat marketing strategies to our benchmark strategy. With the benchmark strategy, we didn't try to beat the market; we sold the same small amount of grain daily, trying to meet the average market price.

In the futures market, Darrel Good and I discovered the same thing that had been discovered in stock mutual fund studies. Numerous studies have shown that actively-managed mutual funds have a difficult time consistently beating the stock market over time.[8] Similarly, of the 25 or so market advisory services we studied, only one of them had a track record of systematically beating the market—and this advisor did it by having farmers take extremely risky moves.[9]

As you might guess, apart from the one firm, we made plenty of enemies among the market advisors. One of our biggest was Richard Brock, whose service fell in the middle of the pack among the 25 services. Ironically, my dad knew Brock, and I met him at a seminar during my undergrad years. Brock advised me to get my master's at Purdue, one of his alma maters.

In 2000, Brock led a group of advisors threatening to sue us to shut down the AgMAS Project, one of the more unpleasant experiences of my entire professional career. The advisors accused us of all forms of bias, and we had to go to a meeting with these guys in Chicago, where they yelled at us for two hours. We had our university lawyers with us and just sat there, listening.

They challenged our benchmark strategy—the one in which we sold a little bit of grain every day. To mollify them, we did alter our strategy some.[10] The change made the lawsuit threat go away, but ironically it didn't change the basic results at all. Although the advisors hated our project, farmers loved it because it gave them a tool with which to evaluate these advisory services.

Despite its popularity, we finally shut down the AgMAS project after the 2004 crop year because it was too labor-intensive and expensive. It took almost all my research time because we were collecting "primary data" rather than obtaining data from another source. Farmers have approached me at meetings for years, asking if we would update our AgMAS project results.

But here's another irony. As Darrel and I constantly discussed and analyzed the data together, I slowly discovered that he was not a true believer in the Efficient Market Hypothesis. Even though the AgMAS project seemed to back up the EMH, my partner in the research effort was chipping away at my total faith in the efficient market.

Darrel influenced me, as did research in the 1990s that began to poke holes in the Efficient Market Hypothesis. Behavioral science literature showed anomalies in the market that smart individuals and large companies with superior information could exploit.

As a result, my views evolved, and I no longer believed that *no one* could beat the market. Now I think a small minority of intelligent traders can consistently do so. After all, one of those 25 advisors—Dan Basse of AgResource—had succeeded, so I couldn't say it was impossible. Even Working did not believe in a perfectly efficient market, and the debate over how efficiently the market processes information continues to rage today.

It comes down to acting on superior data. When I lost big in the market during graduate school (see Chapter 5), I was operating with incredibly flawed information. But I would eventually discover what kind of information was truly valuable. What's more, my journey of discovery began in the most improbable of ways—by towing an "iceberg" around a lake at Iowa State University.

Chapter 7
Towing Icebergs

Three undergraduate students, myself included, gathered in the office of a young, dynamic doctoral student in economics at Iowa State University. He was a wildly popular teacher from the high plains near Dalhart, Texas, so I'll call him "Tex."

Tex knew how to talk a blue streak in his twangy Texas accent, and my friends in the Iowa State agribusiness program loved hanging at his office. He drank Lone Star beer, had a biting sense of humor, and there wasn't a topic he didn't spout off about.

We soaked it all in, like undergraduate sponges—and with about as much sense as a sponge. After all, we were about to embark on what had to be one of the dumbest ideas of my life. It very nearly caused a riot on the campus of Iowa State University.

It was the fall of 1977, and I was a sophomore, which may explain the sophomoric behavior that was about to unfold. Joining me in Tex's office was a friend I will call Rickie, a "city boy" who happened to hail from a small town in Iowa. Because he didn't live on a farm, he qualified as a city boy to me. The other companion involved in our prank was Bob (not his real name), who was actually from a big city—Chicago. We were all heavily involved in the undergraduate agribusiness club advised by Tex.

On this day that will live in infamy, Tex slammed the student newspaper on his desk and exclaimed, "This is the dumbest f*%#ing idea I have ever encountered! *This deserves to be mocked!*"

"This" was a news item about plans to tow icebergs from Antarctica to Saudi Arabia as a way to capture the melting water, using it for irrigation to make the desert bloom. Not only that, but Iowa State was about to host an international conference where this subject would be front and center—the First International Conference on Iceberg Utilization.

For all I know, the idea had merit. But to a smart-aleck undergraduate in 1977, it sounded like one of the most ridiculous proposals ever. A *New York Times* article from October 1977 said the idea had been around for decades. Yet, no one had devised an idea of how "to transport a large iceberg, perhaps a mile wide and several miles long, over thousands of miles of oceans through storms and an equatorial sun."[1]

Even today, the idea continues to hang around. A June 5, 2019, article in *Bloomberg Businessweek* carried the banner, "Towing an Iceberg: One Captain's Plan to Bring Drinking Water to 4 Million People." In this case, a ship captain named Nicholas Sloane hoped to find a way to tow an iceberg to South Africa and convert it into municipal water.

According to *Bloomberg Businessweek*, "Sloane has already assembled a team of glaciologists, oceanographers, and engineers. He's also secured a group of financiers to fund the pioneer tow, which he calls the Southern Ice Project. The expected cost is more than $200 million, much of it to be put up by two South African banks and Water Vision AG, a Swiss water technology and infrastructure company."[2]

With those resources behind him, maybe Captain Sloane will finally prove it can be done. But in 1977, we were certain it was an idea whose time had come—to be lampooned.

The First International Conference on Iceberg Utilization at Iowa State was slated to begin on October 2, 1977. It attracted a host of illustrious dignitaries from the Middle East, including the principal sponsor, Crown Prince Mohammed al-Faisal of the Kingdom of Saudi Arabia.

The event was to be held at Iowa State's Memorial Union. As our undergraduate minds went to work, it dawned on us that directly in front of the Union was scenic Lake LaVerne, which was really just an oversized pond, best known for the lovely pair of swans in residence—Lancelot and Elaine.

I can't recall which of us concocted the insane idea of creating a Styrofoam iceberg and using a canoe to tow it around Lake LaVerne while the conference started. My buddy Rickie knew a guy who finagled a huge Styrofoam sheet. At the same time, Bob commandeered a canoe from the recreation center. We created a floating base, a pontoon on which the Styrofoam iceberg could sit. We carefully cut out the Styrofoam to resemble the jagged shape of a real iceberg. It was maybe 5 feet high at the peak.

On one side of our fake iceberg, we wrote in large letters, "The Real ISU Iceberg—Saudi Arabia or Bust." While most found this funny, the statement on the other side was truly cringeworthy—"Tel Aviv or Bust!" I am embarrassed to admit it, but we were so ignorant it didn't even occur to us that Tel Aviv was in Israel, not Saudi Arabia.

Coming just a few years after the Yom Kippur War in the Middle East, it is hard to imagine saying anything more incendiary. Somehow, even worse, Bob and I, who volunteered to paddle the canoe, decided we should dress as faux sheikhs. Talk about throwing gasoline on the flames! That's how dumb we were.

To top everything off, I wore my high school football jersey as part of my costume, since it was mostly white. My school's lettering on the shoulders made it ridiculously easy to identify me. Our other partner in crime, Rickie, stayed in the background, so I always wondered whether he sensed this would go badly wrong.

The start of the conference on October 2 was a gorgeous fall day—an ideal afternoon for our *Animal House* escapade. Bob and I paddled around the pond, pulling our iceberg behind us as dignitaries began to arrive for the conference shortly after lunch. The Union had a grand ballroom with a huge west window facing Lake LaVerne, which fully displayed our antics. Numerous Mercedes with dark-tinted windows arrived at the Union, and dignitaries would step out, snap a few photographs of us, and then enter the conference flanked by their security detail.

We towed our iceberg for several hours and enjoyed paddling around the lake in the beautiful sunshine. Several of our friends came by to laugh and shout something to the effect that we were crazy. Little did we know!

Around 4 p.m., word reached us that someone had alerted a group of Middle Eastern students, who were rightfully offended and assembling to confront us. I suspect they had a strong motivation to teach us a lesson. Meanwhile, someone had also alerted my Agribusiness and Block and Bridle Club friends, many of whom were country boys and rednecks such as myself, and they were heading to the Union for a showdown.

It was like something out of a movie (*West Side Story* without the finger snapping) as we watched from our canoe. Maybe a dozen or so Middle Eastern students moved through the central campus. Meanwhile, the aggies were also amassing. The two sides converged at the north edge of Lake LaVerne in the area where Bob and I had just exited our canoe.

Immediately, there was a lot of yelling, cursing, and pushing. I could not always tell what the Middle Eastern students said, but it was obvious they intended to beat the hell out of Rickie and me. Our aggie buddies were just as intent on protecting us. To this day, we owe a big apology to those international students, who were understandably outraged at our prank.

We were only a few seconds from an all-out brawl when several Ames police cars, sirens blaring, screeched to a halt where this was all taking place. At about the same time, the local TV station also arrived. The police separated everybody, instructing them to back away and leave. No arrests were made, and both sides somehow quickly melted away.

The cops told Bob and me to get our stuff and to, in no uncertain terms, get the *you-know-what* out of there. But before we left, we were interviewed by the local TV reporter. This, of course, only made us feel like we were even bigger campus celebrities. To top it off, there was a party that night somewhere to celebrate, and Bob and I were treated like heroes.

A little later, back home in Bagley, Iowa, my mom was lying in bed watching the 10 o'clock news when she noticed a short bit about the near riot at Iowa State earlier in the day.

"Jim, will you look at what those idiot students did at Iowa State!" my mom called to my father.

Then, deathly silence...followed by, "OH MY GOSH, JIM, IT'S SCOTT!"

I was on the TV screen in living color, caught red-handed in the thick of things.

Back in Ames, the aggies applauded Bob and me because we had pulled off the prank of the year, and it had impacted an international conference at Iowa State. In our febrile minds, we thought that was the end of it. But it wasn't. The following day, I was heading for class when Bob rushed up to me, breathless and wide-eyed.

"Irwin! Dean Thompson wants to see us! *Now!*"

Professor Louis Thompson, associate dean for undergraduate programs at Iowa State, was a name that struck visceral fear in ag students. Rumor had it that he was a World War II veteran *and* a Marine drill sergeant. Everyone was scared of him. *Everyone.*

The first thing burning through my brain was that we would get expelled. In those days, expulsion could happen as suddenly as a thunderstorm. I still remember being in an animal science class when the professor caught somebody cheating on a test. The professor swooped down, snatched the student's test paper, grabbed him by the back of the collar, and dragged him from class. We never saw that student again. Back in those days, there were no grievance committees, and no one had lawyers. If a professor or dean wanted you gone, you were gone.

Being summoned to Dean Thompson's office was akin to going to the office of Dean Vernon Wormer of *Animal House* fame. Dean Wormer was the one who famously said, "Fat, drunk, and stupid is no way to go through life, son."[3] Two of those descriptions fit me to a tee back in my undergrad years.

So, Bob and I trudged for Dean Thompson's office in Curtis Hall like dead men walking. By smartly staying out of the limelight, Rickie avoided our fate. As we approached the building, Tex was leaving Curtis Hall, having already been raked over the coals by the dean. His face was as white as chalk, and I remember him not saying a word as we passed. He just shook his head. He later said that Dean Thompson told him that he knew Bob and I were not acting on our own. So, he searched for the person he regarded as the real ringleader—Tex.

We tentatively entered Dean Thompson's office, pulling up chairs and taking our lowly seats before the dean's enormous mahogany desk. Then the Marine drill sergeant unleashed a torrent of screaming and cussing like I had never heard. It was the ass-chewing of a lifetime.

He said that we had deeply embarrassed the university and nearly caused an international incident (which was true) and that we deserved to be expelled on the spot (which was also probably true). Bob and I sat, sweat dripping as we were buffeted by the screaming. I had never heard of anybody getting this kind of reaming and surviving without getting kicked out of school.

Then, like the aftermath of a spring tornado, the dean slowly began to calm. His words became more measured, but his tone remained severe.

After letting us marinate in painful silence, Dean Thompson said, "Well...I've looked at the records for you two, and I know you're smart. You both get good grades, and that's the only reason you get to stay at Iowa State."

I blinked, astonished and grateful.

"But if either of you does anything like this again, even remotely close to this before you graduate, don't even bother coming to my office. Just leave campus."

Bob and I began to slink out of his office like death-row inmates who had just received a last-minute reprieve from the governor. But before I could make my escape, Dean Thompson called me back.

"Irwin!" He waved me over. "Irwin, come here!"

Now what? I turned, throat dry and eyes wide.

"I want to show you something," he said. "You're just too smart for these stunts. I want to get you interested in something like this."

Then Dean Thompson began to describe his research, which wasn't anything close to what I expected. He showed me the rough draft of his latest research paper on how to estimate the impact of weather on grain yields in the United States. Dean Thompson was an acclaimed agronomist and among the first to build what we now call crop weather models.

Even today, his research papers are cited regularly.[4] But on that October day in 1977, I had no idea that Dean Thompson was a global talent in this area, a foremost figure in predicting grain yields based on weather. When he handed me that research paper, I didn't realize how groundbreaking it would become. It was like he had given me the Ring of Power, and I had no clue.

"Irwin, you should think about doing more with your life," he told me, and I couldn't argue with that. Dean Thompson asked if I had ever thought about graduate school—which I hadn't.

Looking back at that encounter, I realize this was the first time *anyone* had seriously talked to me about the possibility of going to grad school. My father had always assumed I would return to the farm and the family business after my undergrad years, and so did I. What Dean Thompson did for me, I can never repay. Not only did he *not* expel me from college, but he also took the time to prompt me to think about something more significant, like graduate school. Thank you, Dean Thompson!

In an ironic twist of fate, Dean Thompson also showed me the first statistical regression outputs I had ever seen. I can still see the graph paper with hand-drawn data points and a line with a mathematical equation next to it. I had no idea what I was looking at, but rest assured, I was paying full attention to Dr. Thompson. Little did I know I would go on to generate tens of thousands of statistical regression outputs. Nor did I know the crop yield prediction research he described that fateful day would be an area that partly defined my professional research years later. Somehow, God had turned a near-flunk-out experience into something that would alter my professional career.

Later in life, I had this odd encounter with Dean Thompson tucked into the back of my mind, still fascinated by the idea of predicting crop yields based on weather. I dabbled with it as a professor at Ohio State. When I came to the University of Illinois in 1997, my colleague Darrel Good and I started building simple regression models predicting corn and soybean yields based on crop condition ratings.

Fast forward to a Friday afternoon in July 2004, while working at my desk in Mumford Hall on the campus of the University of Illinois. The secretary in the departmental front office rushed in at about 5 p.m. and told me there was a person in the hall who wanted to talk about grad school. I was the only professor available to speak with him at that time of day, so the fellow strolled in and told me he had a background in meteorology. He also said he had been a fraternity brother with a Kansas City grain trader and an Illinois grain broker, who recommended he find a way to apply his meteorological skills to the grain futures markets. That was why he was interested in talking about graduate school.

I was impressed by the young man. But throughout our conversation, I had the distinct impression I knew or had seen him somewhere. Only after going home did it dawn on me that he had been an on-air weatherman for one of the Champaign-Urbana stations, leaving just six months earlier.

His name was Mike Tannura, and I took him on as a graduate student as he pursued his master's degree in agricultural economics. When the two of us began brainstorming his thesis subject, I determined we needed to find a research topic that would be of interest to a meteorologist. Suddenly, my meeting with Dean Thompson came rushing back. We then read Dean Thompson's old papers, published from the 1960s to the '80s. I discovered the agronomy world had inexplicably lost interest in the type of models Thompson pioneered for predicting corn and soybean yields based on weather.

The literature had dubbed these weather models Thompson-style models, but they badly needed updating—which is precisely what Mike began to do. He was a fabulous student and a tremendous worker. Together, we stumbled onto a topic that perfectly fits a meteorologist. Thank you once again, Dean Thompson!

Our timing was brilliant, and Mike wrote one of the most impactful and phenomenal master theses I have ever supervised.[5] His models were useful for predicting crop yields based on weather and assessing the impact of genetically modified organisms (GMOs) in improving corn yields.

Monsanto, an agribusiness giant, had been claiming dramatic improvements in corn yields because of genetic technology. But Mike's models showed that the big increase in the yield of corn had more to do with ideal weather conditions than the use of GMOs.[6]

Monsanto assigned a scientist to write an article rebutting our results, but in the end, the company had to back down from its claims.[7] They also had to pull away from a massive ad campaign in which they claimed average corn yields would reach 300 bushels per acre by 2030, thanks to GMOs. This prediction was laughable then and still is.

While Mike was finishing his thesis research, he decided to strike out on his own and start a weather forecasting service for commodity traders—a startup company called T-Storm Weather. He is based in Chicago and has carved out a position as one of the world's best weather forecasters when applied to agriculture.

In 2009, Mike and I teamed up with Darrel Good to develop Yieldcast, a service that provides "real-time" forecasts of U.S. corn and soybean crop yields. Commodity traders and others subscribe to receive our projections, which have been invaluable for investment strategies. Since 2010, our track record in forecasting corn yields has been outstanding. Over the years, I believe we have had the best forecasting record for U.S. corn yields in the world.[8]

The irony wasn't lost on me that my earlier AgMAS research had highlighted the severe limitations of advisory services in helping farmers beat the futures market. But now here I was, providing crop forecasting information to help traders.

My re-discovery of Dean Thompson's models reinforced my modi-fied view of the Efficient Market Theory—that it was possible to beat the market, but only if you have the requisite skills and, most impor-tantly, the right information. The futures market is like a powerful, turbocharged racing engine, and information is the fuel that drives it. When trying to beat the market, you're up against a Ferrari, and without the correct information, you might as well be racing on the minibike that Harry and Lloyd rode in *Dumb and Dumber*.

Crop yield predictions became the flip side of my work in the world of commodities. On one side, I studied how the markets work and how policy decisions affect futures trading. On the other side, I worked with Mike and Darrel to provide yield forecasts that help manage people's speculative or hedging positions. And it all started with the germ of an idea planted by an outraged dean, who should have expelled me. Instead, he opened his vault of research and changed my world.

Shortly before Dean Thompson passed away a few years ago, I worked up the nerve to write him a letter. Although he was in his late 90s, he was still active and said he remembered me. Even in one's 90s, how could somebody forget the clown who had towed a Styrofoam iceberg around a lake in front of the Iowa State Union, almost causing an international incident?

Meanwhile, my partners in political incorrectness went on to great success in business, politics, and academics. As our bizarre undergrad-uate incident demonstrates, none of us could have seen the improb-able futures that awaited us after being spared the dean's executioner blade.

Life is unpredictable, and so is the market. For instance, I could never have foreseen the strange things happening in commodity futures markets in the early 2000s. If I had, I would have become wealthy.

During those years, people accused speculators of many things, most of them false. But this isn't to say that speculators are squeaky clean, and markets are impervious to manipulation. So, before we dive deeper into the speculation controversy, let us first explore how people can and have exploited the futures market, primarily through "corners."

I have spent much of my career defending the value of commodity futures markets and arguing for the importance of speculators in keeping the market running smoothly. However, because I defend speculators and free markets, some people accuse me of believing that the markets operate perfectly and that prices cannot be manipulated.

Let me be clear: *I do not believe that in the least.*

After all, I saw the level of cheating in something as wholesome as showing cattle at county and state fairs when I was an impressionable youth. If rule-breaking happens at the county fair, it will happen in Chicago. It's Chicago! Need I say more?

Photos

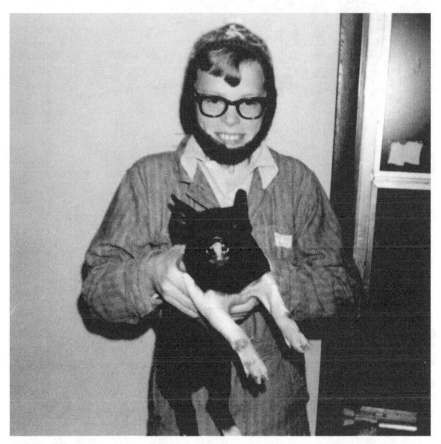

PIG KID—This photo screams "Iowa farm boy." I cannot get over that I am proudly holding a pig *inside* our farmhouse. I am probably ten years old, and the picture was taken around 1968, a year after I was walloped by the Pepsi truck. In fact, I believe the stocking hat is the same one I was wearing when I was hit. (In case you're wondering, I'm not sporting a Mennonite beard. My stocking hat goes under my chin.) *Source: Personal Photo Collection*

X MARKS THE PAIN—In the summer of 2022, I revisited the place where I nearly met my Maker. I'm in front of the now-shuttered grain elevator in Bagley, Iowa, in the spot where I was struck by a Pepsi truck at age nine. This time, I looked both ways. *Source: Personal Photo Collection*

A CLAMOROUS CLAN—My extended family gathers in the early 1960s for one of our legendary Sunday meals at my grandparents George and Lurene's house near Bagley, Iowa. Back row, from left: Grandmother Lurene Irwin (almost out of the picture); Granddad George Irwin; my dad, Jim Irwin (seated); Uncle Don Irwin (standing behind him); me (seated); Aunt Joyce Irwin (standing); my sister Cindy Irwin; Aunt Nicky Hanson; and Granddad Seton Hanson. Front row, from left: my sister Jan Irwin; Grandmother Gwen Hanson; and Uncle Bob Irwin. Source: *Personal Photo Collection*

HORSEPOWER—My Granddad George Irwin tries out our snowmobile and decides he'll stick to his beloved horses. This is the snowmobile I was riding when I almost killed myself driving into the back of a pickup truck in February 1974. Which makes me wonder…Maybe a horse is safer. *Source: Personal Photo Collection*

NATIONAL CHAMPION—Eddie Leavitt wins the 1975 National Sprint Car championship in Knoxville, Iowa, while driving the car co-owned by my dad's best friend, John Ricke. Leavitt won the Nationals again in 1976 (in a different car) and went on to become a Hall of Fame driver. For some reason, my parents allowed me, Jack Hunter, and two other friends to camp at the Nationals in August 1975 by ourselves. Four teenage boys hanging out with a wild sprint car crowd. What could possibly go wrong? *Source: Personal Photo Collection*

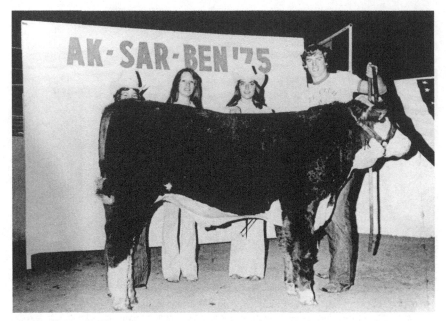

STEER JOCKEY—This is September 1975 just after the start of my senior year of high school, and I'm 17 years old. The steer was the Hereford breed champion at the AK-SAR-BEN '75 Stock Show in Omaha, Nebraska, the biggest win of my steer-showing days. The animal is not El Diablo. He never made it this far. *Source: Personal Photo Collection*

JACK ON THE GAS—My daredevil buddy, Jack Hunter, races his stock car, which bears our family farm name. On this July 1982 night at Stuart Raceway in Iowa, Jack had to drive without the front brakes, which was okay. Jack didn't know the meaning of the word "brake" anyway. *Source: Personal Photo Collection*

A MOTLEY CREW—Jack Hunter, in the New York Yankees jacket, stands at the center of his makeshift pit crew shortly after winning his street stock car race at Iowa's Stuart Raceway in July 1982. This was moments before an all-out riot began, compliments of the legendary Woodard Brothers. From left: my cousin Eric Hanson, me, Jack, the flagman Gail Miller, and Jeff Kempf, a friend of Eric's. *Source: Personal Photo Collection*

THE LAP OF A LIFETIME—My dad, "Diamond Jim" Irwin, is moments away from his first ride-along in a sprint car during August 2004—an event organized by Dave Blaney, a popular racer. My dad was limited to just one lap because of mechanical difficulties, but it was the lap he had always been waiting for. The intense look on his face was not unusual. *Source: Personal Photo Collection*

WINGING IT—If you compare this car with the Eddie Leavitt race car shown earlier, you can see how far sprint cars have come. I went to the Knoxville Nationals in August 2022 and came across this beauty. The large wings use aerodynamics to help the sprint cars go faster while at the same time preventing the cars from flipping over and over, as happened in the past, all too often with fatal results. *Source: Personal Photo Collection*

A FAREWELL TO FARMING—My parents, Jim and Pauline Irwin, stopped farming because grain prices went stagnant in the late 1990s and early 2000s. This is the day of their farm sale in February 2002. Mom and dad stand in front of their last big tractor, a monster four-wheel-drive Ford. It dwarfs the smaller equipment they had when starting out farming. *Source: Personal Photo Collection*

LOST AND FOUND—Speaking of past tractors, my nephew Reilly Vaughan spent thirteen years tracking down the John Deere 4020 that we used when I was growing up on the farm in the 1960s and '70s. Farm families can get very attached to their tractors. This one was originally sold at my mom and dad's farm auction in 2002; then it was sold another five or six times, but we eventually reclaimed it. My family, shown here, help me celebrate. From left: Stacey, me, Jayvon, Matt, Kate, and my wife Kim. *Source: Personal Photo Collection*

STILL CRAZY AFTER ALL THESE YEARS—Jack Hunter and I reunite on the Fourth of July in 2016. We're still standing—proof that God has a sense of humor. By the way, that's a sprint-car decoration we're gripping. *Source: Personal Photo Collection*

HE WHO HAS EARS, LET HIM HEAR—My family still owns some good cropland in Iowa, and my mom, Pauline Irwin, has proven to be a savvy crop marketer. We check the corn prospects during my visit back to Iowa in August 2022. I get my goofy side from her. *Source: Personal Photo Collection*

Chapter 8
Steer Crazy

I sprinted across the soybean field on my grandparents' farm just north of Bagley, running at top speed with a crazed steer bounding after me—a 1,200-pound monster I had accidentally let loose. I was in high school, much too young to die, and this creature was hunting me down.

To understand how I found myself in such a fix, you need to understand a bit about steers. I was a steer jockey for most of my youth, which meant that I showed prize steers, or "club calves," at county fairs, the Iowa State Fair, and a few large, prestigious events, such as something called Aksarben. That last one may sound like something out of Harry Potter, but it's "Nebraska" spelled backward, in case you're wondering who came up with such a crazy name.[1]

But in the world of showing prize steers, the real crazies were the parents who would do anything to win. Think Little League parents, only with extremely dangerous animals.

To understand the level of cheating and rule-bending in steer competitions, you must know how these events run. For all of you urban dwellers, a steer is a male of the cattle species castrated at a young age. (I'll pause to allow all male readers time to cringe.) Kids growing up in 4-H Clubs, such as myself, show these young steers yearly at the county fair—hence the name "club calves."

4-H has noble goals with these competitions. The events give kids the ideal opportunity to show initiative and responsibility by taking care of a young steer. The kids do it all, at least in theory, by feeding, exercising, and grooming their steers, as well as learning the ropes of showmanship. However, when you inject hypercompetitive parents (farm families are no different than anyone else), the outcome is often cheating. Some parents regard it as their life mission to win at the county or state fair.

Farmers typically purchase young steers at several months old, yet they still average about 400 pounds. The goal is to bulk them up like Arnold Schwarzenegger in *Pumping Iron*. In fact, steer competitions may be the closest thing to bodybuilding contests that you'll find in the ag world.

Kids learn to take special care of their steers, giving them healthy diets to maximize their meat. My dad set up a special place in our barn just for our club calves, and I faithfully walked them once a day during the summer. (My sisters also had 4-H steers, but somehow the daily chores seemed to fall more on me.) The goal is to break the steer, much like a young horse, so it will let you lead it anywhere within a couple of months.

To give the steer's coat a brilliant sheen, you wash it regularly and provide special feeds, bulking up the animal. In addition, the steer's hooves must be trimmed—a job better handled by specialists.

On show day at the fair, girls would come by the stalls with hairspray to tease the steer's tail, creating a big ball at the end. Or at least that was the winning style in my day.

Then there's the showmanship portion of the competition, which was always my favorite part. You must encourage the steer to pose with a sturdy stance, like bodybuilders flexing for the judges. I used a show stick to nudge mine into position, with all four legs spread squarely apart. Then I'd poke his belly so my steer would suck in his gut, making the animal look even more muscular and imposing.

Just imagine all the tricks bodybuilders use, and you'll find similar levels of trickery in club calf competitions. Years ago, the Iowa State Fair judges disqualified a Grand Champion steer after discovering the 4-H member's parents had wrapped piano wire around the animal's ribs. When the couple tightened the wire, the steer's rib cage was drawn in, making the animal appear trimmer and stronger. They'd cleverly concealed the wire amidst the steer's hair but evidently not well enough.

In another case, the 2002 Iowa State Fair Grand Champion steer named "Pickles" got disqualified because its "nose-print" failed to match that of the registered steer from the previous December's competition. In the words of state fair officials, the steer at the fair was a ringer. The whole thing ended up in the courts.[2]

In yet another example, "Mongo," the Grand Champion steer at the 2003 Illinois State Fair, was disqualified after the animal tested positive for a banned drug.[3] Farm families take club calf competition very seriously.

When I showed steers, the sale price for a winning animal could be as much as $5,000—big money in the 1970s. I had a high school friend who bought a brand-new Camaro after winning prize money at the Denver Western Open steer show. With the prestige that comes with raising a Grand Champion steer, there is a lot of incentive to cheat.

In my day, one of the tricks used to game the competition was to buy a young steer castrated as late as possible in the year. A later castration means more testosterone and more muscle. And more muscle means a greater chance of winning—not all that different than what goes on in doping scandals in many professional sports. Technically, this was not against the rules, but the strategy carried a risk—the later the castration, the more aggressive the steer.

A typical steer is as obedient as a pet dog once you break it. But a late-castration steer can be hyperaggressive. In fact, to keep the animal under control on show day, some of these animals were fed tranquilizers—which was *definitely* against the rules.

I loved showing steers because I always thought of myself as a bit of a cowboy. I lived in boots for most of my young life up until college and occasionally wore a cowboy hat.

My dad also loved the competition of club calves, so when I was a sophomore in high school, he decided to purchase a late-castrated steer. That animal looked half bull. It was the meanest steer I had ever dealt with and the most expensive.

In those days, most club calves cost about $200 to $300, but a late-castrated calf could set you back $500 or more. While I named all my steers, I can't remember what I called this one, so for this story, let's call him El Diablo.

El Diablo was built like a tank on legs with a beautiful reddish coat and white face. Whenever I washed him, he would try his darndest to kick me to kingdom come. Being castrated, El Diablo couldn't be called a raging bull, but he was definitely raging. I never could break him to lead, and I feared there would be no way to show him at the county and state fairs without tranquilizers.

But we never got that far.

It was mid-August of 1975, shortly before the Iowa State Fair competition, and I had to haul El Diablo to a man in Perry, Iowa, who trimmed hooves. One of my good buddies in high school, Kurt Kenney, agreed to help me load up El Diablo from Grandma Lurene's farm and accompany me. I carefully led the steer through a chute and into the back of a truck—a kind of pickup truck used for hauling small numbers of animals. The wooden rack of the truck bed was extremely high to prevent cattle or horses from leaping out.

El Diablo slammed around in the back the entire way to and from the hoof trimmer. After we returned with El Diablo to my grandma's farm, we should've known to be extremely careful unloading this crazed creature. We were supposed to back up the truck as close to the barn as possible. That way, the portable chute would give no room for error, providing the steer one path to follow—down the ramp, through the barn door, and into his pen.

If we were sane, this is what we would've done. But that day, I had only half a brain and opted for a shortcut. Since correctly positioning the chute was too much of a bother, we decided to stop short of the barn. As a big tough football player (at least in my mind), I decided to take El Diablo into the barn, figuring Kurt and I could handle any steer out in the open, including this one.

I led El Diablo down the ramp and was halfway to the barn when something spooked him, and he came to a sudden and startling halt, resisting my lead. Remember, this was the Arnold Schwarzenegger of animals, weighing at least 1,200 pounds, and it started pulling me across the gravel lot in front of the barn while I hung on for dear life.

My only advantage was that El Diablo wore a halter with a choke chain under his mouth. All I had to do was yank my rope, and the chain would bring the creature under control. At least, that's what it was supposed to do. Unfortunately, tugging on the choke chain made him angrier and more deadly. I had never handled such a furious animal; his eyes were wild, and he pulled, snorted, and tossed his head from side to side. Suddenly, the rope slid from my hands, and the raging steer broke loose and took off running with two high schoolers sprinting after him. Again, not very bright of us. What were we going to do when we caught up with him?

The steer sprinted north, thundering through my grandmother's soybean field. Ahead of the animal were miles and miles of soybean and corn fields, with the nearest town nearly twenty miles away.

Eventually, El Diablo stopped in the middle of the soybean field. Beans do not grow as tall as corn—only about to a person's thigh in August. So, the steer remained in clear view, running back and forth in the field, unsure where to go.

Meanwhile, Kurt and I crept up on him. I figured I'd be able to grab the lead rope and try again to control him with the choke chain, but I should've realized how difficult and dangerous it would be to grab the lead, let alone keep him under control.

The steer stopped. We stopped.

The steer glared. We stared.

When the animal began to snort and paw the ground, the hair on the back of my neck stood. Seconds later, El Diablo charged, coming straight for me.

Kurt and I turned tail and ran across the soybean field, sprinting between the rows with the snorting steer not far behind. I didn't think there was any chance I could make it back to the barn before the steer caught me. Even though we'd removed his horns and there wasn't any danger of getting gored, I was scared witless of being stomped by 1,200 pounds of mobile muscle.

When I finally dared to glance over my shoulder, I noticed El Diablo had given up the chase. I swallowed, saying a prayer of thanks. His charge had done the trick, driving us both away. Realizing the futility of chasing down the animal, we stayed at the farm until dark, hoping El Diablo would get hungry and thirsty and wander back home.

But the animal was long gone, and so was any chance of taking home a top prize at the Iowa State Fair.

My dad was furious at our stupidity, and for the next four days, we kept getting phone calls from other farmers in our area.

"I saw your steer out in our field!" they'd report.

El Diablo never threatened anyone, thank God, but he quickly disappeared after each spotting.

Finally, we got a call from someone who saw him lying down near a fence about two or three miles north of the home farm. So, my dad called Shorty Clipperton, who ran a meat locker in Bagley. We drove to where El Diablo had last been spotted, and Shorty brought his .30-06 deer rifle—a big gun. Once there, Shorty lined up his shot on the hood of his pickup truck and hit El Diablo right between the eyes.

That was the end of my club calf.

Shorty cut through the fence to get to El Diablo's body, using a winch to haul it into his truck bed. (Later, I had to go back and fix that fence, of course.) Then he hauled the steer to his meat locker and turned him into steak and hamburger. We dined on El Diablo for a couple of years—some of the best steaks I've ever eaten. If I could've entered those steaks in the state fair, maybe we would've carried home the top prize after all.

People sometimes do strange and unethical things when it comes to awards and prize money. If these kinds of shenanigans happen at something as wholesome as a 4-H competition, imagine what must have been going on at the Chicago Board of Trade (CBOT) and other commodity futures exchanges since the nineteenth century. Cheating infects every sphere of human activity, and the futures market is no exception.

Manipulations have been taking place since the beginning of the commodity futures markets. Although there are many more safe-guards today, they can still occur. Speculators have been accused of crimes, both real and imaginary, but the real threat of manipulation is through corners.

To understand "cornering the market," consider the card game "Hearts." The object of the game is *not* to win any hearts—or the dreaded Queen of Spades. Each heart is a point, while the Queen of Spades is thirteen points, but in this game, the low score wins.

However, there is something called "shooting the Moon" in Hearts. This is when a player tries to win *every single heart plus the Queen of Spades*. If a player can do that—if he or she can shoot the Moon—then all the player's opponents are given twenty-six points each, and the one who successfully shot the Moon gets zero. Remember, the fewer points, the better.

When you corner the market, you're essentially trying for the same thing. You're shooting the Moon. You're trying to control all the futures contracts for a certain commodity due at a certain time, and you're also trying to take control of the physical supplies.

Take wheat as an example. Let's say there are 100,000 open futures contracts on the market for wheat due to expire in July ("July wheat"). Six months before these contracts are set to expire, a person can quietly buy up the long side (the buy side) of July wheat futures contracts.

To corner the market, you don't have to get all 100,000 contracts—just a significant portion. Let's say, I buy 25 percent of the long contracts or 25,000 July wheat contracts. At the same time, I need to go to the delivery elevators, where the physical wheat is stored, to buy up the wheat supplies. This will give me control over the July wheat futures contracts and the physical grain in the delivery elevators.

As the July expiration date for wheat futures contracts approaches, people on the short side (the sell side) get boxed into a corner. One option for them to escape their short contracts is to find people on the long side and buy their contracts. If they buy the same number of long contracts as they have short ones, the futures contracts cancel each other out, and they've "canceled out their position."

However, if they wait until the July delivery date is close, all they have left are my 25,000 long contracts, which I plan on selling at an exorbitant price. Their only other option is to deliver the physical commodity in July. But once again, they will run into me because I also control most of the physical grain in the delivery elevator, and they'll end up paying a high price. Either way, they lose, and I win.

This example is called a delivery corner and squeeze. Prices rise, forcing my victims to pay inflated prices for the contracts or the grain. The corner and "squeeze" is a particularly colorful term because it conjures images of squeezing a sensitive part of the male anatomy.

Like our poor castrated bull, the victims of a corner are shorn of their manhood. And like a cornered steer, a cornered trader is probably in the mood to trample somebody.

In the card game Hearts, you must successfully shoot the Moon and win all the hearts plus the Queen of Spades—but you must do it on the sly. If your opponents see what you're doing, one of them will intentionally win a point to foil your plans. It's the same with classic corners.

A trader needs to do it on the sly because once others realize what is happening, there are things they can do. For instance, the other traders can get out of their contracts earlier rather than wait until the delivery date when it's too late. But the most common solution is to start shipping more grain to the delivery elevators. As a result, I won't have control over all the product and cannot inflate prices to insane levels.

Corners are more complex today than in the nineteenth century because it is much harder to be secretive. Since the 1936 Commodity Exchange Act, there has been much more oversight of the commodity markets. In the early twentieth century, the commodity exchanges realized the public was out to shut them down, so they had a big incentive to police themselves. The '36 Act created a regulatory agency that now goes by the Commodity Futures Trading Commission or CFTC.

The CFTC's enforcement division keeps an eye out for market manipulation. Returning to our game of Hearts analogy, it would be like having inspectors circle the table, checking people's hands to see if anyone might be trying to secretly shoot the Moon. If they spot it happening, they alert the other players.

Over-regulation is a considerable risk to the market today, but in the early days of trading in the 1800s, the lack of regulation also posed risks. This needs to be recognized in any discussion about speculators throughout history.

In her book, *The Futures*, Emily Lambert offers some juicy examples of historical corners. The most infamous corner, Lambert said, was pulled off in 1888 by Benjamin Hutchinson, or "Old Hutch," whom one reporter described as having the "complexion of a liver sausage and weighed only one hundred pounds."

Old Hutch "stealthily bought up wheat futures contracts," Lambert said. "In the fall, a frost killed off a portion of the year's wheat crop. This worked to Hutchinson's advantage and made wheat even harder to get."

Other traders figured out what he was up to in September of that year, but by then, it was too late. As the contracts neared expiration, sellers couldn't find any wheat to deliver because of the shortage. Hutchinson controlled the futures contracts and the physical grain, so farmers had no choice. They had to buy directly from him.

According to Lambert, "He made millions on the deal, outraged local journalists, and embarrassed his son, who was then president of the Board." (The Chicago Board of Trade.)

Three years later, Hutch tried it again but failed to buy enough corn to corner the market, and he lost $2 million.[4]

A corner takes weeks and months to develop, but today there is a new strategy at work—the "flash boys' manipulation," as described in Michael Lewis's best-seller, *Flash Boys*.[5] These stock traders use the speed of electronic trading to manipulate the market, but because they're operating at the millisecond level, they don't affect prices as much.

The classic corner delivery manipulation is real, and it's a constant threat to the efficient functioning of the markets. For instance, there was the famous Ferruzzi Episode of 1989, which I discuss in Chapter 14. But with these vast markets, it usually takes a large commercial entity or hedge fund, rather than a single trader, to pull off a corner like this.

The risk of manipulation is one reason farmers like my dad deeply distrust traders. As I said in the first chapter, my dad and his farmer friends often suspected that big grain companies, the government, and commodity futures market traders were out to screw them. While many of their suspicions were imaginary, farmers often had a good reason to fret. The 1970s were a turbulent time in the grain markets, with three pivotal events that fueled farmers' suspicions.

The first of these events is the Great Russian Grain Robbery of 1972. The Soviet Union had a series of crop failures in the early '70s and wanted to avoid food shortages and the political turmoil that could follow, so they made massive grain purchases from the United States.

During the summer of 1972, major U.S. grain companies got word of these purchases before they were made public. To no one's surprise, the companies began buying up grain from American farmers on the cheap. Then, after the massive grain sales to the Soviet Union were made public, prices skyrocketed, and farmers who had already sold at a lesser price were outraged because they were cut out of huge profits.

To add insult to injury, the U.S. Department of Agriculture (USDA) subsidized many of the sales.[6] The resulting furor was so intense that the U.S. Congress directed the USDA to create an entirely new export sales reporting system requiring grain companies to disclose sales above a certain size. This reporting system is still in place today.

The second '70s debacle was the soybean export embargo, something for which my dad never forgave President Nixon. In 1973, farmers were riding high in the first half of the year as soybean futures prices went through the roof, shooting from $4 to $12 per bushel in just a few months.

"Beans in the teens" became the rallying cry for high-priced soybeans throughout my high school years. However, fears about a soybean shortage (which never fully materialized) and food price inflation led Nixon to impose a soybean export embargo on June 27, 1973. In a few days, soybean futures prices tanked by over $4 per bushel! I will never forget how angry my father was when he told me what had happened, calling it an unforgivable sin. Nearly all American farmers shared his outrage.

Japan was our number one soybean export buyer at the time because they needed soybean meal to feed their growing demand for meat. In a sense, U.S. soybeans had become a staple of the Japanese diet. As one commentator expressed, a soybean embargo on Japan was like banning hamburgers in America. Embargoes can give a country a reputation as an unreliable supplier, so Japan turned to Brazil, which primarily grew soybeans for domestic use at that time. By October 1973, Nixon lifted his soybean restrictions, but the damage was done. Brazil eventually overtook the U.S. in soybean exports and still remains on top.

"We're really angry at Nixon-san," said Hiroshi Higashimori, secretary-general of the Japan Oilseed Processor Association. My dad echoed those sentiments.[7]

The third pivotal event was the 1977 alleged corner of the soybean market by the Hunt brothers—Bunker and his younger brother, Herbert. As one *New York Times* article reported about the notoriously frugal Bunker, he was "the kind of guy who orders chicken-fried steak and Jello-O, spills some on his tie, and then goes out and buys all the silver in the world."

The Hunts accumulated a total soybean futures position of 23 million bushels by the spring of 1977, more than seven times allowed. They circumvented the position-limit rules by opening different accounts for their children and relatives, but Bunker and Herbert controlled them. They certainly seemed like they were attempting to corner the soybean market, yet all they got was a slap on the wrist for their adventure. The Hunt brothers were not so lucky in their attempt to corner the world silver market later in the decade.[8]

Since the government is interested in preventing corners, they invest much time and resources into doing just that. But the economists' general consensus is that the classic corner is fairly rare due to enforcement mechanisms. We need to separate the real crimes of speculators from the imagined ones, but unfortunately, 99 percent of our attention on speculators is consumed by running after imaginary crimes. Many people confuse the regular operation of a free market with deliberate manipulation.

When crude oil prices escalated from $45 to $148 per barrel between 2004 and 2008, critics blamed speculators, even though the market was reflecting the increasing scarcity of the commodity. Michael Masters, a person who will show up later in my tale, basically said that when he saw these big spikes in prices, he was certain it was a bubble caused by speculators, who pushed prices far away from fundamentals. In truth, unusual supply and demand dynamics were the cause. What's more, evidence shows that in these situations, speculators help prevent price spikes from becoming more dramatic.

There are intelligent speculators, and then there are dumb ones. Those who are clueless can maneuver market prices up or down if they have enough money. But remember, plenty of savvy speculators understand where prices should be. And if the ignorant speculators push prices unrealistically high or low, they will get hammered by the smart ones. This dynamic acts as a constant corrective in the market, keeping prices true.

The bottom line? If people cheat in 4-H steer contests, they'll also try in the markets, so vigilance is necessary. But it's misguided to confuse true manipulation, such as corners, with the typical ups and downs of the markets. What's more, overregulation can throw sand in the gears of normal speculation, making price swings worse.

Therefore, it makes no logical or economic sense to use excessive regulations to castrate the market, especially if your goal is a bull market.

Chapter 9
All That Glitters is Goldman

I never experienced what it was like to trade in the renowned pits at the Chicago Board of Trade (CBOT) or the Chicago Mercantile Exchange (CME), but I spent one Sunday night working in a pit of a different sort. In July 1982, while still in graduate school, I worked on Jack Hunter's pit crew.

Jack was competing in an entry-level stock car race at a small track in Stuart, Iowa. The experience was every bit as wild as the trading pits in Chicago, maybe more so. I will never forget what happened that night, but not just because Jack won his race. I'll remember it as an extreme night of mayhem, thanks to the volatile and eccentric Woodard Brothers from Des Moines.

The Stuart Raceway was a small, quarter-mile, oval dirt track in the boonies, with old, janky bleachers positioned against the protective fence separating the track from the crowd. The bleachers were so close that an out-of-control racecar could easily have leaped the barrier and plunged into the crowd. The track would never pass muster with today's safety inspections.

In the street stock car division, there were limitations on a vehicle's engine and tire size, limiting expenses for low-budget racers like Jack. Our job was to get him amped up for the race and jack up his car whenever it was time to switch a tire. At one point, Jack was about to call it quits when his front brakes began to stick. Fortunately, my dad was there to persuade Jack to let him remove the failing front brakes. Then Jack went out and won the feature race with only his back brakes. He always was a talented wheelman!

Once we were done, we hung around to watch the other races, including the late-model division. In this division, racers could spend to their heart's desire and wallet's capacity to soup up their vehicles for increased speed.

Jack and I, along with my dad, my cousin Eric Hanson, and one of Eric's friends, watched from the pit area on the track's north side. One of the cars spun out in front of the flag stand, colliding with another vehicle. I didn't have a clear view of who was at fault, but one of the infamous Woodard brothers leaped from his car, taking swings at the other driver. Such fireworks weren't unusual in those days because stock car racing was much like hockey, where fans come for a brawl as much as the game. As the old saying goes, people came to see a fight, and a stock car race broke out.

Guys came bolting from the pits as soon as the fighting began. Jack, my dad, and I were among those sprinting across the track.

I still remember my dad shouting, "Fight! Fight! Fight!"

It brought me back to scuffles behind the high school, which inevitably attracted throngs of kids. But then things took a surreal turn when the sound of a late-model stock car roared from the pits.

That's when we noticed the other Woodard brother's car come screaming from the pits and turn around the fourth corner. He was revving the engine loudly as he rolled down the front stretch, looking for a fight.

To our utter disbelief, he drove into the cluster of people brawling on the track. Luckily, he was only going about 15 to 20 miles per hour, but it was enough to knock people in several directions, like bowling pins.

Next, this other Woodard brother slammed his brakes, jumped out of his car (no doors), and emerged with a tire iron. The brothers were a wild sight to behold. Both sported ZZ Top-style beards and could pass for motorcycle gang members; they also might have been mistaken for two dudes in a Viking raiding party.

Thankfully, we had the sense to stop short, unwilling to throw ourselves into a fight where people were swinging tire irons. The three of us stood slack-jawed, staring in astonishment. I had never been this close to an all-out, large-scale racetrack brawl. In the past, a fence had always separated me and the fracas.

I don't think the other Woodard brother ever struck anybody with the tire iron because the combatants retreated when they spotted the weapon. But punches continued to be thrown, with the two Woodard brothers surrounded by an infuriated group of drivers, pit crew members, and who knows who else. This continued until an off-duty policeman hired to work security finally broke up the melee.

Between the car driving into the crowd and the scale of the fight, it was a miracle that no one was seriously hurt. Today, the Woodard brother who had weaponized his car would probably be arrested for assault or worse. But that night, no one was charged, and the race resumed as if nothing had happened.

It was just another night of racing in Stuart, Iowa.

At face value, you might think the Stuart racetrack and the Woodard brothers are worlds apart from those in gleaming offices deep in the New York financial district, and you wouldn't be wrong. The beer and brawling vibe of the racetrack appears to have nothing in common with the high-finance world of New York City. However, there are parallels if you look at it from a different angle.

The Woodard brothers were aggressive, win-at-any-cost wild men, but so are the people you find working at the legendary firm of Goldman Sachs in New York. White-collar investors can be as ruthless and aggressive as their blue-collar, redneck cousins. Like the Woodard brothers, the legendary Goldman Sachs firm has a reputation for cut-throat tactics, except those who work there don't resemble brawlers in greasy overalls and sweaty headbands. Instead, they wear three-piece suits and Rolex watches. Goldman Sachs employees won't be swinging tire irons at you, but they will wield whatever financial instrument needed to get an edge. And while you won't find a single

ZZ Top beard, their financiers can be every bit as intimidating as a Woodard brother.

I got my first taste of the Goldman mystique when I arrived in New York City for the first time in 1984 as a wide-eyed country boy. I was still a PhD student, working on my dissertation at Purdue, and I was visiting the New York offices of the legendary financial institution. My head was spinning.

Goldman Sachs, the granddaddy of American financial institutions, was started in 1869, just after the Civil War, by Marcus Goldman, a 48-year-old German teacher. Goldman initially made money by selling from a pushcart in the streets of Philadelphia but decided he could do better. So, he moved his wife and five children to New York City, which was booming in the post-war period. Goldman hung a simple sign that said, "M. Goldman, Broker and Banker," and he was off and running.[1]

Today, Goldman Sachs has close to 40,000 employees—not bad for a one-time small family business. In 2010, it moved into its sparkling new skyscraper at 200 West Street in Manhattan. But when I arrived there in 1984, Goldman Sachs was still based at 85 Broad Street—a building that the New Yorker magazine described as "one of those bland, squint-windowed, stone-fronted thirty-story monstrosities." Monstrosity or not, to me, it was like going to Disney World for finance geeks.[2]

In the morning, Goldman Sachs sent over a car to ferry me to their headquarters, a perk that graduate students don't often see. I was in New York City to give a presentation in front of the National Association of Commodity Trading Advisors, and one of my PhD advisors, Anne Peck, had arranged for me to get a peek into the world of Goldman Sachs.

Peck was a Stanford professor (on loan as my co-advisor) who was prominent in commodity research, and she had put me in touch with Gary Seevers, an ag economist who had done very well at Goldman Sachs. On that day in 1984, I met Gary at his office, and then a group of younger employees filed in, peppering me with questions. My hands started to sweat. It was as if I had inadvertently stumbled into a job interview that I didn't know about.

The young guys kept bombarding me with questions about "commodity indexes" and "risk premiums," which were entirely out of my wheelhouse at the time. I worked on commodity options, technical trading, and market efficiency, so I had little idea what they were asking. It was like someone dropped me into a room with people who spoke a different language.

It wasn't until years later that I realized what was going on. In the mid-1980s, Goldman Sachs began creating what would become the Goldman Sachs Commodity Index (today known as the S&P GSCI). They were anticipating a growing interest in using commodities as a long-term investment, and their index was the first step in developing commodity investment funds. Therefore, they wanted to pick my brain on commodity investments, but as I said, this wasn't my area, so there wasn't much to pick.

Buying and owning commodities as an investment has been around for thousands of years. For instance, people have been buying gold bullion bars and coins forever. That's a form of commodity investment. However, since gold once backed the United States currency, there were restrictions on how much gold a private citizen could own until the 1970s. People can also invest in agricultural commodities, but there are severe limitations since it's expensive to own a grain elevator to store corn or soybeans or even rent the space for extended periods.

Consequently, the idea arose in the 1970s that investors could buy futures contracts as commodity investments instead of owning the physical commodity. Buying futures contracts was nothing new, of course. What was different was that people were talking about buying them as a *long-term investment strategy*—not short-term speculation or hedging.

Once people began to see futures contracts as long-term investments, it was only natural to create an index comparable to the two most famous stock market indexes—the Dow Jones Industrial Average and the S&P 500. The S&P 500 follows 500 large companies and is regarded as one of the best indicators of the market's overall performance.

The S&P is a weighted index, meaning it doesn't just take the 500 companies and determine an average performance rate across the board. Because investors put more into specific stocks, such as Apple, the S&P 500 puts more weight on them than others—say, General Motors. That way, the index represents the true value of the different companies tracked in the market. Once the index was created, investment funds were developed that aimed to match the performance of the S&P 500.

Goldman Sachs' idea was to do the same thing in the commodity market as in the stock market. They wanted to develop a commodity index that similarly tracked the performance of various commodities, from corn and soybeans to crude oil and gold. Then they would create investment instruments that people could buy to match the performance of this index. Instead of going through the expense and hassle of obtaining 25 different futures contracts in various commodities and managing the cash flows, investors could buy a single index fund that included a variety of commodities.

Index funds in the commodity market would reduce risk, the same way that index funds in the stock market eliminate the risk of investing in individual companies. With a commodity index, you invest in a wide range of commodities rather than putting all your eggs (or wheat, corn, or pork bellies) in one basket.

The first person to develop an "investable" index for commodities was Bob Greer in the 1970s.[3] But his index couldn't compete with the one Goldman Sachs created and announced with much fanfare in 1991.

Just as the S&P 500 gives more weight to specific stocks, the Goldman Sachs Commodity Index, or GSCI, gives more weight to certain commodities. For instance, the crude oil market is enormous compared to hogs, so more weight is put on crude oil futures than on hog futures. Investors seek to own a basket of commodities so they can get a broad diversification, but most portfolios will include more crude oil contracts than hog contracts. The GSCI reflects this diversification as it tracks the performance of the entire commodity market.

However, there is a potentially fatal flaw in all of this. Commodity investments do not operate like stock market investments.

Because of continual economic growth, there is a fundamental tendency for stocks to increase in price. Although stocks experience big dips, historically, the trend is ever upward, which is why the stock market is continually reaching record heights. That's also why stocks are such good long-term investments. The buy-and-hold strategy works wonders as long as you have nerves of steel to wait out the bad patches.

The same cannot be said for commodities. When adjusted for inflation, the prices of commodities have been declining for as long as we have records. The only exception has been crude oil, which has had an upward trend, partly because the OPEC oil cartel artificially reduces crude oil flow, boosting the price. But for other commodities, the trend has been ever-lowering prices.

Take corn, for instance. Its actual price (adjusted for inflation) in my lifetime has dropped dramatically, primarily because of technological improvements. When I was a kid, Illinois farmers would've been lucky to grow 100 bushels of corn per acre. Today, they easily produce 200 bushels per acre. An increase in productivity lowers prices, which is a plus for the consumer, but it's dreadful for anyone who views commodities as long-term investments. I always like to ask, "What's the wind behind the sails for investing long-term in commodities?"

Typically, there isn't much wind—only doldrums.

Because of this trend, there wasn't a lot of initial interest when Goldman Sachs created its commodity index in the '90s and then developed investment funds that tracked the index. Commodity prices were stagnant in the 1990s, so interest as a long-term investment was similarly stagnant. That all changed in the 2000s.

People believe that every twenty or thirty years, there are "supercycles" in which commodity prices skyrocket. We experienced this in the 1970s and then again thirty years later in the 2000s (beginning in 2003 and 2004, to be exact). And although market forces were behind the skyrocketing commodity prices in the 2000s, people blamed it on speculators.

When super-cycles jack up commodity prices, it usually takes a perfect storm of many factors. In the 1960s and early '70s, supply was high, and demand was stable, which kept prices low, so people were not investing in new mines for metals and new wells for oil. But that changed in the early 1970s, as monetary policy was modified due to the collapse of the post-World War II Bretton Woods agreement, stoking inflation across the economy, including commodities. What's more, grain prices spiked because the Soviet Union decided to buy large amounts of grain from the United States for the first time, accelerating demand. We also had a series of bad crops worldwide—again boosting prices.

Inflation + Soviet purchases + bad crops = a perfect storm.

We saw a similar convergence of factors in the 2000s. In same way that commodity prices swooned in the late '60s to early '70s, they stagnated in the late '90s to early 2000s. In fact, that's why my dad decided to retire from farming in 2002; he wasn't making enough money.

However, in the early 2000s, China's economy exploded as it tried to move a billion people from Third-World economic status to middle and upper incomes in a few decades. This translated into high demand for commodities, and prices shot up. In addition, the United States mandated using renewable fuels, which called for corn to create ethanol. Ethanol hiked the demand for corn, and prices soared.

This was followed by poor crops from 2010 to 2012, keeping grain prices high. Specifically, 2010 and 2011 were subpar growing years in the U.S, while Russia and Ukraine had a severe drought in 2010. These woes were followed in 2012 by one of the worst droughts in the United States in the last 100 years. It was a perfect storm that drove high prices.

With commodity prices rising in 2003, the commodity index funds created by Goldman Sachs suddenly looked quite appealing. Commodities were seen as solid long-term investments during this super-cycle. Fueling the frenzy was new research by a pair of prominent financial economists that claimed commodity futures contracts were good investments with "equity-like" returns.[4]

But if the historical trend for commodities has been a steady lowering of real prices, why would any economists say that? We can trace the reason to one of the most famous economists of all time, Lord Maynard Keynes, who speculated on commodities during his life in the first half of the twentieth century. He believed they were good long-term investments because of a "risk premium." He argued that because speculators take on the burden of risk through the futures market, producers compensate them by selling at a slightly lower price.

For example: Let's say the fair market price today for a December corn futures contract is $3.50 per bushel, which means traders believe a bushel in December is worth that value at nearby delivery locations. According to Keynes's theory, to compensate speculators for taking on the burden of risk, producers should be willing to sell commodity futures contracts to speculators for a special deal—$3.45 per bushel instead of $3.50. Therefore, speculators get a reasonable price because of this risk premium. They buy low and sell later at a higher price, closer to the fair market price of $3.50. *Voila!* Buying commodities as an investment strategy pays off.

Keynes's theory has been hotly debated since the 1940s, and my trio of professional heroes—Holbrook Working, Roger Gray, and Tom Hieronymus—led the charge against the existence of a risk premium. Another economist whom I admire, Lester Telser of the University of Chicago, also maintained that there is no such thing as a risk premium. Telser argued that numerous speculators will always be willing to take on a futures contract's long side (buy side) at the "fair" price of $3.50-per-bushel in this case.[5]

In other words, although speculators take the risk from producers and middle operators, they don't get compensated particularly well for it as a group. There will always be a supply of speculators willing to buy at the fair price in a statistical sense. So, the risk premium, as formulated by Lord Keynes, is an illusion. My research partners and I came to this conclusion—based on our work.[6]

At this point, it is essential to understand that I'm not saying speculation is hopeless. My research has shown that some large speculators consistently earn profits in commodity futures markets.[7] But this select group of speculators' profits are offset by others' losses so that, as a group, speculators do not seem to profit over time. Hence, the risk premium is zero.

Without the risk premium, long-term investments in futures contracts do not make good economic sense unless you can predict when one of these super-cycles will occur, temporarily inflating commodity prices. If you get in at the beginning of a super-cycle, when prices are just starting to rise, and if you get out when prices peak, you can make a ton of money. But predicting super-cycles, which occur only about every thirty years, is extremely difficult.

However, leave it to Goldman Sachs to find a way to profit big-time from the super-cycle of the 2000s. When interest in commodity investments peaked, they made a heap of money with their commodity index funds. Then, just when prices began topping out in 2007, Goldman Sachs sold their commodity index to Standard and Poor's (owners of the S&P 500 stock index).

Commodity prices remained high until the bottom fell out in 2014 and 2015, but the super-cycle peaked in 2008. Goldman Sachs rode the commodity investment craze close to the top and then shed its index.

Talk about great timing. That's why Goldman Sachs is Goldman Sachs.

As the old Jim Croce song says, "You don't mess around with Jim." You also don't mess around with Goldman Sachs, the Woodard Brothers of the financial world. They won't hit you with a tire iron, but they'll leave you reeling if you try to outfox them in the market. I would never want to trade if Goldman Sachs was on the other side of the deal. I'd soon be left wondering, "Where did my money go?"

During the super-cycle of the 2000s, Dwight Sanders and I shouted to the rooftops that commodities make poor long-term investments. In 2012, we published a paper saying it just doesn't work. But commodity prices were still high then, so people ignored us. Even though we turned out to be correct, our paper landed with a resounding thud.[8]

After 2012, however, when prices plummeted to normal levels, it suddenly dawned on commodity investors that they were not doing very well.

When I walked into the Goldman Sachs office in 1984, little did I know I was walking into the very heart of the operation that created the index and index funds, leading to the futures market investments boom twenty years later.

What's more, I didn't realize this investment boom—and its alleged impact on prices—would become the focus of much of my research beginning in the 2000s. It also became the center of a controversy that would spawn some of my biggest battles as I defended the futures market from those who blamed speculators for the sudden and startling rise in commodity prices.

But before we dig into that controversy, it's best to get a little more history on the Anti-Speculation Cycle and its greatest victim—the onion futures market. We'll also look at its *latest* victim—futures contracts for movie box-office receipts.

Senator Lindsey Graham of South Carolina once said, "It's one thing to shoot yourself in the foot. Just don't reload the gun." That's a good picture of what happens in the futures markets. Load. Aim at speculators. Shoot yourself in the foot. Reload.

It's almost as ridiculous as shooting arrows at yourself. Believe me, I know. As a high schooler, I did just that.

Chapter 10
The Onion Crying Game

I call it Redneck PE—physical education specially tailored for testosterone-driven, farm-boy high schoolers like myself back in the early 1970s. Our high school was small, with roughly thirty students per class, but hyper-aggressiveness among the guys made us a handful for our teachers, especially the PE instructors. Many of my classmates came from blue-collar families, and their fathers worked at the nearby Oscar Meyer pork slaughtering plant in Perry, Iowa. It was a rough crowd.

Our Redneck PE included boxing, in which I was punched the hardest I have ever been hit. We also played indoor hockey, in which upperclassmen would whack the back of the thighs of unsuspecting underclassmen, leaving stinging red welts. Then there's the ever-popular dodgeball, in which we used overinflated volleyballs—much more painful than the softer official ones used today. We even knocked out a few of our guys. This was Redneck PE at its most ruthless.

Believe it or not, none of these exercises in aggression were as dangerous as archery. It's hard to believe our administration put weapons in the clutches of crazed high school boys.

The idea was to fire at targets mounted on hay bales on the football practice field south of the high school. As guys stood in line waiting for their turn to shoot, several inevitably decided to fire their arrows straight up, yelling, "Run!" Then everyone would scatter as the arrows rained to the ground.

Our classmates were insane, but not crazy enough for my best friend, Jack Hunter.

I'll never forget the beautiful fall morning with picture-perfect clear blue skies, when Jack and I were standing in line holding our big green bows. Our arrows were not as sharp as the ones used in hunting, but they still had metal tips that could do damage. Jack looked at me as we waited our turn and said, *"Watch this, Irwin!"*

Turning toward our school, Jack raised his bow at a forty-five-degree angle, pulled the string back as far as he could, and to my astonishment, he let it rip with a loud twang. The arrow shot like a miniature missile, arching like a rainbow over the building. All of the boys stood in awe as it cleared the school and landed who knows where. We later found out it drove into the ground point-first more than a block away in a little old lady's front yard. She watched it sail into her grass as she sat on her front porch.

That arrow eventually found its way to the principal's office, and so did Jack Hunter. As I recall, they kicked him out of PE for a while, and because we were as thick as thieves, I was too. When one of us was punished, so was the other.

I'm pretty sure no one taught archery in Redneck PE ever again.

I don't blame the school for banning the sport. I would've done the same thing as an administrator. After all, the crazed behavior went beyond the antics of Jack Hunter. We all dabbled with danger by aiming arrows into the air, trying to dodge them as they returned to earth.

Releasing arrows and dodging them as they fall is an excellent picture of what happens when we ban an entire futures market. By banning the onion futures markets in 1958, growers hurt themselves as much as anybody. It's akin to shooting arrows into the sky.

Growers soon become their own targets as the arrows fall on their heads. Although prohibiting teenage boys from bows and arrows during PE made complete sense, banning the onion futures market because of the behavior of a few people was completely counterproductive.

Emily Lambert's book, *The Futures*, nicely lays out the controversy over onions, focusing on Vincent Kosuga, a New York onion grower best known for his colorful escapades in the 1950s. As Lambert said, "He drove stock cars and was frightening behind the wheel. Once, he gave Roy Simmons a ride to Oswego, New York, in his plane and, after dropping him off, continued on until the plane ran out of gas and crashed. Kosuga ended up in a full body cast but insisted on getting out of his hospital bed and going home."[1]

Kosuga carried a gun and billy club, and he made loads of money selling onions to Campbells' Soup and the U.S. Army, only to lose most of it trading wheat at the Chicago Board of Trade (CBOT), Lambert said. Kosuga could also be extremely generous whenever he struck it rich. Once, after a good run in trading, Lambert said he bought new Buicks for some of the other traders at the Chicago Mercantile Exchange (CME), and he even purchased a Cadillac for another broker. One day, while riding with this broker in the car, Kosuga leaned back and put his feet against the canvas ceiling.

The broker friend told him to get his dirty feet off the ceiling of his car.

"*Your* car?" Kosuga scoffed. Then he proceeded to smash his feet through the canvas ceiling.

Kosuga speculated in the onion futures markets and owned and stored heaps of onions in a large facility. According to Lambert, Kosuga once bribed a local weather bureau to issue a frost warning so the price of onion futures would rise, earning him a big payday.

But Kosuga's most consequential manipulation was when he and another trader, Sam Siegel, bought enough onions and onion futures to control 98 percent of the onions in Chicago. They pressured some big growers into buying onions to support the crop price, promising that if the other growers agreed to this, Kosuga and Siegel would continue to buy onions, keeping prices high and benefiting all growers.

If the growers *disagreed*, Siegel and Kosuga threatened to dump their onions into the market at once, driving down prices and devastating the market. Once the onion growers agreed, Siegel and Kosuga broke their word by delivering their onions to market anyway, plummeting prices and making a huge profit.[2]

The consequence of such shenanigans was that outraged onion growers demanded the end of the futures market for their crop. Politicians being politicians, they ultimately bought into the notion that there was no benefit to speculation and obliged. Led by a young congressman from Michigan, Gerald Ford, Congress passed Public Law 85-830 in 1958, which banned futures trading in onions. When President Eisenhower signed the law, it became the first time the U.S. Congress banned futures trading for a specific commodity.

Leaders at the CME, where onion futures traded, were furious. As E.B. Harris, president of the Merc, put it, "Burning down the barn to find a suspected rat is a pretty drastic remedy."[3]

Like the image of firing arrows in the air and watching as they come raining down on your head, Harris's metaphor was spot on. Instead of keeping the rats at bay—instead of trying to rein in people like Kosuga—onion growers burned down their barns by banning futures trading entirely. They hurt themselves more than anyone.

Two of my academic heroes, Holbrook Working and Roger Gray, both released landmark papers pointing out the folly of banning futures trading in onions. The gist of their argument was that by banning futures trading, prices became *more volatile* in the onion market—not less, as producers had hoped. Research has consistently supported this.

Amid the hubbub, Gray, who took up the mantle of Working as a defender of the futures markets, wrote one of the most famous articles in the history of agricultural economics—"Onions Revisited."

In the article, Gray uses the vivid analogy of medieval trials for poachers. In the Middle Ages, citizens would throw an accused poacher into the moat "on the assumption that he would drown if guilty." If he didn't drown, they presumed him innocent.

However, if poaching continued after the alleged poacher drowned, this would be a clue that he might have been innocent all along, although the vindication came a trifle late from his standpoint, Gray said. What's more, what if the accused had been warding off poachers? After he drowned, poaching might *go up*.[4]

In this analogy, speculators are the accused poachers. But instead of drowning them, what if speculation were banned, as was done to onions in 1958? If speculators in the futures market really were guilty of causing volatile prices, the onion market should be much more stable after the futures market was banned—just as poaching should drop if the drowned poacher was guilty.

But this didn't happen. Gray's paper showed that seasonal price fluctuations worsened after onion speculation was banned in 1958. After the ban, onion prices began to make wilder swings from harvest in September to the end of the marketing season in March. The low prices at harvest spelled trouble for producers growing the onions, and the high prices the following March were bad news for consumers. Everyone lost.

Let me remind you of the reason that futures markets kept onion prices more stable. Through the futures market, middle operators can hedge, and this insurance policy reduces their risk. But without hedging in the futures market, they are forced to take on added risk. To compensate, middle operators pay less to onion producers at harvest and charge more to the industries that use the onions. These industries then pass on the added cost to consumers.

Gray's "Onions Revisited" points out that onion prices were most stable from 1949 to 1958, when the futures market flourished. The years before and after this period showed significantly more volatile onion prices—lower at harvest in September and higher by the following March. To exterminate the "rats in their barn," onion growers inadvertently injected more volatility into onion prices. They burned down their barn.

Because "Onions Revisited" was published in May of 1963, five years after the onion futures market was banned, Gray admitted that more time might be needed to see if this trend continued. But "more time" has only reinforced his findings; volatility in onion markets continued to be greater after speculation was banned. The over-whelming evidence shows that speculators reduce dramatic price swings; they don't cause them.

Even today, people continue to reference "Onions Revisited." In 2008, as the economy heated up and oil prices skyrocketed, politicians looked to blame speculators once again. *The Wall Street Journal* responded with "The Onion Ringer"—an editorial that cited Gray's article while making the case against scapegoating speculators for high oil prices.[5]

In addition to this popular journal piece, one of my all-time favorite papers of Working is from 1963, "Futures Market Under Renewed Attack." In it, Working provided evidence that banning futures markets in onions was a blunder. Even now, many producers don't realize what they did to themselves, despite a mountain of evidence.

Working's paper noted that during the years of active onion futures trading, the average fluctuation in price during a season was a measly 20 cents. Before the futures market existed, prices fluctuated an average of $1.19 in a season. And after the government banned the futures market, prices fluctuated 90 cents in a season. In other words, price fluctuations without a futures market were four to six times more severe than with one. His research focused on onion growers in western Michigan, which he said represented onion growers nationally. (Note: Gerald Ford, the future U.S. President who spearheaded the effort to ban onion futures contracts, was from Michigan.)[6]

Holbrook Working took a dark view of the motives behind what happened to onions. He said it was more than politicians buying into the false narrative that futures markets create wide price swings. He hinted that other forces may have been at work because the ban on onion futures trading gave advantages to large dealers in onions.

In a futures market, trading is conducted publicly in open competitive bidding, which is more likely to create a fair price for commodities such as onions, giving an element of protection to every buyer and seller. They can be assured that the prices openly negotiated are less likely to be skewed in favor of the stronger bargainers—the larger onion merchants.

Without open competitive bidding in the futures market setting a fair price, a large onion dealer can throw around its weight and use its power to strike a better deal with a weaker bargainer. Futures markets democratize the system of setting a fair price. Without it, large onion dealers wield much more power over the price. Therefore, Working suspected that large onion merchants may have had some undue influence on banning futures markets because they served to benefit.

I call Holbrook Working the Theorist in defending futures markets, Roger Gray the Provocateur, and Tom Hieronymus the Evangelist. Working provided the intellectual ammunition in the fight to defend the market against those trying to straight-jacket speculation or outright ban it. He was the theorist who explained why the futures markets made sense, performing a valuable function in our economic system. Before Working, few people understood that.

Gray followed in Working's wake, continuing this line of argument, but he did it in a much more provocative way. Hence, I call him the Provocateur. He would show up at meetings smoking a pipe in his tweed coat and mercilessly punch holes in arguments, using metaphors you might find in a literary work. Gray's middle name was Winks. And if there was ever a middle name that fit the personality, that was it!

Gray's economics writing sometimes reads like a piece of literature, not the words of a staid scientist. In his famous take-down of two financial economists, who studied second-by-second price changes in the futures market, he talked about "the liquid sound" of birds. What other academic writer would use poetic metaphors in technical papers or reference playwright Tennessee Williams?[7]

I had my first encounter with Gray as a graduate student giving my very first academic presentation at a CBOT conference—and I was terrified, knowing he would be in the audience, offering critiques afterward. I was well aware of his rapier wit and that he was quick to use it to tear presenters apart.

Gray began work in the 1950s, overlapping with Working for a period at the Stanford Food Research Institute, and he was still active in the mid-1980s. That's why he was in the audience in

December of 1983 when I presented a paper based on my master's thesis at a conference featuring promising graduate student research. I scanned the crowd, looking for Gray, and sure enough, he was there. As I recall, however, he was not in attack mode that day and went easy on me. I imagine he backed down because I was only a graduate student.

Despite my earlier fears of him, I got to know Gray when I became a professor, and he emerged as one of my heroes.

A curious sidenote to the Roger Gray legend is his claim that he saved the futures markets from being closed during the Nixon years. In September of 1982, I was present at another research seminar sponsored by the CBOT, where Gray told the story. During a question-and-answer period, Gray said that John Dunlop, a Harvard economics professor, floated a proposal that Nixon "close the futures markets because speculators had driven up the price." It was the same old refrain.

In response to this looming threat, Peter Flanigan, an investment banker who worked in the Nixon administration, called Gray into the White House for a showdown with Dunlop. Also present were Alex Caldwell, administrator of the Commodity Exchange Authority, and Gary Seevers, then of the Council of Economic Advisors. (Seevers was the guy who invited me to visit Goldman Sachs in 1984.)

Gray had prepared a three-page analysis challenging Dunlop's claim that speculators were raking in money as prices soared. In this report, Gray showed that futures speculators as a group were net short during the grain price spike, which meant they were *losing money* as prices surged.

According to Gray, "I spent maybe fifteen minutes explaining this to Mr. Dunlop, at which point he blew his top. He said he did not believe the figures, and that he wanted us to go back and get the right figures because he knew the speculators in Chicago were not losing money."

When Gray pointed out that he did not work for the government and was not about to "go back and do any further work on this project," Dunlop left the room in a huff. Then Flanigan told both

Caldwell and Seevers that they too would not have to do any more work "because nothing more would be heard from Mr. Dunlop."

Gray, who spent many years at Stanford's Food Institute, concluded in his inimitable way: "When you historians write it up, you can write this as the day that Roger Gray saved the futures market." But he also said there was another important lesson from this incident. "When a Harvard man goes off the deep end," he said, referring to Dunlop, "it always takes a Stanford man to straighten things out."[8]

I had the most contact with my third academic hero, Hieronymus, because he was a professor at the University of Illinois at Urbana-Champaign. When the U of I hired me, it was to fill the same role as Hieronymus, who had retired some years earlier. I also hold the Norton Chair at Illinois, and Larry Norton was Hieronymus' advisor and mentor.

My first personal contact with Hieronymus was as a graduate student at another CBOT conference. He thought a vital part of our education was accompanying him to his favorite Chicago bars. To this day, I've never forgotten hanging out with Hieronymus and a handful of other graduate students at a low-rent cowboy bar in a sketchy part of the city. When there, Hieronymus lit up a stogie and regaled us with colorful trading stories.

I call Hieronymus the Evangelist because his role was carrying the gospel of free markets to the masses. He explained how futures markets worked in a straightforward, down-to-earth manner and churned out a tremendous volume of articles for magazines and industry publications. He also made presentations to many groups. He didn't write as many journal articles as professors such as me, but he engaged with the public like no one else in ag economics. He was the Apostle Paul of futures markets, pushing back against those who tried to scapegoat speculators for high commodity prices. His book on the futures market had a global impact, and it even reached me when I was a high school senior. As I said, I was a hard-core market nerd from a young age.[9]

Thanks to the efforts of economists such as this trio, onions remained the only commodity for which futures trading was banned by Congress—until 2010. You can now add movie box-office receipts to the short list of banned futures contracts.

Finance blogger Felix Salmon wrote on *The New York Times* op-ed pages in May of 2010: "Today, no one is silly enough to ask a member of Congress to simply outlaw futures trading in a certain type of contract—no one, that is, except Hollywood producers."[10]

On June 15, 2010, the Commodity Futures Trade Commission voted 3-2 to approve creating a new futures contract for movie box-office receipts. But the good news lasted only a month. On July 16, 2010, Congress signed the Dodd-Frank Act, which banned futures contracts on movie receipts.

You may be wondering how in the world a futures contract would've worked for movie box-office receipts. After all, we're not talking about corn, soybeans, or cattle here—things you can see and put your hands on. Salmon explained it best:

These futures contracts "...would allow traders to bet on the total box-office receipts of movies in their first four weeks of release," he said. "A contract on *Iron Man* 2, for instance, might be trading at $390, meaning that the market is expecting the film to gross $390 million in its first four weeks. If you think it's going to make more than that, you would go long, or buy, a contract; if you think it's going to make less, you would go short or sell it. At the end of four weeks, the contract would expire at whatever the four-week gross is. If you went long at $390 and the film ended up earning $450 million in its first four weeks, then you'd make $60 for every contract you bought."[11]

This may sound like pure gambling, but as with all futures contracts, a futures market for box-office receipts would've given movie producers a way to hedge—an insurance policy to offset any catastrophic losses. If a movie bombs, the film studio could still make money in the futures market by hedging, offsetting some losses. If the opposite happens and the movie exceeds expectations, the studio would lose in the futures market, but the film's profits would offset the impact. It's insurance against catastrophe.

So, if movie producers are the ones to benefit, why ban futures contracts in box-office receipts? Some of it could be ignorance about how futures markets work or resistance to change. Or maybe producers think it just seems wrong to bet against their film's success in a futures market, even though it's to protect themselves from catastrophic losses. However, they're not betting that their movie will have a poor showing at the box office; they're using the futures market as reliable insurance if the film doesn't perform.

Salmon thinks another possible reason for the movie industry balking at a futures market might be that "top executives at the biggest studios may suspect that smaller and nimbler competitors would get more benefit out of such a market; it's easier to hedge a $10 million project than a $200 million."[12]

He goes on to say, "Hollywood has an entirely predictable predilection for shooting itself in the fiscal foot, so none of this should come as a surprise."

It boils down to the law of unintended consequences. Onion producers wanted to bring price stability to their market, not realizing that futures markets did just that. Onion prices have been more volatile ever since. The arrows they shot into the air, intending to hit speculators, rained down upon them.

In ag economics, much of my work has boiled down to trying to warn people of the folly of demonizing futures markets. I threw myself into defending speculators in the 2000s. As the commodity markets entered another one of those super-cycles, increasing the price of grain and oil, politicians and many producers predictably pointed fingers at speculators as the culprits. The Anti-Speculation Cycle moved into full swing once again, but high prices were not the only problem. There was also an issue of grain prices not "converging," which I will soon explain.

But first, I must tell you about my encounter with the Destroying Angel.

Chapter 11
The Destroying Angel

W hen I strolled into my third-floor office of Mumford Hall at the University of Illinois on a Monday morning in late July of 2008, I spotted a FedEx package sitting on the round table by the window. Examining the label, I confirmed my suspicions that it was from a person calling himself the Destroying Angel—someone who had been emailing me for a couple of months. Did I dare open it? How was I to know whether or not the Destroying Angel was a Ted Kosinski caliber nutcase who had laced the package with some deadly toxin?

Alone in the office, I paced in front of the table, studying the FedEx package from every angle. Then I picked up the hefty envelope and shook it, waiting. Nothing detonated. I could call the university police, but I would feel foolish if the bomb squad descended on my office and spent the morning defusing an envelope loaded with innocuous documents. But wouldn't I be better off looking foolish than dead?

During the first half of 2008, the grain markets (not envelopes) were exploding, with shocking price increases in commodities. What's more, reporters were deluging me with interview requests, thanks to an article that had appeared in *The New York Times* in March of 2008— "Odd Crop Prices Defy Economics," by Diana B. Henriques.[1]

I had been quoted extensively in the article, unleashing a torrent of emails and phone calls. And one of those who had contacted me went by the email handle of "Destroying Angel." I received a string of emails from the Destroying Angel outlining his conspiracy theory about how Chicago corruption was behind the spike in commodity prices. It all culminated with the delivery of this mysterious package.

But before I can describe his conspiracy theory or what happened with the package, you need to understand the strange things that were going on with crop prices around 2008. In addition to the dramatic upward price spike, the grain futures markets were not "converging."

To explain convergence, let me refresh your memory about the two markets that exist for many commodities, which I described in Chapter 4. I'm talking about the cash market and the futures market.

As I explained, farmers use the futures market to hedge against the risk of dramatic price drops in the cash market. The cash market is where trading of the real physical commodity occurs, whereas the futures market trades "paper" commodities except during the delivery period for futures contracts.

The key to hedging is that the futures and cash markets must track each other. If the cash market drops $1 between spring planting and fall harvest, the futures market should also drop about the same for hedging to work. However, the two markets don't move *perfectly in parallel* because the two prices need to converge the closer you come to the commodity delivery date for the futures contract. Suppose you purchased a December corn futures contract. In that case, the price for corn in the futures and cash market should move closer and closer together the nearer you get to the December contract expiration.

You can settle an open futures contract one of two ways. First, you can offset a long position (buy) with a short position (sell)—or a short with a long—in the same contract. Second, you can take or make delivery of the physical commodity during what's called the "delivery period." For December corn, the delivery period is the first two weeks of December.

When cash and futures prices come together during the delivery period, this is called "convergence."

In my chapter on hedging, I simplified the example with Frank and Estelle for clarity's sake. But to demonstrate how convergence happens, let's use a slightly more complicated scenario, this time focusing on Frank. In this example, let's assume that Frank has decided to hedge in the futures market rather than stick to the cash market, as he did in my earlier example. Let's also assume he's farming in Bagley, Iowa, and the grain must be shipped to the delivery elevator on the Illinois River near Peoria, Illinois.

FRANK (SPRING)

Frank sells 5,000 bushels of corn in the futures market in the spring at $5 per bushel. As a result, he controls a position worth $25,000.

Meanwhile, in the cash market, the spring price in Bagley is $4.50 per bushel, while the price for corn at the delivery point in Peoria is $4.80 per bushel.

Because it costs money to transport grain from distant locations to the delivery point, the price per bushel will usually be higher at Peoria than at Bagley. In this case, shipping the corn to Peoria costs roughly 30 cents per bushel, so the higher cash price reflects this difference.

So, here's where we stand in the spring:

- Futures price for December corn: $5 per bushel
- Cash price for corn in Bagley: $4.50 per bushel
- Cash price for corn in Peoria (the delivery point): $4.80 per bushel

FRANK (FALL)

When fall comes around, the price in the futures market has dropped by $1 to $4 per bushel. So, Frank buys back his 5,000 bushels, only this time at the lower price. Because he sold at $5 per bushel in the spring and bought the corn contract back for $4 in the fall, he makes one dollar per bushel in the futures market.

Now he must sell his 5,000 bushels of corn in the cash market, where the price has also dropped because the futures and cash markets generally move in parallel. However, in reality, the two markets don't move *exactly* in parallel. In our example, the futures market dropped $1, but the cash market has dropped only 80 cents, from $4.50 to $3.70 in Bagley and $4.80 to $4 in Peoria.

Here is where we stand in the fall:

- Futures price for December corn: $4 per bushel, down $1 from the spring
- Cash price for corn in Bagley: $3.70 per bushel, down 80 cents from the spring
- Cash price for corn in Peoria (the delivery point): $4 per bushel, also down 80 cents from spring

As you can see, the futures and cash prices for corn at the delivery point in Peoria have converged at $4 per bushel. The only reason the cash price for corn in Bagley didn't *exactly* converge is that it costs 30 cents per bushel to transport the corn to Peoria, which is reflected in the lower price in Bagley. But the $3.70 per bushel is still consistent with the principle of convergence.

In this example, Frank lost money in the cash market because of the price drop between spring and fall, but he offset those losses with his gains in the futures market. He successfully hedged the market.

The "basis" is the difference between the price of a futures contract and the cash price. And since the cash price for corn in Peoria and the futures price stand at $4 in the fall, the basis is zero. Convergence has occurred. The futures price for corn has returned to the cash price.

Convergence assures that the futures market and cash market prices do not wander from each other. You do not want that to happen because the cash price reflects the true price; it's what people agree to pay for the physical commodity and use it for something. But problems can arise, for instance, if cash prices drop to $3.70 per bushel while futures prices soar up to $5 or $6. Something is broken when this happens, leaving Frank to flip his lid and shout, "Serenity now!"

In March of 2008, when *The New York Times* article appeared, this was exactly what was happening. The futures contracts for corn, soybeans, and wheat were expiring at prices much higher than the cash market price during the delivery period. They weren't converging.

"For example, soybean futures contracts expired in July at a price of $9.13 a bushel, which was 80 cents higher than the cash price that day," the *Times* quoted me as saying. "In August, the futures expired at $8.62, or 68 cents above the cash price, and in September, the expiration price was $9.43, or 78 cents above the cash price."

Later that year, the convergence problem worsened, with wheat futures contracts expiring at *$2 per bushel* higher than the cash prices. Something had to be seriously wrong. As I was also quoted saying in the article, "As far as I know, nothing like this has ever happened in the corn market."[2]

What economists call the Law of One Price says that the same commodity selling at the same time and location should have the same price. The futures contract terms are supposed to be representative of the cash market, so futures and cash prices should be the same during the delivery period. But with the price of grain futures contracts consistently coming in higher than the cash price in 2008, this appeared to be a clear and dramatic violation of the Law of One Price.

Both hedgers and speculators base their strategies on the bedrock assumption that futures and cash market prices will converge during the delivery period for futures contracts. When this fails to happen, people question whether the futures market has gone completely haywire.

The March 2008 *New York Times* article proceeded to quote other sources besides me, and some of them made the predictable accusation that speculators were the culprits. The article quoted "veteran traders and many farmers" who complained that speculators are "distorting futures prices by pouring in so much money without regard to market fundamentals."[3] The Anti-Speculation Cycle was beginning to move into high gear.

Actually, the controversy over commodity prices and convergence had begun three years before I was quoted in *The New York Times*. In 2005, I started looking into the problem of the gap between futures prices and cash prices, and my colleagues and I put out a report for the CBOT in the fall of 2006 that, frankly, I'm a little embarrassed about today. It wasn't that our work was poor. We just did not know why convergence wasn't occurring in the grain futures markets.[4]

In contrast to our wishy-washy analysis, however, the anti-speculator crowd was confident they knew what was happening. By the summer of 2006, one theory making the rounds was that speculators, particularly commodity index investors, were artificially inflating futures prices by pouring hot money into the grain futures market. It was causing a bubble in the futures prices, holding them above the cash prices.

The convergence problem kept worsening, causing a firestorm among grain market traders and regulators and within the CME Group (now merged with the CBOT). The problem also began to explode as a public policy issue, and I soon found myself invited to meetings around the world. After twenty-five years of working in relative obscurity as an agricultural economist, I suddenly found myself thrust into the eye of a hurricane.

As I began receiving dozens of emails and interview requests in the wake of *The Times* article in 2008, I dutifully answered them as a good public servant working for the University of Illinois. During this frenzy, the Destroying Angel first emailed me on June 7, 2008, laying out his theory for why grain prices failed to converge.

In one word: fraud.

The Destroying Angel stated, "I believe there is clear and credible circumstantial evidence of criminal fraud by the 'long-only hedge funds' in the commodity futures markets at the Chicago Board of Trade." He claimed the use of fake futures contracts was manipulating futures price expectations. He then dissected this theory over seven pages of single-spaced text, complete with footnotes.

He concluded with: "In the event that you agree with my conclusion that criminal fraud is or may be afoot, please contact Mr. Patrick

J. Fitzgerald, the United States Attorney for the Northern District of Illinois, as soon as possible."[5]

I responded as tactfully as I could to what clearly was an over-wrought theory. However, the Destroying Angel also copied a Department of Agricultural and Consumer Economics colleague who was much blunter with his response: "Look, we are busy people and wonder how you could seriously expect us to look at a message that comes to us from 'the Destroying Angel.' When I see something like this, my first thought is what is wrong with my email filters."

This response ticked off the Destroying Angel, who snapped back, challenging my colleague to a $100 bet on whether he could disprove the conspiracy theory about fake futures contracts. "Of what are you afraid?" the Destroying Angel taunted before adding, "P.S. I have corrected the grammar and punctuation in your first sentence."[6] The Destroying Angel was also a Grammar Nazi.

After the series of emails during June, the Destroying Angel went quiet, and I thought that would be the end. But about a month later, I was on a family vacation at the Wisconsin Dells when I opened my laptop to check my emails.

My stomach dropped when there was another email from the Destroying Angel. I was even more stunned when I read that he was sending me a package via express mail that "may change your mind about the merit of my theory, or it's [sic] worthiness of further investigation."[7] I kept quiet about the disturbing email, trying to put it out of my mind to enjoy the rest of our vacation.

My dread only increased as I drove to the office on Friday morning, knowing that the package from the Destroying Angel was waiting. When I walked into my office on that bright morning in July of 2008, I saw the Destroying Angel's FedEx package staring at me from the table in my office. I eventually worked up the nerve (or the stupidity) to open it. Later, people were horrified when they learned I decided to open a package sent from a Destroying Angel.

Maybe it was my nerves, but as I ripped into the package, I fumbled things, spilling everything onto the floor. One of the papers floated like a feather in the brilliant sunlight, and when it settled on the carpet, it appeared to be a check. I plucked it from the floor and could not believe my eyes.

The Destroying Angel had sent me a cashier's check for $10,000. Yes, that's right. A valid check for $10,000! In a detailed document, he said that if I could disprove his "New Theory of Commodity Price Convergence Failure," I would win what he had dubbed the "A. bisporigera prize." I could cash the $10,000 check.

"It's the honor system," he wrote. "Since you've got the check, I'll have to leave the decision over whether you've successfully refuted it [his conspiracy theory] up to you. I can't even force you to refund the prize money to me if you decide to do absolutely nothing. I have no contractual leverage. You're your own referee."

He went on to say he wasn't crazy, "nor am I a crackpot. I am deadly serious." He claimed he wasn't worried about losing the challenge (or the money) "because I'm certain you can't refute the theory —simply because I'm sure it is correct." He also said he wasn't worried I would take the money and run because, "the nature of your academic pursuit tells me you're a stand-up guy, and your photographs on the UIUC and *farmdoc* websites look like those of an honest man. (Besides, I know where you work, so I can come and picket your offices, bleed the air from your tires, or take all your office supplies while you're at lunch.)"[8]

I assumed that the last sentence was a joke. Or so I hoped.

I emailed back, telling him I received his package and that "you certainly have a way of getting someone's attention. You surmised correctly that I am not going to cash the check."[9] There was no way on earth I would risk what might follow if I cashed it.

Another series of emails started in which the Destroying Angel tried to convince me about his ideas for cracking the case of non-convergence in grain futures markets. He argued that if his theory of fake futures contracts was true, the conspirators must also be faking the delivery of thousands of tons of grain. He believed warehouses were being used as a front to make it look like people were delivering grain, as promised by the fake futures contracts. He even went as far as throwing out the idea of borrowing a pickup truck, dressing up in ratty old clothes, and driving by one of these potentially phony warehouses to "take a gander."

His plan sounded like something out of a hard-boiled detective novel about Old Chicago, as he laid out possible ways that he could scope out any suspicious warehouses. To begin with, he said he could watch to see if there was any activity at the various warehouses.

"Is there anyone around the place?" he wrote. "What kind of fences, gates, and security system does it have? If it has a lot of technological security—automated cameras and so forth—and no people, that's a red flag."

Also, if the warehouse looks too well-kept, this too would make him suspicious that the warehouse is just a front for phony shipments of grain; an active warehouse would not be tidy.

"Are there any fresh truck tire tracks?" he continued. "Do the gate hinge and lock look used or rusty? Does the gate look like it's been swung open lately? The free end will often drag on the ground creating a circular gouge."

This fellow had watched way too many detective shows.

Once again, the Destroying Angel concluded that if any of this detective work raised serious suspicions, "then you definitely have probable cause and can go immediately to the U.S. Attorney with our theoretical and factual findings."[10]

He had said "our" findings. This was getting seriously creepy.

I was more and more concerned about how to bring this episode to a close, so I wrote, "I do not believe that we have access to the necessary data to disprove your hypothesis. It would require access to the trade-by-trade records of the exchanges, which are closed to us like most everyone else."

Nevertheless, the Destroying Angel persisted, trying to coax me to rise to the challenge, so I wrote back, "Perhaps this is a good point to call this a 'no decision' on the bet. I can return the check, or you can simply put in a stop payment order."[11] I returned the check and prayed that the Destroying Angel episode had come to a close because I wasn't about to answer his challenge and spend my time running around Chicago riverfronts hunting for fake warehouses like some grain gumshoe.

Much to my relief, I never heard from the Destroying Angel again.

I should note that the crisis during those years wasn't just that grain futures prices were not converging. Commodity prices were also skyrocketing, especially since the second half of 2006.

China was emerging as a major importer of soybeans, sending prices for that crop soaring. Demand for corn was also through the roof, thanks to the new mandate that ethanol be added to gasoline.

Ethanol is produced from corn, so the new requirement ignited demand—and prices. In 2008, corn prices went over $8 per bushel, an unfathomable number just a few years earlier, when corn was hovering around $2.

As farmers' income in the Corn Belt shot up, it was reflected in the annual Farm Progress Show held in the Midwest. I recall walking through the 2008 Farm Progress Show amid the boom and seeing various ag industries offer pricey incentive gifts to farmers—including off-road vehicles. In the past, incentive gifts consisted of baseball hats and bags, not ATVs. In addition, as farm incomes rose, so did farmland prices. In the immortal words of Kenny Bania from *Seinfeld*, "That's gold, Jerry! Gold!"

Meanwhile, crude oil, which had been below $20 a barrel in the early 2000s, reached $145 a barrel by July of 2008. When gasoline prices at the pump shot over $4 per gallon in the United States, serious people were saying that crude oil would reach as high as $200 a barrel and gasoline would crack $6 per gallon. That's the kind of thing that catches a politician's attention, so some began to promote the theory that speculators were artificially pushing up prices. I should not have been surprised when, in May of 2008, I received my first request to testify before Congress.

With all the attention flooding in my direction and conspiracy theories rising from the likes of the Destroying Angel, I was in for a wild ride. But during the whirlwind, I made a momentous decision that would change the course of my career.

As I said several times earlier in this book, I have always had a deep admiration for the great agricultural economists of the past who defended the futures markets in the face of unwarranted attacks from the 1930s through the 1970s. Although I have never thought of myself as being in their league, I made a fateful decision in the summer of 2008 to step forward and take on the public role of defending commodity futures markets, confronting reasoned and bizarre theories.

So, the strange things happening in the commodity markets inspired me to rise to a challenge. I needed to determine what was happening in the markets and explain it as well as I could to the public. It would take me several years, but I finally managed it with the assistance of several outstanding colleagues, including Dwight Sanders, Phil Garcia, Darrel Good, and Aaron Smith.

In the early stages of this work, I testified before a U.S. Congressional hearing and learned first-hand what a circus D.C. can be. It was the first of two testimonies that I wouldn't soon forget. And as you will see, I knew a thing or two about being grilled.

Chapter 12
Ferris Irwin's Week Off

I n the immortal words of Ferris Bueller, "Life moves pretty fast. If you don't stop and look around once in a while, you could miss it."[1]

Those are wise words, although I don't recommend using them as an excuse to be as irrepressibly irresponsible as Ferris Bueller and his buddies in the classic John Hughes movie *Ferris Bueller's Day Off*. And I certainly don't advise anyone to be as reckless as I was during my undergraduate years at Iowa State. (My kids might read this.)

Perhaps my most reckless action of all came during the spring of 1980, the final quarter of my senior year. My good buddy, Jeff Hemer, and I decided to "stop and look around" when we should have been studying.

The result was a grilling by a professor almost as nerve-wracking as the one I received from Dean Thompson after my earlier incident with the fake iceberg at Iowa State.

Jeff and I met as freshmen at Iowa State in 1976 and became fast friends. Among other things, we shared a passion for automobile racing. I told him about my love of dirt track sprint car racing at Knoxville, and he shared with me his affinity for Formula One road track racing. It took only one trip to Knoxville to hook Jeff on sprint cars, and he rarely missed the Knoxville Nationals for the next thirty years.

I'm not sure who came up with the idea—me or Jeff—but one of us floated the notion of driving to California to watch the United States Grand Prix West at the end of March 1980. Formula One races are the most glamorous of all types of racing in the world and feature single-seater, needle-nosed, high-speed race cars in various Grand Prix events worldwide. (Formula One refers to the rules that govern Grand Prix racing.) Although I was a sprint car guy, I had long followed that series as well.

But there was a catch to our planned Grand Prix pilgrimage. If we intended to watch it, we had to go smack in the middle of our classes during the final quarter of my senior year. (Jeff still had another quarter to graduate.) It would become our version of the "senior skip" —or better yet, it would be our version of Ferris Bueller's Week Off.

The 1980 United States Grand Prix West was in Long Beach, California, on March 30, so I arranged for us to stay with my relatives in nearby Laguna Beach. Jeff lived in Kansas City, so that's where we would start our venture in his little blue Toyota Celica, which he called Fred. The Celica wasn't quite the same as the 1961 Ferrari 250 GT from *Ferris Bueller's Day Off*, but it was plenty fast.

We started the road trip in the early hours, driving the distance from Kansas City to Laguna Beach (over 1,600 miles) as if we were in a race. We stocked up with sandwiches and pop, so we never stopped except for fuel, flying west like a proverbial bat out of hell. We rarely dipped below 80 miles per hour the entire trip, which was insane, but so was my decision to make this ten-day trip in the middle of my final quarter in college.

I would miss a week and a half of what was only a ten-week quarter. It certainly was not my brightest idea because I was on track to go on to grad school the next fall, and I couldn't afford to flunk my last remaining required course.

Impervious to common sense, Jeff and I floored it to Laguna Beach in well under twenty-four hours. My enduring memory of the drive is coming down the mountains for Albuquerque, New Mexico, in the middle of the night with the Celica speedometer absolutely buried. It seemed like we were indeed flying. I will never comprehend how we were spared a speeding ticket or some sort of accident. Angels once again.

My relatives had a place on a craggy rock overlooking the Pacific Ocean, and they put us up in what to us were very luxurious digs. Jeff and I had the time of our lives at the Grand Prix, running around town, going to the practices, visiting the tents where we met the drivers and mechanics, and coming away with a healthy collection of autographs. Added to that was a bit of girl-watching. I was in gearhead heaven.

The 1980 Grand Prix West was an 80-lap race, covering 151.60 miles on a temporary course set up on the city's streets. That year, it was considered one of the most star-studded races ever held in Long Beach, but the winner was a relative newcomer at the time.

Nelson Piquet of Brazil came away with what would become the first of his twenty-three victories in Formula One racing. Our personal favorite was the French-Canadian driver, Gilles Villeneuve, who had to retire from the race with transmission problems. There were several accidents, but the most horrific was on lap fifty when Clay Regazzoni's brakes failed, and he hit Ricardo Zunino's car abandoned on the track.

Regazzoni smashed into a concrete wall, the accident paralyzing him from the waist down. His career was over, and his life had also nearly ended. But it was quite a day for Brazilians. In addition to Piquet's victory, his fellow Brazilian and two-time world champion, Emerson Fittipaldi, finished third.

After a dream-like week in California, Jeff and I hopped into the Toyota Celica named Fred and raced back to Iowa State. As Fred carried us closer and closer to home, reality began to set in. I had a growing sense of doom.

Back then, if you were a graduating senior, you didn't have to take a final exam if you had an A or B in a course. However, I had a low C or high D in my only challenging course, tax accounting, which my agribusiness major required for graduation. There was a severe risk of flunking if I had to take the final, and if I failed this final required course, it might jeopardize graduate school the following fall. With a low grade in such an important course, you are probably wondering why I spent ten days traveling to sunny California and back rather than studying in Iowa. But by now, you must have caught on that my judgment in those days was, at times, shall we say, questionable.

My tax accounting course was taught by a curmudgeonly old professor nearing retirement. As the finals loomed, I trudged into his office, which looked like the stereotypical cluttered workspace of an absentminded professor—books and papers stacked on every possible open surface. I sat down and looked across the desk at my professor, waiting to get grilled.

"Irwin!" His gravelly voice boomed. "I haven't seen much of you this semester."

"Yeah, that's true. I'm graduating and all that." As if graduating was a legitimate excuse to blow off his course.

"What are your plans next year?" he asked.

"I'm going on to grad school to get my master's degree in ag economics at Purdue."

"Good to hear that. Good! You must be a pretty smart guy."

Was there sarcasm in his tone?

"Let's look at your grades," he said, flipping open his grade book. As he studied them, he sighed, then muttered, "Irwin, hmmmmmm." Slyly, he looked up at me. "Are you *really* going to grad school?"

I shrank in my seat. "Yes, sir, I'm going to grad school."

He returned his gaze to his grade book and stroked his chin before looking at me again. He exhaled like an exasperated parent whose kid had just spilled his entire meal on the floor.

Then...

"You don't deserve it, Irwin, but I'm going to give you a B. Now get the hell out of my office!"

I raced from that room before he could change his mind. I couldn't believe it! He had given me a B, absolving me from taking the final—which might have doomed me.

To this day, I have been paying it forward for what that professor did for me—as undeserving as I might have been. I will do almost anything to help my seniors graduate. I help students study, some-times allowing extra projects to bump up their grades. All because of what that curmudgeonly old professor did for me.

Those who think my professor should have let me suffer the conse-quences have a solid argument. But what he did was the picture-perfect example of grace—undeserved forgiveness. In my case, his grace led to good, and I didn't become a lifelong slacker because of his generosity.

During my college days, I had been confronted *two times*—first by a dean and then by a professor. And in both cases, I received surprising doses of grace and unmerited understanding. Instead of expelling me, Dean Thompson offered a peek at his landmark research. And instead of flunking me, my tax accounting professor made it possible to advance to grad school.

Grace is in short supply in the world, but especially in politics, where your enemies will dredge up anything they can to destroy you, where cancel culture reigns supreme.

Going back to my days at the Irwin dinner table on Sunday after-noons, where our extended family had spirited political discussions, I have rarely shied away from strong, healthy debates. And as you'll soon see, I relish academic sparring. However, I take issue with the politics of personal destruction, where the goal is not to win an argu-ment but to destroy a person. Today, it's everywhere, as Twitter mobs descend on their victims like the feathered demons in Alfred Hitch-cock's *The Birds*.

I got a taste of the politics of personal destruction when I stepped into the public square to defend futures markets in the controversy over speculation. But that unpleasant episode didn't come until later when *The New York Times* wrote a hit piece on me and my colleague, Craig Pirrong. Initially, the debate generally stayed on topic without getting personal—although I quickly learned things sometimes get surreal when politics enter the picture.

In July of 2008, I entered, for the first time, the three-ring circus of a Congressional hearing. This hearing was a supersized version of the grilling that I got from my tax accounting professor—although I didn't expect the same amount of grace from politicians as I got from my professor.

D.C. doesn't do grace.

This was my first time in front of a Congressional hearing, but it wasn't the first time I had been invited. Earlier that year, in April of 2008, the office of Senator Carl Levin, a Democrat from Michigan, asked me to testify on the question of what was driving up crude oil prices. However, a few days before I was due to testify in early May, with my airline ticket already in hand, I suddenly received an email from Senator Levin's office, politely saying they no longer needed my testimony. I thought it would be a great honor to testify, and then poof! My invitation went up in smoke.

It didn't take long for me to get wind of the politics behind my disinvitation. Somebody must have discovered I would NOT be providing testimony implicating speculators in the run-up of crude oil and grain prices. I was too pro-market, so I had to go. I didn't fit the preset narrative: Speculation was bad.

Later in July 2008, however, I received another invitation to testify, this time before the U.S. House Agriculture Committee. In this case, no one retracted my invitation, and I found myself heading for Washington, D.C.

There were five of us on the panel—two academics and three from industry. The topic of commodity prices and futures trading was all over the news, so reporters packed the place, which was standing room only. It was a Friday, and about fifteen to twenty House committee members were present, with many shuffling in and out of the room. Although it's called a "hearing," many politicos made it clear they were more interested in talking, not hearing. They would pop into the room, make a statement about the evils of speculators, and then just as quickly vanish. The grandstanding was shameless.

Sparks flew at the hearing, thanks partly to my fellow academician, Craig Pirrong, a University of Houston finance professor. Craig and I were on the pro-free-market side, while the other three represented trade organizations—Robin Diamonte from the Committee on Investment of Employee Benefit Assets, Paul Cicio from Industrial Energy

Consumers of America, and Jeffrey Korzenik from VC & C Capital Advisors, LLC.

Those three were convinced that speculators were a significant source of the rise in commodity prices. None of us would give an inch to the other side, but I marveled at how Craig was particularly aggressive—quick to jump in and point out the mistakes of the industry folks. "Pugnacious" was the word I'd use to describe him. One of the industry guys was equally fiery, and I sat between them, caught in the crossfire and marveling at the theatrics.

Craig and I argued that there were logical reasons behind the behavior of the futures market, pushing prices up. But one of the panelists pushed back, trying to prove how irrational the markets were behaving. He said that when the Saudis announced they would increase oil production, the price of oil didn't decrease as expected.

"What do you have to say about that, Dr. Pirrong?" one of the congressmen asked pointedly. Craig then went on to explain to the congressman the difference between sweet crude oil and sour crude oil. Most people don't realize there is a range of crude oil types that vary in chemical characteristics and uses. In this case, the Saudis planned to increase the *sour crude* output, which did nothing to address the shortage of *light sweet crude oil*. And it was the light sweet crude shortage that was contributing to the rising prices.[2]

In another instance, Craig quickly pounced when a panel member attempted to come up with a folksy analogy, comparing the increase in speculation in oil futures trading with the rise in the water when many people jump into a pool. It was a very flawed analogy, and Craig ripped it to pieces. He explained that speculators are "out of the pool" once oil futures contracts get to the point of the commodity's delivery. They've already sold and are out of the market. So, if the speculators are out of the pool, how could they be raising the water level, so to speak? How could they be causing the price of oil to rise?[3]

Each of us got about five minutes to have our say. Then came the Q and A from the congressional committee, which was evenly divided among Republicans and Democrats. The chairman of the panel became extremely frustrated that the two sides couldn't agree on anything, saying something to the effect that he couldn't believe experts had such diametrically opposed viewpoints. He was so upset with us that he sent us away with homework. He ordered the five of us to call each other over the weekend to determine whether we could hammer out some compromises.

It never happened, although we exchanged a few emails. In the end, none of us changed our views.

Shortly after this panel testimony, my research partner, Dwight Sanders, and I wrote an op-ed for *The New York Times*—"Futures Imperfect," published on July 20, 2008.[4] When I first suggested to Dwight that we try to get an op-ed published in the *Times*, he thought it was a very long shot. Even my department head at the time told me, *"The New York Times* is never going to publish your stuff, Irwin."

But the op-ed did appear, and we began the piece by laying out the situation: Some people were asserting that high volumes of buying in the futures markets had created a bubble in which market prices far exceeded fundamental values. As a result, members of Congress were proposing to limit speculation in commodity futures markets.

Dwight and I went on to point out that this was nothing new. "The history of United States futures markets is riddled with confrontations between politicians and speculators," we said. "Just after World War II, soaring grain futures prices, especially for wheat, attracted political attention. President Harry Truman proclaimed that 'the cost of living in this country must not be a football to be kicked about by gamblers...'"[5]

It was the same old refrain.

Toward the end of our op-ed, we laid out three primary reasons why the recent price increases did not fit neatly with the bubble theory.

1. Livestock and meat futures markets did *not* experience dramatic price increases, even though the highest concentration of speculative buying had been in those markets. If speculation was boosting prices, why not in livestock and meat futures?

2. The high prices had also affected commodities that didn't have futures markets, such as edible beans.

3. When a bubble is present, commodity inventories should build, but for the previous two years, inventories for most commodities had remained stable or had fallen sharply.

Dwight and I went on to argue that the energy and grain markets were experiencing higher prices because of United States monetary policy and market forces, such as strong demand from China, India, and other developing nations. Moreover, the lack of growth in crude oil production affected the energy markets by boosting prices, while the grain markets saw higher prices due to greater demand for corn for biofuel production and unfavorable weather that hurt harvests.

"Regulation of commodity futures markets is at an important crossroads," we concluded in our op-ed. "Have we learned from our mistakes, or will we repeat them?"[6]

Many politicians in that Congressional hearing were more than happy to repeat their mistakes by proposing to overregulate the market. Welcome to D.C., where mistakes are not only made; they become preserved in bureaucracy, like mosquitoes trapped in amber for millions of years.

One curiosity about our Congressional hearing is that the three people on the anti-speculation side of the argument worked in the private sector, not academics. That's because, in the United States, most academics unite in their support of speculation, whether the professors are politically on the right or left.

Paul Krugman, the left-leaning economist who writes for *The New York Times*, gets just as frustrated with what he calls "the speculative nonsense" as I do. In his column on June 23, 2008, Krugman wrote, "the mysticism over how speculation is supposed to drive prices drives me crazy, professionally."[7]

To make his case, he used a hypothetical situation involving two people, Joe Shmoe and Harriet Who. Joe and Harriet have no direct involvement in oil production, but they like to bet. Joe bets that oil will cost $150 per barrel, but Harriet says it won't. Krugman points out that their bet has nothing to do with the spot price of oil; it does not affect "the actual price people pay to have a barrel of black gunk delivered."

In the same way, a futures contract is a bet about the future price of a commodity. If you think the price of a commodity is going up, you buy a futures contract. If you think it is going down, you sell a contract.

Both sides of the contract are placing bets on what the price will do, and Krugman concludes that this "has no, zero, nada direct effect" on the spot price of oil. He also says this is true no matter how many Joe Shmoes are placing bets on the price change.

Krugman noted there could be an *indirect* effect if someone who owns oil decides to sell a futures contract to Joe Shmoe. This person might hold oil off the market so he can meet the contract by delivering oil when it comes due. But as Krugman pointed out—and so did I— there wasn't any evidence from the inventory data that oil was being kept off the market. There was no hoarding going on.[8]

While American economists, both left and right, are fairly united in their disdain for the anti-speculation theories, that's not as true in Europe. Anti-speculation is more prevalent among European economists for reasons that escape me. For some, it has even become something of a moral crusade. Joachim Von Braun, a German economist, went as far as saying that speculation kills people. His simplistic logic went as follows: speculation raises food prices and, therefore, more people starve.[9]

In 2008 and 2009, it seemed like every government or quasi-government agency remotely connected to food released a report about the food price crisis—from the United States Senate to the World Trade Organization, the United Nations, and Oxfam. Many central banks got in on the act as well. Some went after speculators with a vengeance, proposing sweeping market regulations.

The report that caused the greatest stir by far came from Senator Carl Levin's Senate subcommittee. Released in late June 2009, it had the ominous-sounding title, "Excessive Speculation in the Wheat Market." Ironically enough, committee staff members had contacted me earlier in the year, and we began extensive conversations about the impact of speculation in the grain futures market and, more specifically, about non-convergence problems in wheat.

I was probably more than a little naïve, given the politics of the situation, but I believed Levin's subcommittee was receptive to my arguments. I was honestly shocked when the report turned out to be strongly anti-speculation. It supercharged the debate about speculative position limits in U.S. commodity futures markets, which had been simmering since the price spike of 2007-08.[10]

A few days before the Senate report was released, the committee staff kindly provided me with an embargoed copy. I discovered that to pull it together, the subcommittee had turned to the Commodity Futures Trading Commission (CFTC), which tracks data on commodity index traders. The subcommittee obtained CFTC data on commodity index trader positions in the grain futures market back to 2004, just before strange things started happening in the market, which made the data potentially very valuable.

Dwight and I decided we needed to get our hands on that data for our research, so I reached out to my Senate subcommittee contacts and asked if I could use the new data for academic research.

To my surprise, someone sent me a spreadsheet within a couple weeks, which was a good thing considering that later in the summer, I wrote a scathing commentary on the Senate wheat report along with other University of Illinois colleagues. That was the end of favors from the committee staffers.

The anti-speculator crowd argued that there was an immense growth in commodity index trader positions in the futures market during 2007 and 2008, pushing prices sky-high. But the CFTC data from the subcommittee contradicted this claim. The new data showed that, at least in the grain futures markets, the big growth in index positions happened in 2004 and 2005. If these trading positions were responsible for the price spike, the impact should have occurred immediately. There would not have been a two-year delay. In fact, the data showed that the growth in commodity index positions in the grain markets was flat during 2008.

This information was a gold mine. Dwight and I could go to town, using the newly acquired CFTC data and the publicly available statistics. Before this, we had gathered a lot of data and made our pro-speculation arguments over and over, but we hadn't done much in the way of formal statistical analysis. We now had a chance to dig in and do rigorous statistical tests ourselves.

In a fortunate confluence of events, I was contacted in late summer of 2009 by an economist, Linda Fulponi, who worked for the Organization for Economic Co-operation and Development (OECD). She asked if Dwight and I would be interested in writing a report and doing some original research on the speculation controversy. The OECD, founded in 1961 and based in Paris, was a relative bastion of economic rationality in Europe. The OECD's goal is to promote democracy and market economies, and its membership includes over thirty countries. As position papers started flying out of offices of one organization after another, the OECD decided to contribute its two cents to the debate. In the fall of 2009, while I was speaking at conferences and meetings in Europe, including at the OECD, I met with Linda to talk about the contract to do this report.

It was a hectic time for me because my dad was sick and struggling in the final stages of Alzheimer's. But Dwight and I saw an opportunity. We could use this contract to do the formal testing we were itching to get started on, especially now that we had our hands on the additional data from the Senate sub-committee. It also did not hurt to have the backing of a prestigious blue-ribbon organization like the OECD.

While our contract didn't offer much money, it was enough to jump-start our research. In fact, the OECD got more for their money than they ever could have imagined. Dwight and I worked for six months and conducted an exhaustive empirical analysis looking for clues to whether there was any statistical correlation between the positions of commodity index traders and price movements in both the ag and energy futures markets.

When we turned in our report to the OECD, Linda and her colleagues were stunned. They had expected a standard twenty-page report, and we delivered a 131-page, five-pound behemoth. Thirty pages were devoted to an extensive literature review. Dwight and I had basically written a dissertation on the topic.

Our statistical analysis was exhaustive. We took all the available CFTC data on index fund positions and tested whether there was a relationship to price movements in a wide range of commodity futures markets. No matter how we conducted the tests, we kept coming up with the same answer. There was no correlation between index fund positions and the rise in commodity futures prices. We concluded that index funds did not cause a bubble in agricultural, energy, or metal futures prices. As a result, we argued that the evidence did not support new regulations limiting index investors' participation in commodity futures markets.[11]

Linda, our OECD contact, was not afraid of our conclusions. Standing a little under five feet tall, she was a fierce fighter and championed our research at the agency. But as the report went through revisions and worked its way up the chain of command, some at the OECD were less enthusiastic about releasing it. Linda argued that if we did the analysis correctly, the OECD shouldn't be afraid of the conclusions. But the report was so controversial that it was unclear if it would ever be available to the public.

Before they could consider releasing anything, I had to participate in yet another hearing. This time, I appeared in front of an OECD working group, a high-level policy-making committee that would be influential in deciding if the public would have access to our data.

So, in May of 2010, I found myself in Paris again (tough duty) to testify on the results of our report. OECD officials prepped me for my testimony because the French would jump all over our conclusions, and the Germans weren't any happier about our findings. The testimony was to take place at the OECD headquarters, a gorgeous chateau on the outskirts of Paris. As my dad used to say, I was "walking in tall cotton."

Soon, I found myself in a vast room, which looked a bit like the United Nations, with officials wearing headsets to translate my testimony. As I faced yet another grilling, I tried to ignore my nerves but found it hard to do. I had to appear before the assembled governmental representatives from around the world, some of them openly hostile, and I didn't have the pugnacious Craig Pirrong to give me cover.

At the time, I wasn't sure our findings would see the light of day, but, remarkably, a condensed version was finally released in June 2010.[12] It was like a bomb going off in the bureaucracies of Europe. Dwight and I thought our results were so obvious that no one could disagree with them. But leave it to the Europeans. I'm unsure if I have ever produced anything that caused so much consternation among so many people as that OECD report.

Immediately, the OECD started getting pushback. For instance, Sir Richard Branson, the founder of the Virgin Group and a good buddy of President Obama, co-wrote a letter to the editor of *The Economist* in direct response. The criticisms leveled by Branson and others essentially took issue with both the data and our methods.[13]

Dwight and I decided that if some people didn't agree with the way we conducted our tests, we'd do them differently by gathering more data and looking at the issue from new angles.

So, over the ensuing years, we continued refining our data and methods, but we kept coming to the same result. There was no correlation between index fund positions and the rise (or fall) in commodity prices in ag and energy futures markets.

If index funds really were driving price movements, it should have been obvious in the data. It was not. After reviewing the empirical evidence, one observer wryly noted, "If we claim that elephants were playing in the backyard, then we would expect to see their footprints."[14]

We stuck to our guns, but so did our opposition, and conflict over this issue kept escalating. During this time, I also came to the surprising discovery that I had a nemesis. His name was Michael Masters.

Chapter 13
Bubble Boy

No one messed with the rodeo guys, not even the Iowa State football players, during my undergraduate years in the 1970s. The rodeo guys rode bulls—for fun!

These were the guys who sat on the backs of animals that weighed 1,500 to 2,000 pounds—beasts that could stomp you to sawdust if they hadn't already gored you. These were the guys who would start fights at the drop of a hat, and most of the time, they were the ones dropping the hat.

The 1970s were well before bull riders wore Kevlar vests to protect themselves from being gored, so these guys played with death all the time. I was neither a rodeo guy nor a tough guy, and I didn't get into many fights. However, I had several friends in the rodeo crowd from my earlier days as a steer jockey. These were the same folks that came to my aid during the infamous iceberg-towing incident.

Toward the end of my final quarter at Iowa State in late spring of 1980, one of my rodeo friends invited me to a local bar in the Radisson Hotel in Ames, Iowa, after the annual Block and Bridle Club banquet. Nothing of note happened while I was at the bar with my girlfriend and future wife, Kim—just a bunch of people shooting the breeze and having a few beers. So, imagine my surprise the next day when I opened the newspaper and read a headline about a brawl at the Radisson Hotel bar, which required the services of state troopers to get it under control.

Incredibly, it all unfolded about fifteen minutes after Kim and I left, and it was like something out of the Wild West. In fact, old Western movies inspired the trigger for the melee.

As the story went, one of the rodeo guys, a fellow I will call Bud, apparently was getting quite inebriated. I did not know him very well, and Kim and I were not sitting with his group when we were there. The Radisson had a huge mirror behind the bar—like the ones you see in Western movies.

In Western barroom brawls, a cowboy inevitably hurls a chair at someone who ducks, and the chair shatters the enormous mirror.

Well, Bud always wondered what it would be like to heave a chair at a bar's mirror. So, on this night, he suddenly stood, picked up a big stool, stepped in front of the bar, and hurled it as hard as he could against the plate glass, shattering it into thousands of shards. The bouncers pounced on Bud, and that's when all hell broke loose.

Bud was like one of the bulls he rode, lashing out wildly. Even though he was in the wrong, rodeo club ethics required you to have each other's backs. So, other club members jumped into the fray, and it became an all-out brawl. Once the Ames police arrived, the bull riders proceeded to pick a fight with them. It was a John Wayne movie come to life, and I was so glad I had gotten out of there in the nick of time.

As I said, I was not one to get into fist fights. Professional squabbles, however, were a different thing. I was never one to shy away from conflicts of a more intellectual variety—polite disagreements or white-collar wrangling, you might say.

In 2008, all hell broke loose in the economy, including the commodity markets. Suddenly, I found myself in the academic equivalent of a barroom brawl, although nothing was broken except for maybe a few egos.

For me, it all started when I opened *The Wall Street Journal* in May of 2008 and read about the Congressional hearing to which I'd been disinvited. Someone I had never heard of made an outrageous claim that speculators were almost solely responsible for driving up crude oil prices. I couldn't believe anyone was taking these claims seriously, but they were.

One evening, I was venting about this at the dinner table, particularly about the man making the wildest claims, when my oldest son, Matt, declared, "Dad! You have a nemesis!"

I had never looked at it that way but realized Matt was right. I did have a nemesis, and his name was Michael Masters, a hedge-fund manager. As *The Wall Street Journal* wrote in September of 2008, Masters had "stumbled into the spotlight after sending an email to acquaintances earlier this year, complaining that institutions were driving up the price of fuel, food and metals." The villains driving up prices were "index speculators," Masters said in this email, and they had to be stopped.

According to *The Wall Street Journal*, this email eventually reached Senator Joseph Lieberman, an independent from Connecticut, and then it "ricocheted to other legislators. Mr. Masters soon testified before Congress and began informally advising legislators."

As Senator Claire McCaskill reportedly told Masters, "You may be the most powerful guy in Washington right now."[1]

Crude oil had just gone over $140 a barrel, boosting gasoline prices at the pump and rattling motorists. A villain had to be found, and Masters, of course, pointed at evil speculators. He essentially argued that commodity index investors (speculators) had overwhelmed the normal supply and demand function in commodity markets, causing a massive bubble in the grain and crude oil futures markets. Masters claimed the price of crude oil should be closer to $60 or $70 per barrel. So, he wasn't just claiming that speculators had inflated prices by one, two, or three percent. He was talking about prices being 50 percent above what they should be. In his way of thinking, speculators had unheard-of power to move the market.

He provided no rigorous evidence to back up these claims besides some slick charts and his hedge fund trader experience. But he captured the imagination of politicians using colorful language, and his charts made everything seem so simple.

I'll give him credit. He effectively spoke to non-economist groups, offering a story that seemed to fit the facts. As another *Wall Street Journal* article put it: "'Speculators' were spotted everywhere this side of the grassy knoll."[2]

Among Masters' famous charts was one showing a dramatic increase of index investments in futures markets (a trend I described in Chapter 9). He was correct in pointing out that the investors behind pension funds and university endowments were taking large positions in commodity futures markets.

Pension funds, university endowments, and sovereign wealth funds were looking to add commodities to their portfolio to manage risk. Returns from commodities tend to be uncorrelated to returns from stocks. Therefore, if you added them to your portfolio, the idea was that if your stocks take a hit, your commodities could remain unaffected, giving you protection.

Masters claimed these large investments in commodity futures markets created the massive bubble, pushing oil and grain prices to ridiculous levels. What was truly ridiculous was that some people bought this argument.

I should point out that Dwight Sanders and I have said, from the start, that large orders from index funds can affect prices in the commodity futures market. But our research over more than fifteen years has consistently shown that the effect these huge orders have on prices is at most *small and short-lived*—maybe a week or two at the most.[3] Masters claimed the consequences were huge and could last years.

In theory, there should be *no impact* of large orders on price because there are always two sides to every sale of a futures market contract. There is someone on the buying (long) side and the selling (short) side. The two parties must agree on a price that satisfies both, so in theory, the price should reflect a reasonable value. Therefore, no matter the trading volume, there should be no impact on prices—*in theory.*

In reality, there could be a small impact from large orders. Let's say an investor wants to make a considerable order in the corn futures market, with the price of corn being $3 per bushel. Those on the sell or short side might look at this huge order and say, "I'm not quite willing to sell at $3 per bushel. The size of the order is just too big." However, if those on the buy side give the short side an incentive, the deal might go through. The trader on the short side might say, "I'm not willing to sell to you at $3 per bushel. But I will make the deal if I can go short (sell) at $3.05 per bushel."

When a lot of these deals occur, the price of corn could increase— but only slightly and only for a brief time—maybe minutes or hours, or days in extreme cases. But not for years.

Although Masters claimed that the futures price for crude oil was as much as 50 percent too high due to speculators, today we know normal supply and demand forces pushed crude oil prices to $145 per barrel.

As *The Wall Street Journal* indicated in June 2008, one of the significant factors driving prices up "is supply and demand, as prosaic as that might seem amid today's political agitation. Energy consumption is surging in China and India, and global supply is not growing fast enough to keep up. Congress could do something useful if it opened up America's vast natural resources, which are blocked by environmental romanticism. But then, it's so much easier to shoot the price messengers."[4]

In other words, in 2008, it was so much easier for a host of politicians to buy the Masters' argument hook, line, and sinker.

Masters became the public face of the speculation debate, and he was called to testify before Congress repeatedly. As Masters made his mark, Congress began to assemble a myriad of proposals to slow the speculation train. Essentially, the idea was to limit the size of positions speculators could take in commodity futures markets.

For instance, one of the ideas floated was for the Commodity Futures Trading Commission (CFTC) to distinguish between "legitimate" and "non-legitimate" traders. Legitimate traders owned grain, like farmers, while non-legitimate traders were those evil speculators who traded contracts but didn't own the physical commodity. We were back to early twentieth-century attitudes when politicians complained about traders in "wind wheat." It was the same old misunderstanding.

People failed to understand that although speculators may not own the physical commodity, they brought liquidity to the market. They offered a greater pool of traders who could take the opposite side of a futures contract.

If you drive speculators from the market through regulation, people wanting to take a short position (sell), like hedgers, might find themselves in trouble when they need someone to take the opposite long side (buy). Without speculators, fewer traders are available to take the other side of futures contracts. This predicament is referred to as reducing the liquidity of the market.

Think of a small futures contract order as a pebble dropped into a body of water which causes tiny ripples to settle quickly. The large orders that Masters was concerned about were like dropping a large stone into the lake. Its ripples will be bigger because larger orders can have a modest impact on prices. But Masters talked about huge impacts that lasted for years, like tsunamis that circumnavigate the globe and keep going.

Driving speculators from the market and thereby reducing liquidity only exacerbates the problem. The impact is negligible if you drop a giant rock into a large body of water like Lake Michigan. But drop one into a small swimming pool, and the effect is much greater.

When you reduce liquidity by driving away speculators, it's like shrinking your pool of water; you run the risk of increasing price volatility. To use the words of mothers around the world, "You're cutting off your nose to spite your face."

Masters summed up his ideas in a report that was ingeniously called "The Accidental Hunt Brothers." His clever reference was to the Texas oilmen who attempted to corner the silver market in the late 1970s. Although they failed, this was a genuine attempt to buy up the world's silver and corner the market. Masters argued that speculators were "accidental Hunt brothers" because the big orders from commodity index funds were inadvertently driving up oil and grain prices, as would happen in a real corner.[5]

During this controversy, my research collaboration began in earnest with Dwight Sanders, an agricultural economics professor at Southern Illinois University. We already had a long and profitable partnership because our skills are complementary.

Dwight is a great data man and a much better statistician than me. He will take the lead in data analysis and often write our first draft while I act as the closer, taking what we've got and being an absolute bulldog about refining everything on paper and getting the details just right. Dwight prefers to stay in the background, while I'm more visible when impacting policy with our work. We make a great team.

Dwight hails from the Branson area in southwest Missouri, where he grew up on a small 80-acre farm. Their land was not suitable for a large-scale grain farm, so his parents were part-time farmers; his mom kept chickens, while his dad managed 35 to 40 cows. According to Dwight, his grandparents lived next door, the properties separated by a 10-acre field. This field was lorded over by a strutting rooster ready to attack anyone who dared invade his territory.

"Me and my friends practiced our sprinting when we crossed that field," Dwight recalled. "It was a mad dash to get across the field before the rooster got to you. We learned to get over barbed wire fences pretty fast."

The rooster would never quite reach Dwight, but the bird once sank its spurs into a friend's calf. "No stitches were required, but it did require some peroxide and a little bit of TLC from my mom," he said.[6]

That rooster makes a fitting metaphor for Michael Masters, who ran around the proverbial farm field making a fuss about speculators without a shred of solid evidence. Like a rooster, Masters was a lot of show and feathers.

Dwight said the number one thing people get wrong about speculators is the notion that everybody is getting rich.

"They don't understand that speculation is a zero-sum game," he said. Because there are two sides to every contract, one makes money while the other doesn't.

Dwight and I published our first academic paper on the speculation controversy in 2009. Since then, we have co-authored over 20 others —more than one per year. Whenever Dwight and I would write something on commodity index trading and futures prices, a flurry of criticism would arise, and we'd respond, kicking up another wave of criticism to which we'd react.

It was an endless feedback loop. Publish. Receive criticism. Respond. Publish again. Receive criticism again. Respond again.

Even my colleagues noticed our persistence. Whenever I would see my good friend Wade Brorsen, a distinguished ag econ professor from Oklahoma State University, he would exclaim in his southern drawl, "Scott, you're just writing the same paper over and over and over. Write something new!"

It's true. Dwight and I were covering the same ground. But in the process, we were refining our methods and digging deeper into the data. It paid off, especially when I found myself tangling with another opponent—Chris Gilbert, a British economics professor, now retired.

Gilbert produced one of the first academic papers purporting to show that commodity index traders were at the center of the controversy over price spikes in 2007 and 2008. When he published it in 2009, Dwight and I were skeptical of his results.[7] This was when we started making similar formal statistical tests for our OECD report (see Chapter 12), but we had very different results. Even when we used the same data that Gilbert used, we didn't deduce the same answers. This was very curious.

The differences were mainly due to Gilbert's use of an index to average commodity index trader positions across agricultural futures markets (an index of index positions). It was never entirely clear to either of us why you would take an average of index positions for statistical analysis when you have the actual index positions for the individual agricultural markets. But I am pretty sure it was because good data on index trader positions were hard to come by for the crude oil futures market.

Gilbert thought the average of index positions in agricultural markets should correlate with index positions in other markets, like crude oil, for which actual data were limited. We now know this was a flawed assumption and skewed the statistical results.

I don't believe Gilbert fully embraced Masters' ideas, with his insistence on a massive bubble caused by large purchases of index funds in commodity markets. But Gilbert certainly saw these index funds as part of the problem. So, he and I developed a friendly rivalry on the issue because the anti-speculation side often used his papers. We even jointly headlined an international conference on commodity markets in Germany during the summer of 2014. A nice time was had by all.

My duels with Gilbert were mainly fought in research journals. Every research paper must run a gauntlet of reviewers before it's accepted or rejected. Once accepted, it is often contingent on certain changes.

The reviewers, while supposedly anonymous, are also not supposed to know the author they're reviewing. But in our small circle of economists working on the commodity futures market, it's not hard to suspect who is offering up reviews and who is writing what paper. We know each other's style too well. After a while, I even recognized Gilbert's font type.

While it's more challenging to determine one's reviewers, when Dwight and I submitted one of our early papers on the commodity price crisis and got rejected, I suspected it was due to Gilbert's influence. However, we eventually published it in the *Canadian Journal of Agricultural Economics*. I assume Gilbert was not a reviewer for that submission because it's unlikely that we'd have gotten it past him. After the paper released in 2011, it wound up becoming one of that journal's most cited papers during the remainder of the decade.[8]

For that paper, we used the data obtained with the help of the friendly Senate staffer noted in Chapter 12. This information showed that trade positions in the index funds for four major grain markets— corn, soybeans, and two types of wheat—grew most rapidly in 2004 and 2005 *before* prices began to spike. Trade positions were flat in 2007 and 2008, when they supposedly created a bubble that distorted prices. Gilbert didn't have access to this crucial data in his work.

As I said earlier, European economists, like Gilbert, seem to have a bias against speculators, but most American economists do not. Ken Singleton, a prominent finance professor from Stanford, was a rare exception. His research appeared to implicate commodity index investors as an important cause of high crude oil prices. Singleton is a brilliant finance professor, but he's not a commodity futures person, nor has he spent his career studying the futures market. Among economists, he was something of an outlier on this subject.

So, in August 2011, the Commodity Futures Trading Commission (CFTC) sponsored a major academic conference in Washington, D.C., on speculation and commodity futures markets. Singleton and I were headliners, taking opposite viewpoints. Singleton, whose name carried a lot of authority for those in the room, delivered his paper first.[9]

Dwight and I were confident that Singleton had fumbled his analysis. He used a method of projecting index positions in crude oil futures borrowed from Mike Masters—similar to the problem that plagued Gilbert's research. This was an enormous clue that something was wrong with his data and that his statistical results were not to be trusted. The method essentially used index positions in tiny futures markets, such as feeder cattle and Kansas City wheat, to project positions in the mammoth crude oil futures market. Using small markets to make projections for huge markets is not exactly a formula for success. So, when I stood to give my presentation, immediately following Singleton, I began by essentially saying that everything he just stated was wrong.

As I noted earlier, I may not be drawn to barroom brawls, but I didn't shy away from academic dustups.

I was nervous as I made my presentation because I was taking on a bright star of the academic community. I was picking a fight with someone way above my pay grade. Moreover, I based my analysis on Dwight's and my new work, and this was my first time presenting our findings.

Our paper needed a catchy title—at least catchy by academic standards, where documents have dry, somber ones. So, I convinced Dwight we should call it "Testing the Masters Hypothesis in Commodity Futures Markets."

By journalistic standards, this, too, may seem mundane. But what set it apart was giving the theory a name—"the Masters Hypothesis." In academic circles, this was the equivalent of hurling a wooden chair at a plate-glass mirror behind a bar.[10]

When I pitched the title to Dwight, he hesitated to call the theory the Masters Hypothesis. It seemed too in-your-face. Too aggressive. Too provocative.

Perhaps I was behaving like the over-aggressive rooster in Dwight's 10-acre field, but he reluctantly conceded. Looking back, it was a brilliant move. The name stuck, and to this day, the idea that commodity index investors can wield so much power over commodity prices is called the Masters Hypothesis. To drive home my point, I began my presentation with a photo of Masters and images of some of his infamous charts.

But I wasn't ready for what happened next. It was like receiving a sucker punch right out of the blue.

The CFTC, which sponsored the conference, consists of politically appointed commissioners balanced between Democrats and Republicans. However, the CFTC director is appointed by the president, so then President Obama named Gary Gensler, a pro-regulation appointee sympathetic to the Masters Hypothesis crowd.

Perhaps that explains what happened after I finished tearing into Singleton's research. The chief economist at the CFTC was Andre Kirilenko, the conference's main organizer. After I presented, Kirilenko stood and said they had a special guest to respond to my presentation before the scheduled break.

I had no idea this was coming. I had not been informed.

Imagine my shock when Kirilenko introduced Michael Masters, asking him to comment on my presentation. They set me up. Masters had been sitting in the back, waiting to counterpunch me and my research.

To this day, I really cannot remember much. The only part I recall him saying was, "Scott, you've got to get a new photo of me." He didn't think much of the one from my presentation.

It was the first time I met my nemesis face-to-face in public. I talked to Masters during the break once the dust settled after our presentations. It was an awkward and brief encounter, and I could sense he was unhappy I had named his ideas "the Masters Hypothesis."

Despite our sharp difference about the markets, he seemed genuinely decent. This was academics, not the WWE, so our exchange was polite. Any trash-talking took place in our minds, not out in the open. Ours was intellectual combat. No one needed the state police, and no one broke any giant mirrors.

But this was only the beginning. Things were just heating up.

Chapter 14
The Hatfields and the McCoys

L ike George Washington, I have a story that involves a tree and an axe—although Washington's tale revolves around a cherry tree, and mine is all about an apple tree. Washington's story underscores unfailing honesty, whereas my tree-and-axe escapade accentuates my propensity to do stupid things growing up. My family loves the "dumb Scott" stories in circulation (who runs in front of a truck?), but their all-time favorite has to be this one.

Just south of the garage on our farm stood two lovely apple trees, which sprouted beautiful white blossoms in the spring. My mom loved those trees. So, when I saw that a large branch had fallen after a storm, leaving an ugly stub, I decided to do something about it. As a favor to her, I would cut off the remaining branch stub, which was at least six inches in diameter.

While my motives were good, my execution was not. It was the summer of 1971, just after my seventh-grade year, so I was the ideal age for doing dumb things. My first mistake was deciding to attack the branch with an axe. I can't remember why I didn't use a chainsaw, but my father had probably banned me from going anywhere near such a dangerous tool.

The stub was about eight feet off the ground, so I needed something on which to stand. Did I use a ladder? Nope.

Remember, I was a seventh grader. I hauled out a bench but standing on it wasn't enough to put me within reach. So, I placed a box on the bench and clambered on top.

You can probably see where this is going.

I was a tall, gangly kid—about 5 foot 10 inches, weighing around 130 pounds: all legs and arms and uncoordinated movement.

I swung the axe and barely made a dent in that thick branch. The blade was dull, so it would take some extra oomph. I kept at it, slowly chipping away, but my unsteady foundation wobbled as my swings became more vigorous. As I pulled back with the axe, my legs suddenly went out from underneath me.

I can still see it to this day—a moment imprinted forever in my mind. My feet slipped, and the tool flew from my grasp. I sprawled backward while the axe soared straight into the air. I can still visualize it falling—straight for my head!

Just before I landed on my back on the solid ground, the axe struck me with a glancing blow to the noggin. The sharp end had hit me! I might've died if it hadn't been dull.

After falling and realizing the axe nailed me on my forehead, something wet trickled toward my eyes. When I regained my senses, I rose to my feet and sprinted to the house, blood streaming down my face. As I appeared in the doorway, I must've looked like a blood-covered Sissy Spacek from the movie *Carrie* because my mom was horrified. What had her son done now?

She and my sisters wrapped my head in a towel before we hopped into the car for Jefferson, Iowa, and drove to the same hospital my dad had taken me to after I was hit by the Pepsi truck four years earlier. In fact, I was probably treated by the same doctor—our family physician, Dr. Thompson.

Since head wounds bleed profusely, my injury probably looked worse than it was. But the damage was deep enough that I came away with about fifteen stitches. To this day, I can still feel the scar—and my sisters have never let me forget the incident. Dr. Thompson gave me a stern lecture about the stupidity of trying to chop a branch with an axe while standing on a box perched on top of a bench. I wouldn't have been surprised if he had scrawled it on a prescription pad and told me to tape it to my bathroom mirror.

The image of me standing on a box on a bench while swinging an axe over my head is ridiculous. But it's also the picture-perfect metaphor for systemic risk.

In 2008, while controversy heated over the impact of speculation on commodity prices, much of it centered around systemic risk. One side claimed speculators added risk to the system, while other economists, such as myself, said speculators lessened it.

When we discuss systemic risk in an economic sense, we're talking about the threat to the system as a whole, such as the banking system or the futures industry, including the trading exchanges. When a system is unstable, risk has a way of cascading through it, increasing rather than being managed and minimized.

When one large futures brokerage firm fails, it takes out another with it. And then that firm takes out another. Risk crashes through the system just as my bench-and-box ladder flew from underneath me, and I came crashing down. Systemic risk is all about inherent instability.

One of the best examples of the dangers posed by systemic risk in a commodity futures market occurred in 2022, when the price of nickel skyrocketed in the wake of the Russian invasion of Ukraine. Russia is a major producer of nickel, but the war disrupted production, raising the price of this precious commodity dramatically. Nickel is a key industrial metal essential for electric car battery production.

Xiang Guangda, founder of the Tsingshan Holding Group Company in China, did not see this spike coming, putting him in a precarious position. Guangda is also known as "Big Shot" because of the power he wields as one of the major nickel producers and investors. (What is it about commodity traders and their nicknames?)

Big Shot expected nickel prices to decrease because, according to *Bloomberg News*, "He had a rule of thumb that whenever prices rose above $20,000, he would consider shorting nickel...because his production costs in Indonesia were as low as $10,000 a ton."[1]

So, he massively shorted nickel—he *sold* nickel contracts—assuming prices would go lower. He planned that when the prices dropped, as anticipated, he would settle, or offset, his short contracts by buying nickel at a lower price than he sold. Buy low and sell high, raking in gobs of money.

But things did not go as planned. Instead of dropping, nickel soared by 250 percent in two days because of the invasion of Ukraine, *Bloomberg* reported.[2] Big Shot's position was suddenly as shaky as a seventh-grade boy standing on a box on a bench with an axe in his hand. Big Shot had a "Big Short" problem, and he struggled to cover his "margin calls," which reportedly were in the billions.

To understand a margin call, you need to realize that when traders buy or sell a futures contract, they only have to pay upfront about 5 to 10 percent of the face value of the contract to the futures exchange. This is the "leverage" that many commodity futures traders find so attractive. The "initial margin" is a good-faith deposit to cover a portion of future losses, if any occur.

A "maintenance margin" occurs after losses have eaten into your initial margin, and the exchange requires you to restore the initial balance. For example, if the price of nickel rises by $100 per ton and you have sold (short), you have to put an additional $100 per ton into your account to restore the initial balance. This is commonly known as a margin call in the futures trade.

A bedrock principle of futures trading is that you must settle all accounts by the day's end before trading resumes the next day. Therefore, buyers (the longs) and sellers (the shorts) must make good on their margin calls each and every day; that's why the price at the end of the day is called the "settlement" price. Margin calls must be met, with the losers paying the winners.

In the case of nickel, things came to a head on Monday, March 8, 2022. Big Shot and other large traders tried to get out of some of their short positions by buying back futures contracts, which caused nickel futures to explode to over $100,000 per ton, a new all-time high price. As a result, the shorts (sellers) like Big Shot, who were already big losers, suddenly faced catastrophic losses and mammoth margin calls.

This is when the exchange that has operated the nickel contracts for decades—the London Metal Exchange (LME)—stepped in and changed the rules of the game.

Rather than making the losers pay out, the LME extended credit to traders such as Big Shot (he wasn't the only short in a fix, but he was the biggest), which violated the bedrock principle that the losers pay up to the winners. Then the LME compounded the problem by simply canceling numerous contracts on March 8, taking Big Shot off the hook for a considerable sum. This also meant that people on the winning side (the longs) would not reap their payday. Finally, the LME suspended nickel futures trading altogether for the week following March 8.[3]

All of this was unprecedented in the modern-day history of commodity futures trading. A futures exchange must honor all trades executed per its existing rules to maintain marketplace integrity. Not honoring the trades would be like the NCAA stepping in and canceling March Madness if Duke were losing big time to the University of Illinois in the final minutes. Allow me to fantasize for a moment with my Illini.

In this scenario, there is neither a winner nor a loser, and Duke walks away with its record intact. No one would be happy except Duke fans.

This is essentially what the LME did for Big Shot and his powerful trading company, the Tsingshan Holding Group Company. But why would the London exchange take such a drastic step? Did they fear that the Tsingshan Group would be unwilling or unable to pay the billions of dollars it owed? Were they afraid if Tsingshan went bankrupt, it would take down several important banks? Could it even bankrupt the LME clearinghouse, which was ultimately responsible for covering the billions owed to the winners—the longs—if Big Shot could not or would not meet his margin calls? Such a scenario could start a contagion of bankruptcies, the kind of systemic risk that people fear.

In other words, the fear of systemic risk may be what drove the LME to self-immolate over nickel. I don't see how their nickel contract can rebound from this debacle. There is already clear evidence that liquidity for the contract (the volume of trading) is drying up. Who would ever take a risk with the LME's nickel contract if those on the winning side worry that their contract might be nullified to protect a prominent investor? This is the most spectacular example of the fear of systemic risk leading a 145-year-old futures exchange to take such unprecedented actions. Other exchanges are already circling, thinking about starting their own futures contracts for nickel.

It also means those who got shafted (the longs) will be filing lawsuits that could stretch for a decade or more. If this happens, my colleague, Craig Pirrong, will be very busy. Craig, the University of Houston finance professor who testified alongside me before Congress, has made a career out of studying systemic risk in futures markets and other financial markets. As a result, he testifies in these kinds of cases regularly.

Studying systemic risk wasn't part of Craig's original plan, however. He received his PhD from the University of Chicago, studying industrial organization. He didn't get involved in commodities until 1986, when Fred Arditti, former chief economist for the Chicago Mercantile Exchange (CME), hired him to work at GNP Commodities. When Arditti had a falling out with the GNP owner and left the firm, things also turned sour for Craig, who decided to leave. So, on the morning of October 19, 1987, Craig hopped on an early train, reached the office at 30 S. Wacker Drive by 7 a.m., and dropped a resignation letter on his boss's desk.

One-half hour later, the markets opened, and prices crashed. It was Black Monday when stock markets worldwide went into a freefall, declining by anywhere from 20 to 39 percent. Some feared it was the beginning of another Great Depression.

"I was watching this and wondering, 'Is the world going to come to an end?'" Craig recalled. "I figured that the 19th wasn't the best day to resign." When his boss told him that the CME clearinghouse almost failed that morning, Craig said, "That was my first clue about systemic risk and the kinds of things that could go wrong."[4]

Black Monday was pivotal for Craig. But the most significant event that drew him into the world of commodities and risk was the Ferruzzi scandal. In May 1989, an Italian conglomerate, Ferruzzi, SA, cornered the soybean market. Then they attempted to do it again in July, triggering an emergency order from the Chicago Board of Trade (CBOT). The order required all firms holding July 1989 soybean futures contracts above a certain limit to reduce their speculative positions over five business days. The emergency order applied to "all firms" that exceeded this speculative limit, but in reality, it was aimed solely at Ferruzzi.

Eventually, farmers sued the CBOT over the Ferruzzi corner of soybeans, which tanked the price of their crop after it ended, and they even went as far as dumping truckloads of beans at the Board of Trade's door in Chicago. The farmers' lawsuit was decided in the CBOT's favor in 2002. Meanwhile, a class-action suit was filed against Ferruzzi and settled in 2006.

Craig Pirrong acted as an expert witness in both cases.

As Craig explains in his "Streetwise Professor" blog, "Ferruzzi was a rather outlandish company that eventually collapsed in 1994. Like many Italian companies, it was leveraged out the wazoo. Moreover, it had become enmeshed in the Italian corruption/mob investigations of the early 1990s, and its chairman, Raul Gardini, committed suicide in the midst of the scandal. The traders who carried out the corners were located in stylish Paris, but they were real commodity cowboys of the old school."[5]

When commodity prices exploded in 2007 and 2008, Craig Pirrong and I became the leading defenders of the futures market. But, as I mentioned earlier, Craig tended to be more combative than me. As the controversy heightened, he began a feud with Gary Gensler, head of the Commodity Futures Trading Commission (CFTC)—the government agency overseeing commodity futures markets. Today, Gensler is head of the U.S. Securities Exchange Commission (SEC), which enforces laws against stock market manipulation, in the Biden Administration.

But no one should be surprised about the Pirrong/Gensler feud. Craig, after all, was a descendant of the Hatfields—one half of the

Hatfield and McCoy feud, the most famous feud in American history. Craig's grandfather was raised in the hills of southeast Ohio, and his great-grandmother was a Hatfield through and through.

Ironically, the Hatfield and McCoys' conflict started with a commodity—a pig, to be exact. In 1878, Randolph McCoy accused Floyd Hatfield of stealing one of his pigs. A Hatfield relation, Bill Staton, testified on behalf of the defense, and as a result, Floyd Hatfield got off scot-free.

The McCoys blew their lids, and two years later, Sam and Paris McCoy murdered Staton, the trial's star witness. Then, a couple of months after that, a Hatfield boy and McCoy girl started a Romeo-and-Juliet romance with a slightly different outcome. The Hatfield boy abandoned the very pregnant McCoy girl and took up with her cousin —another McCoy.

Thus began the infamous Hatfield and McCoy feud in the hills of Kentucky and West Virginia.

Things got even uglier in August 1882 when three McCoy brothers stabbed Ellison Hatfield and shot him in the back. After Ellison died, the Hatfields apprehended the three McCoy brothers, bound them to pawpaw trees, and fired more than fifty shots into them.

Craig's great-grandmother, a Hatfield, lived deep in the coal country of southeastern Ohio. To illustrate just how ferocious she could be, he told me about when she gave birth to his grandpa. After going into labor, she sent out her younger brother to fetch the doctor, but it was a stormy night in April, and the physician refused.

Furious and undeterred, Craig's great-grandmother then sent her older brother, Frank, who stuck a shotgun in the doctor's face, which is much more persuasive than a co-pay. The doctor wisely relented and delivered the baby. Almost forty years later, when Craig's grandfather discovered the family never paid the doctor his $5 shotgun delivery fee, he settled the debt with the doctor's widow, priding himself on not having anything outstanding, even a five-dollar note.

When Craig's great-grandmother learned that her son had paid the widow the five bucks, she blew up. "You paid the widow of that son of a bitch?" she exclaimed. "I told Frank he should've killed him!"

Frank considered killing him at the time of the birth, but they wouldn't have had a doctor if he had.

Craig said his grandfather was a full-blooded hillbilly whose father had skipped out on the family; the replacement was an abusive stepfather who used to "shoot oil wells." He would lower nitroglycerin cans into a well shaft and blow it up, releasing gushers of oil—a kind of proto-fracking.[6]

Craig's grandfather enlisted in the Navy to escape his abusive stepfather and brutal poverty, even though he was only sixteen years old. His mother made the deception possible by signing a paper saying that he was eighteen. Craig's grandpa thrived in the Navy and even became part of a submarine crew during World War I.

In these early days of submarines, locking yourself in a vessel and submerging was as close to serving in a floating coffin as you could get. (Talk about systemic risk!) It didn't help that he had an incompetent captain. The crew, fearing that the captain would get them all killed, decided to deliberately surface their submarine during an exercise when they were supposed to practice sneaking up on a battleship. Not only was the captain embarrassed, but he got fired—which was the crew's intention.

Craig's grandfather wanted to make the Navy his life's work, so he applied for the Naval Academy. But a commanding officer told him, "You're just a hillbilly. If you want to make it in the Navy, you have to have family connections and money. You're not going anywhere in the Naval Academy. You'll be unhappy."

To his eternal regret, Craig's grandfather gave up his Navy dream and spent the rest of his life working for the phone company, becoming head of the northern division of Illinois Bell. (He once fixed the phone of Al Capone, who gave him a hat as a thank-you gift.) But although Craig's grandpa did not live out his Navy dream, Craig's uncle did. Craig recalled attending his uncle's Naval Academy graduation at four, saying, "I was entranced. I was predestined to go into the Navy."

Sure enough, Craig went on to attend the Naval Academy, where he said he learned two important lessons. "First, I found out that I was a libertarian and not a conservative," he said. "Second, I found out that I had issues with authority. I didn't like giving orders, and I didn't like taking orders."

It was probably the loud genes of his great-grandmother making themselves known.

So, in 1979, Craig resigned and enrolled in economics at the University of Chicago, the epicenter of the economics world. The bohemian campus was the polar opposite of the military, and Craig found the lifestyle and the academics "intoxicating." As he described it, "The intellectual excitement around economics at Chicago was absolutely unbelievable. It's hard to describe the University of Chicago in that era if you're in economics."

One of the first lectures he heard was by Milton Friedman, renowned winner of the 1976 Nobel Prize in Economics. Robert Lucas, Jr., who won the 1995 Nobel Prize in Economics, piqued Craig's interest in economic growth. During Craig's senior year, he took a price theory class from Gary Becker, winner of the 1992 Nobel Prize in Economics. You couldn't walk a hundred feet on campus without bumping into another Nobel winner.

It was a long, winding road that brought Craig into the commodity world. But it set the stage for Craig's personal 'Hatfield-and-McCoy feud' with Gary Gensler of the CFTC. That same battle sucked me into the fray, thanks to my research with Dwight Sanders.

Amid the controversy over speculation in the futures market in 2007-08, I also got to know Jeff Harris, the chief CFTC economist. Harris experienced a lot of political pressure to support reining in speculators, so he found himself between a rock and a hard place. Independently, Harris's position was the same as the vast majority of American academics like me. He didn't think speculators were the villains, but because he was an appointee to a federal agency, he had to be balanced and fair to both sides of the debate. It was an impossible job, and I admired what he tried to do.

Harris conducted a special survey to get at the market positions of crude oil speculators. Then in September 2008, he released the results of this survey, which showed that the commodity index traders' positions in the crude oil futures markets had not gone up at the time of the price increase; therefore, they couldn't be the spark that ignited price increases in crude oil.[7]

Harris's report enraged Democrats in Congress because it failed to provide the smoking gun, implicating speculators. He wound up not being reappointed as chief economist of the CFTC under President Obama, but that probably would have happened regardless of this report. Harris had been a Bush appointee.

As I mentioned in the previous chapter, the CFTC consists of four commissioners—two Republicans and two Democrats—all presidential political appointments. The fifth person is the chair of the CFTC, also appointed by the president.

Since this position is a voting tiebreaker, the chair usually changes with each presidential administration. President Obama appointed Gensler from Goldman Sachs, who was perhaps the most ambitious chairperson ever to lead the CFTC. He had close ties with the Clintons and served as Hillary Clinton's chief financial officer for her 2016 campaign. If she had won the election, there was a good chance he might have wound up with a cabinet position.

But this was 2008, not 2016, and Gensler had big plans at the CFTC. After the crash of 2008, there was pressure to regulate all financial markets, so Gensler helped to lead the regulatory charge in the futures markets. Normally, the CFTC was the sleepy backwaters of Washington's regulatory land. But not under Gensler. He hired dozens of new CFTC employees and at least doubled the budget.

Gensler's goal was to use regulations to put position limits on non-agricultural commodities, such as crude oil. Agricultural commodities already had speculative position limits, dating back to the 1930s, when there were only futures markets for ag products. It wasn't until the 1970s and 1980s that the exchanges added futures markets for many other commodities, such as gold and crude oil. Gensler planned to expand position limits to speculators in these other markets, particularly energy.

But, as I pointed out earlier, when you tightly limit speculation activity, you risk taking away the lubrication that makes the markets run smoothly. Setting limits that truly pinch would be like going to an auto garage and saying, "I need five quarts of oil in my engine," but the garage tells you, "Sorry. You're only allowed four quarts." There is no logical reason for limits like this. Only politics.

In the wake of the 2008 crash, there was pressure to regulate all financial markets, so nobody was sure what would happen. Then, in 2010 the massive Dodd-Frank legislation passed in response to the crash. One part of this legislation gave the green light to limit speculation in futures markets for all physical commodities. The law also gave Gensler and the CFTC the authority to develop these restrictions.

A battle was brewing as the futures exchanges, trade organizations, and other groups banded together, lobbying the CFTC, citing Dwight's and my research in many cases. Suddenly, I became a public face for the effort to stop the implementation of the restrictive position limits.

Craig Pirrong was also in the public eye, probably even more so than me, due to his feisty blog, "Streetwise Professor." Craig loved to get under the skin of Gary Gensler, whom he nicknamed "GiGi," He also called the monstrous Dodd-Frank Law "Frankendodd," and he dubbed Gensler "the Igor of Frankendodd."

In one of his blogs, Craig wrote, "Gensler and his ilk believe that they are somehow superior to those who manage financial firms. They are oblivious to the Knowledge Problem and can see the speck in every banker's eye but don't notice the log in their own. People like Gensler and Hillary, who are so hubristic as to presume that they can design and regulate the complex financial system, are by far the biggest systemic risk. Frankendodd was bad enough, but Son of Frankendodd looks to be an even worse horror show and is almost guaranteed to be so if Gensler is the one in charge, as he clearly aims to be."[8]

And then there's this sampling of titles of various blog posts by Craig:

- "Gary Gensler, Naked and Exposed"[9]
- "Gary Gensler's Plan to Take Over the World"[10]
- "Igor Gensler Helps the Wicked Witch of the West Wing Create Son of Frankendodd"[11]

- "Cleaning Up After the Dodd, Frank & Gensler Circus"[12]

Based on these titles alone, is it any wonder that Gensler banned Craig from stepping foot in the CFTC building in D.C.? Craig learned of his ban while arranging a meeting with one of the CFTC commissioners. When he suggested they meet at the CFTC office, the commissioner said, "Sorry, but you can't come to my office. We'll meet in a coffee shop down the street." The Craig-ban held firm until the Gensler reign ended.

With D.C. Democrats ruling the roost, I, too, became a persona non grata and was no longer invited to testify. Then, in the fall of 2011, the new speculative position limit regulations came up for a vote. The two CFTC Republicans voted against them, of course, but one Democrat began to waver and threatened to side with the Republicans. It took a bit of arm-twisting to get him to vote with Gensler and the Democrats, and the new regulations squeaked by. The rule-making document provided an incredibly skewed, one-sided literature review on the topic. Therefore, Dwight and I submitted official comment letters explaining our disagreement and putting ourselves out there publicly as being opposed.[13]

Since the Commodity Exchange Act passed in 1936, one cannot impose new position limits on traders unless regulators meet something called "the necessity condition." This means lawmakers must have evidence that the trading group in question is creating unwarranted or artificial price movements before imposing limits on them.

The regulators were in a bind. The preponderance of evidence strongly showed that speculators in the commodity index funds could *not* be connected to unwarranted or artificial price movements. The vast majority of the evidence showed that the necessity condition had not been met.

So, how were regulators going to get around this problem?

They say that necessity is the mother of invention, and in this case, the "necessity condition" was the mother of invention. But I must give Gensler credit for an ingenious idea; he argued that the Dodd-Frank legislation told the CFTC they *had* to impose limits on speculation. In other words, "Dodd-Frank made us do it" became their defense. They argued that Dodd-Frank trumped the Commodity Exchange Act of 1936.

But the battle was only beginning. It takes time to implement such massive changes, so in 2011 and 2012, the CFTC issued all sorts of rules. Meanwhile, the various futures industries took the unprecedented step of banding together and suing the CFTC in federal court to stop the position limits.

While the Democrats lined up behind the regulations, Republicans were against them, and I was clearly on the Republican side. The futures industry argued that the CFTC still had to meet the necessity condition. They pointed to the evidence showing that the necessity condition had not been met, with Dwight's and my research as a prominent example.

In this kind of civil case, there is no trial. A federal judge reviews the arguments from both sides and then delivers a ruling. So, the political stakes were high when, in the fall of 2012, United States District Judge Robert L. Wilkins declared that the 1936 Act overrode the Dodd-Frank legislation. The CFTC and Gary Gensler had failed to meet the necessity condition.[14]

Judge Wilkins went further than expected by vacating all the new regulations. In legal terms, the regulations ceased to exist. They were vaporized. Gone.

Many thought he might modify the regulations, but they were not expecting him to toss out the rules entirely. Gensler and the Democrats, hot under the collar, started to appeal but soon dropped it, probably because they received legal advice that it wasn't worth the effort. Judge Wilkin's decision was so strong that it would have been a waste of time.

Because of this, I made some significant political enemies. I didn't realize, though, that I had also made some enemies at *The New York Times*.

I was about to face a humiliation much greater than my Parade of Shame through my hometown streets.

Photos

PIGS ALIVE!—This is the opening day for the live hog futures trading pit at the
Chicago Mercantile Exchange (CME) in February 1966. Two leaders at the CME
take the phrase "live hog futures" literally, as they lug live hogs into the exchange.
The person on the left holding a pig is Gerald Hirsch and the one on the right is R.J.
O'Brien, who was on the CME board of directors at the time. Note that prices were
displayed on enormous chalk boards back then. *Source: CME Group, Inc.*

IN THE PITS—This is the main trading room at the Chicago Board of Trade (CBOT) in 1974. It's very close to what I would've seen when I paid my first visit to the CBOT in 1978. I would have observed the ordered chaos from the visitor's gallery in the upper right-hand corner. *Source: U.S. Department of Agriculture*

TRADING PLACES—The climactic scene of *Trading Places* captures the frenzy of the
trading pits as well as anything. These are actual futures traders in the World Trade
Center in New York City. In the movie, street hustler Eddie Murphy is given a
chance to prove that even he could be a successful trader, given the right
circumstances. Before futures trading went electronic, people from many walks of
life learned how to become pit traders. In Chicago, more than a few were ex-cops.
Source: Alamy

THE SPIRIT OF THE TRADER—This photo shows a trader in the wheat options pit at the Chicago Mercantile Exchange (CME) throwing up his arms as other traders toss confetti at the closing bell for the year on December 31, 2009. The scene perfectly captures the spirit of the trading floor—the excitement, the energy, and the jubilation (at least when you score big). Those days are sadly gone. *Source: Alamy*

HANDWRITING ON THE WALL—Leo Melamed shows me the hand-drawn chart he created to convince traders that electronic trading would not initially conflict with regular trading in the pits at the Chicago Mercantile Exchange (CME). The raucous, colorful pits would inevitably give way to the much more efficient electronic trading system that Leo championed—Globex. *Source: Personal Photo Collection*

A PROPHETIC VOICE—Terry Duffy, CEO of the CME Group, Inc., chats with me
in Chicago after a meeting of the Agricultural Markets Advisory Council in
September 2022. This was the day after Terry testified in D.C. about crypto
markets, and he was very direct about his concerns with the assembled group.
Little did we know that a big chunk of the crypto world would blow up only a few
weeks later. Terry was one of the few who sensed this was going to happen. *Source:
Personal Photo Collection*

SOMEONE GET THIS GOPHER TO REHAB—Rinny the gopher, a puppet with a serious drinking issue, showed up at my office unexpectedly in September 2018. Rinny wears a speaker's badge and displays the alcohol-scented remains of his breakfast, lunch, and dinner. The speaker's badge is for an upcoming OPIS Biofuels conference, where I was one of the keynote speakers. *Source: Personal Photo Collection*

PARTNERS IN CRIME—When my co-author, Doug Peterson (left), made his first
visit to the Chicago Board of Trade in October 2018, the scene was a far cry from
what I witnessed during my first visit in 1978. Only a few pits remained open. The
place was mostly empty. I am still happy that Doug got to witness firsthand a little
of the magic of the futures trading pits. *Source: Personal Photo Collection*

Chapter 15
All the Smears That are Fit to Print

When I was at Iowa State, my father purchased a brand-new, 16-row rotary hoe, which does not come cheap. I'm sure the unit had to have set my dad back thousands of dollars, but for some reason, he put this new equipment in my hands one day while I was home from college.

Not only did he put me in charge of a new rotary hoe, but the tractor that I used to pull the hoe was my dad's pride and joy—his "hot-rod tractor." Back in the 1970s, farm machinery companies were not keeping up with the power demands of the most aggressive farmers. People like my dad wanted to pull larger tillage equipment at faster speeds, which required greater horsepower engines.

Enter the legendary John Kinzenbaw.

In 1965, 21-year-old Kinzenbaw was fresh out of the Army, so he started a welding shop in Victor, Iowa. He soon found his calling by "repowering" John Deeres. He replaced 130-horsepower tractor engines with 300-horsepower Detroit Diesel engines. As he explained to one reporter, "We could really make a plow move."[1]

Of course, this caught the attention of my hot-rod father, and we made a pilgrimage to Kinzenbaw's machine shop on Thanksgiving Day of 1971. (I remember the exact date because it was the same day as the college football "Game of the Century" between Nebraska and Oklahoma.)

My dad arranged the visit through my Uncle Dick, who went to school with Kinzenbaw and worked for him in the early days. I recall going with them to the shop and marveling at projects in various stages of completion. But what I most remember was my dad's schoolboy excitement over these revved-up tractors with exhaust pipes that extended into the air on either side of the engine. My dad desperately wanted to get his hands on one of Kinzenbaw's repowered tractors. He was like a car enthusiast in the 1960s who dreamt of getting his hands on a Shelby GT or Shelby Cobra Mustang. Carroll Shelby was the legendary car designer played by Matt Damon in the movie *Ford vs. Ferrari*, and John Kinzenbaw was the Carroll Shelby of hopped-up tractors.

My dad finally got his Kinzenbaw repowered tractor in 1978, a massive two-wheel drive 5020 John Deere with the heads of the big Detroit Diesel protruding from the sides and dual chrome exhaust stacks. My mom hated that tractor, and I believe she refused to drive it. She didn't think it was safe to operate, and boy, was it loud. Without a cab or mufflers, driving that tractor was like tailgating a huge semi blasting down a highway with a full load at 75 miles per hour. The sound was deafening.

The irony is that the Kinzenbaw repowered 5020 may have saved my life on this fateful day back in college when I used it to pull our brand-new rotary hoe through the fields.

After farmers plant corn, a pounding rain can cause the ground to cake over, making it difficult for corn seedlings to emerge. So, the solution is to use a rotary hoe, which has a long toolbar hooked to the tractor's rear, and ours extended across sixteen 30-inch rows. Hanging from it are fingered wheels, which pop off the top layer of caked soil, making it easier for corn seedlings to emerge from the ground. But for this to work, the rotary hoe should be pulled at a relatively high speed.

By entrusting me with this new, expensive piece of machinery, it was obvious my father hadn't completely given up on me being a farmer, even though I'd set my eyes on graduate school. But what happened next must've given him second thoughts, as well as third and fourth thoughts.

Mosquito Creek ran through my grandparents' property, and it was an unpleasant name for an unpleasant stream. As kids, we were ordered never to swim there because the town of Bagley dumped raw sewage into it. On the east side of Mosquito Creek, my grandfather built a fence strong enough to last 100 years. However, it had a slight bend that followed a curve in the creek, and Grandpa George had driven a ten-inch fencepost into the ground at this spot as an anchor. Getting past the post was always tricky since there was little space between the fencepost and the first row of corn. My dad eked yields out of every last inch, so he planted as close as humanly possible to the fence line. He was famous for profit maximization.

So, I climbed onto our hot-rod tractor and set to work, pulling the rotary hoe behind this beast of a machine. I started along the end rows, which is where you always begin. As I said, a rotary hoe should travel at a good clip, and for farm machinery, that's about 10 to 12 miles per hour. The fingered wheels spin fast but shallow because the last thing you want is to dig up your young corn plants, which are about two to three inches in the ground.

I had the tractor in sixth gear as it raced down the row, pulling the rotary hoe behind, traveling north along the western side of the field beside Mosquito Creek.

But there's one thing I didn't consider as I pulled that rotary hoe down the end row near the fence. Jutting from one end of the toolbar is a hitch used to transport the rotary hoe down the roadway, and it extended the bar a bit farther than I thought. Another thing I forgot is how much that big post protrudes where the fence line bends to accommodate the creek.

WHAMMM!

The hitch struck the post with a tremendous, bone-rattling force, and I was hurled forward.

The rotary hoe jerked so violently to the right it nearly threw me from the tractor, which was an old-school machine without a cab.

While I held on to the steering wheel, my legs dangled between the tractor's side and its wheels. If I hadn't been able to hang on to that steering wheel, I would have fallen beneath the repowered tractor. And if those enormous wheels didn't crush me, I would have been chewed to pieces by spinning blades.

The reason the repowered 5020 might have saved me is its weight. A lighter tractor might not have been able to absorb the shock, and it could have hurled me beneath the tires and blades. My other saving grace was that the tractor's engine died instantly. If it hadn't, the equipment would have kept moving forward, making me lose my grip, only to be run over and chopped to bits by the rotary hoe. It could have been an ugly death, but my guardian angels were still at work, saving me from yet another tragedy.

I shook like a leaf as I came to my senses, climbing back into the tractor seat. I looked over my shoulder and stared at the toolbar, a massive, thick steel rectangular tube, unable to believe my eyes. I had done the impossible.

The force of the impact had bent that toolbar at a roughly 45-degree angle. Think about the kind of force needed to bend a steel tube, and you get some sense of the incredible power at work.

The toolbar on my dad's brand-new, expensive rotary hoe had bent like a straw. Since the accident also destroyed the hitch, I had no choice but to shamefully drive the equipment home along Highway 141 with the twisted toolbar sticking out to one side, blocking both lanes because the thing was so wide—a dangerous thing to do. I crept down the road, and when I reached town, I turned left onto Main Street. Unfortunately, this was my only option because Main Street was the only road wide enough to drive to our farm shop on the other side of town with the rotary hoe extended.

This was my Parade of Shame.

People gathered on the side of the street and gawked. I doubt any had ever seen a toolbar bent like that. As if the visuals weren't bad enough, the repowered 5020 probably sounded like an airplane landing on Main Street. With Bagley being a small town, word spread lightning fast about what the Irwin kid had done now. I never lived it down.

Of my many accidents, this one scared me the most because of how close I had come to death. Perhaps that accident is what finally convinced my dad I was better off as an agricultural economist working behind a desk rather than anywhere near his expensive and dangerous farm machinery. My dad and his shop foreman managed to heat the toolbar and reshape it, pulling at it with another tractor, but the rotary hoe never moved straight again. He had to trade it off shortly afterward.

Parading through town and pulling my destroyed rotary hoe behind me was one of the most humiliating experiences of my young life. But I deserved it, you could argue; I had foolishly run my dad's machinery into a fencepost.

Later, I would face a much worse public humiliation, only in this case, it was completely undeserved. *The New York Times* targeted me and University of Houston professor Craig Pirrong with a hit piece. Our crime was defending the futures markets. *The Times* wanted to neutralize both of our research with the politics of personal destruction. So, they went after us with a front-page story in their business section in December 2013—a late Christmas present I'll never forget. A Parade of Shame on a national scale.

I remember exactly where I was when I received word that the article was released. Stacey, my 10-year-old daughter, had just set a 60-meter-dash record at an indoor track meet, but it was difficult to savor the moment. While driving her the five hours from the late-December track meet in northeastern Indiana, I spent much of the time on the phone with Craig. The article "Academics Who Defend Wall St. Reap Reward" tried to make the case that Craig's and my research had been compromised because of the source of funding for some of our work.[2]

It was complete nonsense and reeked of politics. Gary Gensler and the Commodity Futures Trading Commission (CFTC) were in the midst of resubmitting the position-limit rules for speculators, which Judge Wilkins had thoroughly dismissed in the fall of 2012. The piece's timing was undoubtedly suspicious since Craig and I were the two most outspoken academic opponents of the position-limit rules and defenders of the futures market.

In my almost thirty years in academics up to that point, no one had ever seriously questioned my integrity. And now here I was, on the front page of *The New York Times* business section. If my neighbors back in Bagley had caught wind of it, they would've been saying, "What has that Irwin kid done this time?"

Craig was clearly the paper's number one target. The article began by focusing on him for about two-thirds of the story. But don't think the final third left out any punches. I did not escape their scrutiny, and the rest of the article was just as searing.

Today, destroying people's reputations through social media or traditional media has become almost a sport, like big-game hunting, except the trophies are the heads of those who disagree with you politically. Now, it was happening to me.

The experience also taught me about dealing with the press. I had been hopelessly naïve when *The New York Times* reporter David Kocieniewski first showed up unannounced at my office at the University of Illinois in the fall of 2013. My secretary said the reporter had appeared out of the blue, and when I got there, I found that he'd left a note, asking to talk with me.

Although I had done plenty of interviews before, I had never spoken to an investigative reporter. My experience at this point had been primarily with ag reporters, who are almost universally friendly. So, I went into the interview thinking it would be much the same.

As I said...incredibly naïve.

Amid all this, I received a Freedom of Information Act (FOIA) request asking me to supply all my emails going back ten years. As you might guess, this amounted to thousands of emails—a royal pain. Fortunately, the university had an office to help me comply with the FOIA request.

What was even more ridiculous was that I complied when the newspaper asked if they could take my photograph, scurrying to campus the day after Christmas, a frigid morning. *The New York Times* photographer had me pose in the College of Business atrium, which should have raised some red flags.

I don't work in the business college and have no formal connection with it. I work with the ag college, a completely different unit in a different location on campus. However, the photo fit the narrative they wanted.

In the article, Kocieniewski stated, "The business school at the University of Illinois has received more than a million dollars in donations from the Chicago Mercantile Exchange and several major commodities traders to pay for scholarships and classes and to build a laboratory that resembles a trading floor at the commodities market."[3]

In other words, because the Chicago Mercantile Exchange (CME) and commodity traders donated to the business college, my research on commodities was suspect—even though I have no connection with the business college and zero collaborative research with its professors. I didn't even know the CME had donated money to the business college until years after the fact when I was talking to my college's development staff.

Kocieniewski made his insinuation in the very first paragraph in which he mentioned me. It wasn't until the last few paragraphs that he finally pointed out that, by the way, none of the CME's money had gone to me or the Department of Agricultural and Consumer Economics, where I worked. Anyone who didn't read the end wouldn't know I had no connection to the business college.

But there was my photo, where I was posing in the College of Business building. Craig Pirrong couldn't believe I had been so cooperative. It was as if I were assisting in my own execution. Can I polish your rifles before you shoot me?

I should note that I have had a long working relationship with the CME Group, and before that, with the Chicago Board of Trade (CBOT). This, after all, is my research area. To say I shouldn't have any relationship with the CME Group would be like expecting computer engineers to have no working relationship with IBM, Apple, or Hewlett-Packard or expecting aeronautical engineers to have no dealings with Boeing.

As discussed in Chapter 11, the CME commissioned two colleagues and me to write a white paper in 2005, when the grain contract convergence problem first arose. They paid us a total of $15,000, split among three professors. I also accepted a position on a new Agricultural Advisory Council that the CME Group started in late 2013. The council serves as a sounding board on the main issues in agricultural futures markets, and I received a $10,000 annual stipend for this position, as did other council members.

That is the sum of my financial ties to the CME Group. To try to connect me with the millions of dollars in funding that went to the College of Business was ridiculous and deceptive.

As Peter Klein, a professor at Baylor University, wrote in my defense: "The result is a preposterous article with 'jaw-on-the-floor' errors, mendaciously edited, so the unfounded accusations come first, and the self-contradictions revealed only at the end of the piece."[4]

In addition to trying to make the patently false connection between me and the business college's funding from the CME Group, Kocieniewski tried to get at me through my consulting activities. Consulting is widespread among professors in all areas, from engineering and chemistry to environmental science and agriculture. Universities require you to follow specific rules and disclose your consulting work to check for any potential conflicts of interest. I followed these rules to a tee, and I dutifully disclosed all my consulting work.

Nevertheless, the article's goal was to toss around strong suggestions that my research was compromised and hope that insinuations alone would be enough to do me in.

The New York Times also mentioned a consulting job with a company that developed and offered commodity index products to investors. This company hired Dwight Sanders and me during the controversy over whether commodity index positions dramatically influenced market prices. The company asked us to examine whether their commodity index positions affected market prices.

Given the political sensitivities surrounding speculation, we gave considerable thought to whether we should pursue this consulting project. However, it would provide us access to detailed data previously unavailable to researchers, so we thought it worthwhile to take it on. Dwight and I later used that data in several journal articles.

The company paid Dwight and me $50,000 (split two ways) for this short-term, six-month consulting job, not a small amount, but also not that large compared to the total funding that goes into a professor's research. In our report, we found that the firm's commodity positions did not affect market prices, which was entirely consistent with our broader research.[5] However, *The New York Times* wasn't interested in the merits of the research. The article was all about smear tactics. The idea was to imply that this short-term consulting job tainted all my research.

Long before the consulting job, I consistently argued against the Masters Hypothesis, which claimed that speculators had a massive impact on prices. I didn't suddenly change my tune to satisfy one consulting customer. In fact, I ensured the *Times* reporter was well aware of the op-ed piece that I had written in *The New York Times* of all places in July of 2008. He made no mention that my opinion on the Masters Hypothesis had been unchanged for years because that would be evidence that my consulting job hadn't swayed me to alter my opinion. Such information would go against his storyline.

What's more, it's not just my research that came to these conclusions. Even in 2013, academic research had been overwhelmingly negative about the Masters Hypothesis, so my findings were no surprise. Of those studies that link speculation with commodity price changes, the majority say the effect is small and short-lived, which I do not take issue with. Properly stated, almost no academic research backed up the massive, long-term impact on prices being claimed by Masters and many politicians. Any possible short-term, minimal effects were not justification for new regulations of commodity futures markets.

If my speculation research was tainted, it sure fooled a lot of academics who served as journal editors and reviewers. Between 2009 and the 2013 *New York Times* smear article, I published thirteen papers dealing directly with the speculation controversy in nine academic journals. Articles are not published unless they pass muster with reviewers and each journal's editor. Over that span, it is safe to say that I had dealt with twenty to thirty fellow academic researchers. Are we to believe that my "biased" research ran this gauntlet of editors and reviewers, and the bias managed to go undetected the entire time? Give me a break.

My approach has always been to go where the data leads me. Dwight and I have sliced and diced the available data in many ways, and we cannot find the smoking gun implicating speculators. As I like to put it, if the Masters Hypothesis were true, the relationship between index positions and commodity futures prices should jump off the page. But the relationship just isn't there. In truth, the real shock would have been if our report found a connection between the firm's index funds and the massive upward swing in commodity prices in 2007-08.

Today, very few academics argue that speculators were responsible for this dramatic increase in commodity prices; that theory has been thoroughly debunked. But in 2013, the hypothesis was still being taken seriously in some non-academic circles, and *The New York Times* had only to hint at a conflict of interest to try to neutralize our research. Because there was no smoking gun, they figured all they had to do was blow smoke of their own. And if they destroyed our academic reputations in the process, then Craig and I were just collateral damage.

The University of Illinois, at both the departmental and college levels, backed me all the way. Many other academics leaped to my defense, calling the article a nasty hit piece.

Felix Salmon, a financial journalist, wrote, "Kocieniewski has missed the mark. Neither Pirrong or Irwin is mendacious or venal, and indeed it's the NYT which seems to be stretching the facts well past their stretching point...Once you realize how much of an axe Kocieniewski is grinding, then the rest of his article rapidly starts to crumble."[6]

Jim Hamilton of the University of California in San Diego wrote, "David Kocieniewski of *The New York Times* is guilty of some outrageously bad journalism in the form of a groundless ad hominem attack on the reputation of two professors for the sole purpose of reinforcing the prejudices of his misinformed readers."[7]

Despite the much-appreciated support of colleagues, Kocieniewski's article was a punch to the gut. I recall attending an economic association meeting after the story came out, and I was chatting to a woman about software. She stared at my nametag and said, "Your name sounds awfully familiar. Do I know you?"

I figured I might as well own up to it, so I told her about *The New York Times* article targeting me and Craig Pirrong. "Oh yes, that's where I saw your name," she said.

Craig wasn't as naïve as me when the *Times* first contacted him. "When I got this call from the reporter, I was immediately suspicious," he told me. "The reporter was asking a lot of gotcha questions, and he was asking personal financial questions. It was pretty clear that it was going to be a hit piece, so I was circumspect in my answers, and I waited with trepidation for the article to appear."[8]

The way the *Times* targeted Craig was similar to how they approached me, with the reporter implying that industry funding had swayed his research. Once again, the reporter failed to note that Craig's findings on speculators had been consistent over the years and hadn't suddenly changed to please those funding his research. In fact, one of the research papers cited by the *Times* went completely *against* what the people funding Craig's project wanted from him.

According to Craig, the Global Financial Markets Association, a banking industry trade group, asked him to study the systemic risk of commodity traders—a topic that interested him. The banking group believed commodity traders posed systemic risk, and therefore, should be subject to the same regulations as banks. They hoped that Craig's research would back their claims.

"But I came up with the wrong answer," he said. "I found that commodity trading firms didn't pose systemic risk and therefore didn't need to be regulated like banks do."[9]

Because Craig's research was not what the banking group wanted, the paper was never released. However, a commodity trading group by the name of Trafigura got wind of the research and asked Craig to write a white paper for them. So, Craig expanded his work and wrote it.

The New York Times tried to argue that this paper was proof he was in Trafigura's pocket, implying he skewed the results to make them happy. The paper failed to point out that a banking group initially funded the research and that the results were *opposite* to what the group wanted.

Ironically, Craig said this paper "is the most read thing I have ever written. It's become a standard source for bankers who don't understand the commodity trading business and want to understand the basics."

Like me, a host of economists came to Craig's defense, including one of his intellectual heroes, Thomas Sowell. "So basically, I thought the right people got it, and the wrong people didn't, and that was fine with me," Craig said.

In the long run, he added, the hit piece didn't do any damage to his career, "and in some respects, it's been beneficial because it's established some cred. One way that I put it is that if you don't matter, they don't come after you."[10]

I am happy to say that, in the long run, I, too, never received any long-lasting blowback from the article, at least none that I'm aware of. It all blew over in a couple of months. But even though the controversy was short-lived, it was still a very unpleasant experience. I can only imagine what it must be like for those unfairly targeted by waves of never-ending articles published for months. The one thing I truly regret is taking that stupid picture for the article in front of the business college. Self-inflicted wounds are sometimes the most painful.

Although the article aimed to neutralize Craig and me, it didn't work. We continued our research, and our findings still confirmed that speculators did not have the massive impact on prices that the Masters Hypothesis claimed. Craig doubled down on his research, writing a series of fierce responses.[11]

But, most importantly, the position limit rules were put on ice. Over the next few years, the rules went through multiple iterations, and in December 2016, Gensler and the CFTC finally completed the 300-page set of rules. But by that time, President Obama was on his way out. They decided to let the new Trump administration do whatever they desired with the rules, so the regulations languished.

To my surprise, the CFTC resurrected the position limit rules and passed them in a split 3-2 vote in October 2020. While this latest iteration of the rules appears much less draconian than those proposed a decade earlier, my view on expanding position limits has not changed. They do not meet the necessity test and are not needed.

I was embarrassed by my journalistic Parade of Shame in *The New York Times*, but I survived with no lasting damage—which is more than could be said about my dad's brand-new rotary hoe during my earlier Parade of Shame. *The Times* experience was painful, but it was gratifying that the evidence and the truth ultimately won out in the public square.

However, this battle will have to be fought again. Like a zombie, the Masters Hypothesis will eventually try to crawl out of the grave, and the Anti-Speculation Cycle will resume again. As Craig likes to say, "Bad ideas never die."

Chapter 16
The Market Finds a Way

G rowing up, I loved going to the Knoxville Raceway so much that if I had a girlfriend in high school, I would break up with her before summer because I preferred spending weekends at the race-track with my dad and Jack Hunter. Seriously.

The two-hour drive (at the speed limit) to the Knoxville Raceway on the weekend was an Irwin family summer tradition, and I savor memories of taking back roads to the track. In the 1970s, when the national speed limit dropped to 55 miles per hour, we found various shortcuts, allowing us to drive like crazy men.

We nicknamed the most famous shortcut the Dawson Speedway, a long, straight stretch of paved country road where we could push well over 100 miles per hour without worrying too much about the highway patrol. By some miracle, I don't recall any of us ever getting a speeding ticket on these drives.

When I was a kid in the 1960s and '70s, Taylor "Pappy" Weld and his three sons were the biggest winners at the Knoxville Raceway. They were known as the Kansas City Mafia because they dominated the racetrack as crime families once controlled the Chicago streets.

During the early 1960s, when we lived in Oklahoma, my dad became friends with a wheat farmer who had grown up with Pappy

Weld. This farmer told him how Pappy would drive his Indian motorcycle from the barn's "hay mow," a wide opening with big doors under
the roof peak where farmers haul in the hay. In other words, Pappy
Weld rode his motorcycle out of a two-story window—for fun. Even
Jack Hunter was impressed.

This farmer introduced my dad to Pappy, and whenever we went to
Knoxville, my dad would take us to the pits after the races to look at
the cars and chat with the Welds. Sprint car racing is one of the most
accessible sports, allowing close contact between fans and drivers. My
dad was casually acquainted with Pappy, who always asked, "How's
the Iowa corn farmer doing?" Pappy was very kind to me, but he was
also your classic tough guy, with a butch haircut and rolled-up shirt
sleeves revealing powerful biceps.

The Weld that my dad seemed to know the best was Pappy's son
Greg, who won the Knoxville Nationals in 1963 at only nineteen. The
Nationals are the Indy 500 of sprint car racing and THE event every
summer. His brother Jerry finished second that year. However, the
most famous race involving the Weld brothers occurred in 1964 when
a dispute over rules nearly led to a riot.

All three brothers were racing that year—Greg, Jerry, and Kenny.
During qualifying on Friday night, Greg Weld—the defending champion—recorded the fastest lap time, which gave him the inside track
for the coveted pole position in the national championship race on
Saturday. However, even with the best time, drivers couldn't qualify
for the main race unless they finished in the top five of their heat race,
which was also on Saturday night.

As it turned out, Greg got into a minor accident in his heat with a
local driver named Earl Wagner. (The rivalry between the locals and
the Kansas City Mafia was intense.) The Welds claimed that Wagner
hit Greg's car on purpose to knock him from the heat race and,
thereby, out of the main race.

When an accident like this occurs, the yellow caution flag is waved,
and the other drivers slow and continue to circle the track. The drivers
in the accident have a certain amount of time to try to repair their

vehicles. Since Greg still had a chance to stay in the race, his pit crew went to work.

As the time ticked by and the other cars continued to drive around the track, waiting for the race to restart, the officials finally declared that time had run out. The race would resume without Greg Weld.

The Welds were furious, and they put up a major stink. I talked about the incident with Bob Wilson, an official Knoxville Raceway historian. While he didn't know what the Welds said to the track officials during this dustup, it was enough to get Greg Weld, the defending champion, disqualified from the entire event for poor sportsmanship.[1]

Racers who didn't qualify in their heats still had a chance to get into the main race by finishing in the top two in a consolation race. However, by being disqualified for poor sportsmanship, Greg couldn't drive in the consolation race and lost his last chance.

The Welds weren't having any of this. Like a force of nature, they would find a way, somehow, to skirt the rules. Though disqualified, Greg had his car pushed onto the track before the start of the consolation race, telling his crew not to move it under any circumstances.

When a tow truck came to drag Greg's car off the track unceremoniously, a standoff ensued between the Weld family on one side and the tow truck driver and track officials on the other. The crowd surrounding them mushroomed as word filtered through the pit area. The conflict began to boil over into the stands. Thousands of people took sides, and it looked like there would be an all-out riot if the officials didn't intervene soon.

The track promoter, a guy named Marion Robinson, tried to settle the dispute. To tamp down tensions, he suggested a compromise that must have riled the track officials who had disqualified Greg Weld. Robinson decided to leave it up to the other drivers in the consolation race to vote on whether to allow Greg to compete or not. When the voting finished, the other drivers gave Greg the green light to participate in the consolation race. Greg had to start at the back of the pack, a terrible disadvantage, but he managed to fight to a second-place

222 Back to the Futures

finish—good enough to qualify for the championship race that followed.

Just as with the consolation race, Greg would have to start the big race at the very back. But despite this position, he once again fought to the front during the championship race—an almost unheard-of feat. He wound up finishing in second place, while his younger brother Kenny took first, despite never having won a feature race at Knoxville in his life. Kenny was only eighteen, making him the youngest Nationals champion in history.

But the story doesn't end there.

Because of the chaos, the Marion County Fair Board, which operated the track (and still does), unanimously voted one week later to bar all the Weld brothers from racing at Knoxville for two years—a severe blow to the most powerful racing family in the region. But the Welds being the Welds, they always seemed to find a way around rules and restrictions.

One week later, another driver from Kansas City, Bob Williams, arrived at the track with the same number 94 super-modified sprint car in which Kenny Weld had won the Nationals. Williams provided evidence that Pappy had sold him the car for *one dollar*, making it eligible for the race. Because the Fair Board banned Pappy and his sons from stepping foot on the racetrack, they watched from the roof of the livestock sale barn across the street. Remarkably, Bob Williams won the feature race that night. The stuff of legends.

As if that wasn't enough, their two-year ban was nullified the following summer, so the brothers wound up missing only a couple of months of racing.

The Welds always seemed to find a way.

Where there are rules, there will be endless contention and controversy. The same is true in commodity trading, and nowhere was this more evident than in the great mystery of non-convergence in grain futures markets, which we first explored in Chapter 11.

While the outlandish conspiracy theories of the Destroying Angel about non-convergence were just plain wacky, I still could not explain what was driving the historic episodes of decoupling between cash and futures prices. As my colleagues and I eventually discovered, non-convergence had everything to do with the market's ability to find a way around the rules—in this case, obscure grain storage rules.

In *Jurassic Park*, Dr. Ian Malcolm, played by Jeff Goldblum, famously said, "Life will not be contained. Life breaks free. It expands to new territories and crashes through barriers, painfully, maybe even dangerously...Life finds a way."[2] He was talking about the dinosaurs' ability to propagate, even though all creatures on the island were female. Life will find a way.

Malcolm could have used the same words to describe the Welds—and the market. The market will not be contained. It finds a way, crashing through barriers and creating new pathways. Non-convergence is the market's ability to "find a way" around storage rules.

To recap the controversy, for commodity futures markets to function properly, the crop price in the cash market at delivery locations should be close to the same as the futures price at the time of delivery specified in the contract. This is called "convergence." With December corn, for example, the closer you are to the delivery date in December, the closer the cash price for a crop should be to the futures price.

Beginning in 2005, however, the rates for corn, soybeans, and wheat at delivery locations were not converging. The prices were not just missing convergence by a small margin. By September 2008, the cost of wheat on the Chicago futures market was more than $2 per bushel higher than in the cash market at delivery time, when prices are supposed to come back together. The gap between soybean futures and cash prices was about 80 cents per bushel—a clear violation of the Law of One Price, which says the price of the same commodities at the same location at the same time should be the same.

Non-convergence made it much more difficult for farmers and other ordinary traders to hedge or facilitate price discovery—two of the primary functions of a commodity futures market. Major traders understood how to compensate for non-convergence in their calculations to ride the roller-coaster, but this was still a persistent and puzzling problem.

Before digging deeper into how we solved the mystery, it's essential to know more about how the grain market system works. If you recall from the first chapter, farmers had their grain trucks weighed when they went to the elevator in Bagley, Iowa. Then they dumped the grain, weighed the empty vehicle, and received a ticket saying how much their crop weighed.

That scale ticket was known as a "warehouse receipt" and could be bought and sold. For example, if corn was $2 per bushel, and you purchased 5,000 bushels, you would write a check to the elevator for $10,000. Then you would receive a warehouse receipt—a small certificate showing that you owned 5,000 bushels.

The Chicago Board of Trade (CBOT) used these warehouse receipts in grain futures delivery for almost 150 years. Beginning in 2000, the CBOT utilized a different instrument for delivery, a shipping certificate, and it's now all digital.

A shipping certificate and a warehouse receipt are similar, so we can assume they are interchangeable for our purposes. The key is that when you take delivery on a grain futures contract, you receive a piece of paper representing grain rather than the grain loaded on a truck, barge, or railcar. This minor detail seems of no practical significance, yet it makes all the difference when explaining non-convergence.

Because the 5,000 bushels of grain represented by the warehouse receipt are sitting in an elevator, the receipt owner has to pay a storage fee. If you sell the warehouse receipt to someone else, then they pay the storage cost. The other option is to unload the grain from the elevator for use or export, which is called "canceling the warehouse receipt by load-out."

As non-convergence continued to puzzle the experts, one of the solutions promoted by some in the grain industry was something called "forced load-out." According to Fred Seamon, the CME Group's agricultural markets executive director, the exchange feared that this so-called solution would kill their wheat contract.[3] (Remember, by July of 2007, the CBOT, which created the wheat futures contract, had merged with the CME to form the CME Group. The CME Group now managed the wheat contract.)

So, what is forced load-out?

Under this system, when traders who are long (buyers) in the futures market take delivery, they are forced to load out the physical grain. They no longer receive a piece of paper representing the grain in storage. Instead, they must have the grain loaded from the storage elevator in the next few days.

This idea, by definition, would have solved the convergence problem in wheat because if traders are forced to load out the grain, the cash and futures prices are forced to converge. But at what cost?

It might solve non-convergence, but Fred, myself, and others were almost certain it would kill the wheat futures contract in the process. In other words, the medicine to cure non-convergence would kill the patient.

The problem with forced loadout is that the market power of typical buyers (longs) and sellers (shorts) in the delivery market is not equal. If the buyers taking delivery of physical wheat must load out over a short time, they may be hard-pressed to negotiate a fair selling price with the large grain companies that own most of the delivery elevators and shipping stations.

The buyers face the prospect of owning "captive" wheat supplies that can be sold only after negotiating with a few large grain companies. No wonder these grain companies like forced load-out because they believe it could give them a competitive advantage in futures delivery. An advantage in the futures delivery market can ripple far and wide through cash wheat prices since the CME Group's futures market is a global benchmark.

So, the CME Group was in a bind. They had to find a way to solve the non-convergence problem before the grain industry pressured them into implementing an idea like forced load-out that could alter the competitive balance in the delivery process. This issue could ultimately have led to the demise of the wheat contract.

I took three swings at solving this great market puzzle, the first attempt coming in 2005 when our University of Illinois team was asked to write a white paper about the non-convergence problem. As I said in Chapter 11, this first swing was a whiff.

When non-convergence became an even greater problem in 2008,

our team took a second swing at it. The group included me, Phil
Garcia, Darrel Good, and Gene Kunda, all from Illinois. We focused on
structural problems with futures contracts, strongly hinting that the
wheat non-convergence was because the futures contracts didn't
specify enough delivery locations in the right places. This theory
turned out to be wrong.[4]

We also started collecting a vast amount of data to assess the issue
better, developing the world's best database on everything that has to
do with convergence. The information included "spreads" between
futures prices. The spread is the difference between prices for different
contracts, like May and July wheat futures. We found that non-convergence seemed to be related to the level of price spreads, but we
weren't sure why.

So, as I did presentations all over the world, people kept asking the
same things: What is going on with wheat? Were the index funds
causing this problem? I would answer by waving my hands in the air
and saying that the cause is something structural in the markets. But I
wasn't very convincing. I couldn't even convince myself.

In the fall of 2009, the U.S. Department of Agriculture (USDA)
was still under heavy political pressure to determine the underlying
cause of non-convergence. This was in no small part due to a U.S.
Senate report issued in July 2009—"Excessive Speculation in the
Wheat Market."[5] This report, discussed in Chapter 12, made no bones
that the cause of non-convergence was a series of price bubbles
created by index-fund buying in the wheat futures market—the
Masters Hypothesis.

In response, the USDA's Economic Research Service (ERS) dished
out some money to our group at the University of Illinois, a team at
the University of California, Davis, and a few others around the
country to discover the cause. Each research team, including ours,
worked on the issue separately, yet no one seemed to make much
progress during the first year.

Therefore, Sally Thompson, a former Illinois colleague leading the
ERS project, decided something finally had to be done. She said the
USDA would give us a second round of funding, but only if the Cali-

fornia people worked with the Illinois people. It was an inspired decision.

For the first time, Phil Garcia and I collaborated with Aaron Smith from UC Davis. Smith hails from New Zealand, where he grew up raising livestock and small grains on the Canterbury plains. He's also a rabid rugby player, but most importantly, he might just be the best ag economist in the world.

Aaron is a great theorist, a math expert, and a sharp market thinker. We made a good team because Phil and I had strengths with data and basic economics. We also shared a fundamental belief that people were wrong to blame non-convergence on commodity index funds. Like us, Aaron suspected the problem was related to something in the futures contracts—such as storage rates.

Here is the critical part. The CBOT (and later the CME Group) sets the storage rate on warehouse receipts obtained through grain futures contract delivery. For almost 25 years, starting in the early 1980s, the maximum storage rate allowed for CBOT warehouse receipts was 5 cents per bushel per month, except in the early 2000s when the rate was briefly lowered. The storage rate had been set at a maximum of 5 cents per bushel per month for so long that very few people gave it much thought.

It turns out that was a huge mistake.

The next thing to understand is that the market provides an incentive for storing grain, allowing its use throughout the year. This is done with the "carry"—the cumulative storage return over time.

If you look at a wheat futures contract today, it might say that the price for a July 2022 contract is $6.04 per bushel. Assume that's for the current delivery. But if you look at the price projections for a year later, you might find the cost for a July 2023 wheat contract is $6.34 per bushel. This price increase—30 cents—is called the "carry" or the "spread." It covers the cost of storage, providing the incentive to store grain for future use.

If the July 2023 futures contract price had been *lower* than the one in July 2022, then no one in our example would want to store grain from one harvest to the next. And if you don't store grain, supplies may run out before the next harvest. You might just run out of wheat to make bread in March.

A 30-cent increase in the wheat price over one-year boils down to two and a half cents per bushel per month. It's the market's way of forecasting that we can get adequate wheat storage if the cash price rises two and a half cents per bushel per month. In this example, that's all the incentive needed to get producers and grain merchants to store their wheat. Think of the two and a half cents per bushel per month as the market rental rate for the storage facilities. It balances the *demand* for storage with the *supply* of storage.

Now, let's return to that cap on storage rates specified in the grain futures contracts—5 cents per bushel per month. Let's look at two examples—one when the market carry is below 5 cents and one when the market carry is above the cap.

NEWMAN!

A trader by the name of Newman has purchased a July wheat futures contract. The current cash price for wheat at the delivery location is $5 per bushel in July, and the expiring July futures price for Newman's contract is also $5. Because the cash price equals the futures price, convergence is perfect.

What's more, let's say that the market carry is 4 cents per bushel per month. In other words, the futures price in mid-July for a contract expiring two months later, in September, will be $5.08 per bushel—a rise of 4 cents each month to cover the storage cost. This also means the December contract price will rise another 4 cents per month, or 12 cents, to $5.20, and so on.

In this case, the 4-cent market carry each month is no problem because the CME Group allows a storage rate of up to 5 cents per bushel per month for futures contracts.

However...

NEWMAN, WE HAVE A PROBLEM!

What if the market projects that the carry will be *above* 5 cents per bushel per month? For example, what if the market says the carry should be 10 cents per month to cover grain storage costs, but the futures contract rules say it cannot exceed 5 cents per month?

In this situation, the paper used for futures delivery—the warehouse receipt—becomes more valuable than grain in the elevator because the storage rate is lower. There is a disequilibrium. The carry for wheat in the futures market needs to be 10 cents per bushel per month to match the demand for storage with the supply of storage— but it can't get there because the storage rate for futures wheat is capped at 5 cents. Meanwhile, there is no cap on the storage rate in the cash market so it can rise to 10 cents.

Suddenly, the Law of One Price no longer holds because "futures grain" and "cash grain" are no longer the same commodity. The storage cost for futures grain is cheaper than the cost for cash grain. It's as simple as that.

THE MARKET FINDS A WAY

In response to this problem, the markets will force an adjustment. Like the Welds and those pesky dinosaurs in *Jurassic Park*, the market will crash through the artificial barrier of the storage rate cap.

In our example, the market projects that the carry—the monthly increase to cover storage costs—should be 10 cents per month. For example, July wheat at $5 needs to increase to $5.20 two months later in September. But if the storage rate increase is capped at 5 cents per month, wheat in the futures market will be only $5.10 for September contracts—not high enough to cover storage costs.

How does the futures market respond? How does September wheat get to $5.20 in the futures market?

The storage rate in a futures contract may be capped, but the price of wheat is not. Therefore, the market finds a way around this problem by increasing the current price of July wheat in the futures market to $5.10—10 cents higher than the cash price.

- September futures price for wheat—$5.10 July futures price, plus 10 cents per bushel for storage (5 cents per bushel over two months) = $5.20 per bushel
- September cash price for wheat—$5.00 July cash price, plus 20 cents per bushel for storage (10 cents per bushel over two months) = $5.20 per bushel

In such a scenario, the July futures price is 10 cents higher per bushel than the cash price at the same delivery location. Non-convergence has occurred.

This is a simplification, but it captures the basics. The very heated political debate about non-convergence assumed that the market must be broken and some external force, such as index funds, was causing grain futures prices to go haywire. But we realized that the grain futures markets were simply adjusting because the storage-rate cap on the futures contract was too low. To make up for the low storage rate, futures prices compensated by going up relative to cash prices. The market found a way.

This example explains a discrepancy of 10 cents between the futures and cash prices at delivery locations, but in 2008 the price of wheat futures was *two dollars* more than the cash price at delivery. How did we explain that kind of difference?

The previous example was from July to September. But what if the market expects the storage rate to be 10 cents per month, not 5 cents, *for an entire year?* In this case, the wheat futures price needs to increase by 5 cents per month for twelve months to return everything to equilibrium.

In other words, the futures price for the expiring July wheat contract in the previous example now has to be 60 cents higher than the cash price at the delivery location. So, our model not only explained why non-convergence happened but also why it was so massive.

In late 2011, Aaron, Phil, and I finished the first version of our paper, outlining the math behind this solution, and eventually published the final version in 2015.[6] By the time it appeared in print (things don't move quickly in academic publishing), market conditions had changed, and non-convergence problems had already ended in 2010 and 2011. But we now had the answer to the great mystery of what caused the historic episodes of non-convergence. It was not bubbles caused by index funds. The market made a way when futures contract rules did not keep up with changing conditions.

This knowledge is crucial so we can take steps to prevent a similar situation from reoccurring, and it raises an obvious question.[7] Why had this level of non-convergence never happened before?

The last time commodity prices skyrocketed, as they did in the mid-2000s, was in the 1970s when I was in high school and running off to the Knoxville Raceway at every chance. So, Phil, Aaron, and I decided to find out if there had been a non-convergence problem in the '70s. We were stunned to see that as grain prices increased during the 1970s, the storage rate marched up in parallel, staving off any threat of non-convergence. The storage rate started at one and three-quarters cents and steadily increased as the cash and futures prices rose. By 1981, the storage rate was about a nickel per month, where it stayed until 2005. The CBOT never changed it.

For twenty-five years, the nickel-per-month worked fine, but in 2005 it needed to go higher—yet futures contract rules made it difficult to make this adjustment. It looked like the exchange had forgotten how to manage storage rates during grain price booms to avoid non-convergence.

In 2018, while researching this book and introducing my co-author to the few trading pits still open, we met with the CME Group's Dave Lehman and Fred Seamon at the legendary Ceres Café in the old CBOT Building at LaSalle and Jackson in the heart of downtown Chicago. I asked about futures storage rates in the 1970s, and Dave pointed me toward Glenn Hollander, an old trader who had been at the CBOT during the '70s. I contacted Hollander, who said he had been a long-time member of something called the CBOT warehouse committee.[8] Among its annual duties, this committee reviewed the storage rates that warehouse elevators charged cash grain customers to see if the storage rate on grain futures contracts needed to be adjusted.

At this time, the storage rate was not written into the futures contract rulebook, Hollander said, so the exchange could quickly and easily change it. He also told me that when they adjusted the storage rates upward during the 1970s, it *wasn't* to fend off the threat of non-convergence. No one was even focused on that problem.

During this period, the USDA often owned and stored grain as part of the operation of price support programs. The USDA would determine the "fair" storage rate they would pay and then publish it. (The government can do that.) The CBOT committee looked at the USDA storage rates, and whenever the USDA rates went up, so did theirs. They kept bumping up the storage rates because of inflation, which was rampant in the '70s. They didn't realize that by doing this, they were also preventing non-convergence. They did the right thing without knowing it!

Before the 1990s, a gentleman's agreement among the major grain companies ensured they would charge the same storage rate on warehouse receipts used for futures delivery. If they didn't, chaos would erupt. But in 1991, Cargill announced they would no longer honor the agreement and would increase storage rates unilaterally. This caused consternation among the other big grain companies, which successfully lobbied the CBOT to change the rules to block Cargill's move.

To do this, the CBOT had to write the storage rates into the official rulebook for grain futures contracts. This stopped Cargill from creating chaos, but it also significantly reduced the flexibility to change storage rates in the future. Because the CBOT wrote the rates into the futures contract rulebooks, no one could change them unless first approved by the Commodity Futures Trading Commission (CFTC), a complicated and time-consuming process.

All of this led to the perfect storm that was non-convergence from 2005 through 2010. The CME Group needed to increase storage rates beyond 5 cents per bushel per month, but they had much less flexibility to make the change due to that little-known episode back in the early 1990s.[9] A classic example of the Law of Unintended Consequences.

I pride myself on being part of the team that solved the "Crime of the Century" in grain futures markets. I believe this will stand as the best and most important work of my academic career. Fred Seamon of the CME Group stated it this way: "Illinois research was the linchpin for us solving the wheat convergence problem. I think forced load-out would have killed the wheat contract. So, when your research came out, it gave us the opportunity to come up with another way of addressing non-convergence, and it saved the wheat contract."[10]

The CME's "other way" of addressing non-convergence was to create a variable storage rate (VSR) system. Whenever price spreads reached a certain threshold, the storage rate would automatically rise by three cents per bushel. Some grain owners weren't happy with the VSR system because their storage costs could increase in certain situations, but it prevented non-convergence.

There is still one missing piece of the puzzle. We do not yet fully understand why storage rates needed to be so much higher starting in the mid-2000s. I suspect rates needed to hike because of the ethanol production boom. Ethanol led to a massive increase in the demand for corn and, therefore, storage space. With greater demand for storage space, the prices surged. I have not proven conclusively that this is the correct explanation, but I am confident this is moving in the right direction.

Today, Aaron Smith maintains a non-convergence monitoring website, which estimates the storage market rate, comparing it to the one specified in grain futures contracts. It does this in real-time, watching for warning signals of future threats of non-convergence.[11]

So, can non-convergence in grain futures markets happen again? It's not likely, but I can never say never. After all, the market may somehow find a way. It has a knack for doing that. I also have to wonder whether the Destroying Angel is still out there and whether he would be willing to give up his conspiracy theories after reading our paper. I would not bet on it.

Chapter 17
Trading Spaces

I never saw the dominance of electronic trading coming. Like so many others, I thought trading and price discovery required nose-to-nose bargaining, as you once found in the raucous pits of Chicago. Even after the Chicago Mercantile Exchange (CME) introduced electronic trading in 1992, it wasn't evident that the new system would catch on, let alone take over.

For me, it wasn't until May 1999 that a light bulb finally went off. It happened while attending yet another conference sponsored by the Chicago Board of Trade (CBOT). In the lead paper— "Is Sound Just Noise?"—Joshua Coval and Tyler Shumway probed the question of what would be lost from the pits if all trading went electronic.

Coval and Shumway zeroed in on the role played by noise in the pit, sending traders signals that something was happening. When trading electronically, you can't experience this "hive"—the dramatic rise and fall in noise that accompanies the waves of trading activity. Does that put electronic traders at a disadvantage? Exactly how important is the sound that comes with pit trading?[1]

One of the best depictions of this hive activity, this collective cacophony, is the final climactic scene of the classic 1983 comedy *Trading Places*, starring Dan Aykroyd and Eddie Murphy. The filmmakers originally wanted to set the final scene in one of the Chicago exchanges. But no matter how hard they tried, they could not get approval, according to a 30th-anniversary *Insider* retrospective about the movie. The director, John Landis, didn't specify which Chicago exchange had refused them.

As a result, they filmed the pit scenes at the commodities exchange in the World Trade Center in New York. "About 90 percent [of the floor traders in the movie] were actual traders, and a great deal of it I shot during actual trading hours," Landis said. "I was quite taken aback at how physically rough it was—they really elbowed one another...It was like a contact sport."[2]

In addition, the traders in the movie were very, very noisy. It was a spot-on depiction of pit behavior—with all of its sound and fury.

In the climactic scene, we see the nefarious Duke brothers working through their floor trader, buying up contracts for oranges before the crop report would be released that morning. They had a jump on everyone with inside information about a bad orange crop, which they knew would send prices even higher. (Unbeknownst to them, however, they had been fed false data.)

As soon as other traders saw the Duke brothers snatching up contracts, they knew something was up. The hive spurred into action, and noise levels skyrocketed. In turn, this alerted everyone else, triggering a buying frenzy.

At the eye of the storm were Aykroyd and Murphy—the only ones with the knowledge that the orange crop was actually good, and prices would plummet as soon as the U.S. Department of Agriculture (USDA) announced this. Knowing the prices were about to drop, Aykroyd and Murphy decided to sell.

Suddenly, everyone wanted to cut a deal with them, buying up their contracts. Virtually all of the traders wanted to buy, buy, buy, while Aykroyd and Murphy wanted to sell, sell, sell. Not until the crop report was announced did the Duke brothers and other traders realize they had been duped. Suddenly, everyone wanted to sell to cut their losses.[3]

The *Trading Places* scene is a wonderful example of how noise fed the frenzy in the pit. When the Duke brothers started buying, others picked up on this, and the buying madness swept through the pit—spurred on by the noise.

To document this kind of impact by sound levels, Coval and Shumway took second-by-second recordings in the CBOT Treasury bond pit over two months in 1998. Then they compared it to price and trading volume data during the same period. The data carried precisely synchronized time stamps to match the noise volume with the trading data. Among their findings was that a change in sound level was a good predictor for price volatility, signaling dramatic swings in price several minutes ahead of time.[4]

Hearing this paper delivered at the CBOT conference was a seminal moment. It was the first time I took electronic trading seriously. After all, the CBOT had commissioned this study, so they were obviously serious about it. They wouldn't be backing the research if they weren't concerned.

At the time of this study, resistance to electronic trading was fierce, especially from those who stood to lose their jobs—the floor traders. To find out how electronic markets fought through this formidable opposition, I visited the man who helped to make it happen—Leo Melamed of the CME Group.

My co-writer and I traveled to Chicago to the newly remodeled CME building, a glass-dominated structure that looks like something you'd find in Silicon Valley. One floor is devoted to recreational pursuits for CME employees—everything from pool and ping-pong tables to foosball and even Bocce ball, an Italian game dating back to the Roman Empire. The only thing missing were young employees rollerblading or skateboarding along the hallways. We met Leo in his beautiful, spacious office, a museum in miniature with numerous photos of the old CME trading pits.[5]

Leo Melamed's life is a story of risk—taking risks as a trader, as well as by introducing innovative new futures markets and pioneering electronic trading. But the high-risk tensions in his life go back even further to September of 1939 when he was seven years old. He remembers being at the barber shop in Bialystok, Poland, when his world turned upside down. He perched on the children's bench, raising him to an adult's eye level. As the barber draped him with a white smock, shouting erupted outside on the street.

A man darted past, screaming that the Nazis were approaching. Melamed said he never saw his mother move so fast. She grabbed his hand, and together they began running.

"There were many others in the street, slamming shutters, closing doors, pulling down window shades, drawing curtains," Leo wrote in his memoir, *Escape to the Futures*. "The entire city was in a crouching lope."[6]

Leo and his mother fled to a brick, two-story building at the city's edge, where his father had grown up. His father, a member of the Bialystok city council, was already in hiding because inside information revealed that the Nazis planned to hold the city leaders hostage.

Because they lived on the edge of Bialystok, Leo's family was among the first to see the Nazis enter the city.

"The tanks came first," he said. "You could hear their thunderous roar long before you saw them. There were countless numbers of them moving slowly into Bialystok like so many alien robots. As they passed our building, they made a strange squealing and eerie noise."[7]

Bialystok became a political football between the Germans and the Soviet Union as World War II exploded on the continent. The Germans invaded Poland from the west, while the Soviets rumbled in from the east, thanks to the treachery of the Molotov-Ribbentrop pact, in which Stalin and Hitler divided the country. Initially, the Germans controlled Bialystok. But after a new border was established, Bialystok became part of the Soviet empire. And as the Nazis departed, Soviet soldiers flowed into the city.

"Two of the most repressive and cruelest regimes in history had been shoved down Bialystok's gullet," Leo said.[8]

While the Nazis and the Communists pursued his father, his family spent the next two years on the run. First, they fled to Wilno, Lithuania, where life started to return to some form of normalcy. But in 1940, Stalin decided to take back Lithuania. So, their only hope of escaping was to obtain transit papers to Japan.

Officially, Japan disapproved of issuing transit papers to fleeing Jews. Yet, the Japanese consul general in Lithuania, Chiune Sugihara, defied his government's orders. He issued transit visas to Jews, who then rode the Trans-Siberian Railway across Siberia to Vladivostok. From there, they could take a ship to Japan.

According to Leo, historians credit Sugihara "with saving the lives of over 6,000 Jews in that frantic month of August 1940. Unfortunately, it still wasn't enough." As the last train left the station, hundreds more stood on the platform without visas and "watched their last hope pulling away." Sugihara could only bow to them and say, "Please forgive me. I can't write any more [transit visas]. I will pray for your safety."[9]

Leo's family was among those who received transit visas. What followed was a grueling journey across Siberia, followed by a voyage to Japan. They reached Japan in early 1941, and on April 18, they arrived in Seattle. All this unfolded before Pearl Harbor when the United States and Japan became bitter enemies.

Because of these pivotal experiences, "the idea of risk penetrated into my being," Leo told us when we sat down with him in early 2020, just before the COVID-19 pandemic. "My mother told me that in her mind, she never let go of my hand for the entire two years on the run. She used to say to me that disaster was just around every corner. She lived with risk, and I think it generated in me how to handle risk."[10]

By now, you've noticed the central theme of risk.

There's risk in working on the farm, as my knack for nearly killing myself repeatedly demonstrates so clearly. And there's price risk in the markets, which can be managed with the aid of futures contracts.

Up to this point, I have focused on the history of futures markets, how the markets work, and why speculators play such a vital role in establishing prices and managing risk. In the final chapters, I turn to the future of futures markets, and there's no better person to begin with than Leo Melamed.

Leo's ability to handle risk enabled him to become what he describes as a "pretty good trader" in the futures market of Chicago. Today, he is over ninety years old and has become a legend. He helped usher in two of the most significant changes in the history of futures markets—the expansion of futures contracts beyond agriculture to include financial contracts in the 1970s (which you'll read about in Chapter 20) and the electronic trading system that transformed futures trading worldwide.

According to Leo, brokers trading in the CME and CBOT pits during the 1990s were earning about a billion dollars a year, divided among them, so the idea of being replaced by an electronic trading system was a threat. But Leo could understand their fears. After all, he also had been a floor trader, beginning in 1953. However, that wasn't his original plan.

Being raised in a Jewish family, he says fathers often pressured their sons to become a doctor, a lawyer, or an engineer, so he chose law. At that time, he didn't know a thing about futures trading. It was serendipity that brought him to the trading floor of the CME in the early 1950s.

Melamed hoped to land a law clerk job while working on his degree. "It was a Sunday morning, and my buddy calls me up, telling me there is a perfect job for me at a Chicago law firm," he recalled.[11]

So, Leo immediately picked up a copy of *The Chicago Tribune* and found an ad saying they were looking for runners at Merrill Lynch, Pierce, Fenner, and Beane. With a name like that, he figured the company had to be a law firm looking for a clerk.

The next day he applied at their office, which happened to be inside the CBOT building. He thought nothing of it, assuming it was their employment office. The people there told him to show up at 110 North Franklin Street the next day.

"I figured Franklin Street must be where the law office is," he said. So, he arrived the following morning, fully expecting to enter a law office. But instead...

"I walked inside, and it was like Alice in Wonderland," he said. That address—110 North Franklin Street—was the CME building. And the group he assumed to be a law firm was actually a company working on the trading floor.

When Melamed walked into the madhouse of the CME, he said, "I fell in love with the movement and the sight of the people shouting at each other. I could tell they were trading something that was obviously very important."[12]

Like myself, Terry Duffy, and so many others, the energy of the trading floor enthralled him. Also, like Duffy, Leo started as a runner, dashing around carrying trade orders from brokers manning the phones to traders in the pit. He did this job while simultaneously working on his law degree. After getting a taste of the futures markets in action, he decided he wanted to become a trader, so he asked his father to loan him $3,000 to buy a CME membership, giving him the right to trade on the floor. His father, who had saved $5,000 since the end of the war, agreed to loan him the money under one condition. He had to finish his law degree.

"I kept my promise," Leo said, finishing his degree and then working in law (while also trading) until 1965.

In 1967, he joined the CME board and became chairman of the board two years later. The irony is that someone who fell in love with the futures market after witnessing the trading floor frenzy went on to envision the system that would eventually spell the end of floor trading.

Initially, Leo was like most people (including me), who believed futures trading could not work unless done in person in the pits.

"Back in 1977, I said the only way a transaction system for futures trading could work was through open outcry. You've got to face each other and compete eyeball-to-eyeball. It's the only way you're going to get liquidity. But I was wrong."[13]

Leo said he was standing in front of the CME trading pit for S&P 500 futures in 1984 when the advantages of an electronic trading system suddenly became clear.

"I'm standing at my desk on the floor of the exchange," he recalled, "and what do I see? I see runners take orders, run to the pit, give it to their broker, and run back to get another. And this is going on throughout the exchange, people running back and forth."

Leo realized the system would be much more efficient if handled electronically through the computers revolutionizing society in the

1980s. "I knew we were going to be an antiquated joke if we did not accept the changes happening all around us."[14]

At the time, he happened to be writing a science fiction novel, which would be published in 1987 as *The Tenth Planet*. In this novel, he creates an advanced civilization of about 50 billion people, running on the power of a single computer.

"This computer could do everything," he said. "If you broke your finger, the computer could tell you what to do. A Hollywood producer connected to Steven Spielberg told me I had made one mistake with the book. He said I should have called the computer 'Google.'"

With the promise of computer technology humming in his mind, Melamed assembled a committee in 1986 to find ways to respond to globalization—with electronic trading being one of those ideas. Four or five committee members were successful, intelligent traders who were open to the idea of electronic trading.

"Counting votes, the committee was optimistic that the CME board could be won over," Leo wrote in his 2021 book, *Man of the Futures*. "On the other hand, to pass a membership referendum was a near impossible task; *hell no*, was the most likely response."[15]

According to Leo, people told him, "There is no way you're ever going to get a majority of members to say yes to electronic transactions. No way. You're wasting your time."

Why would floor traders vote for a system that could doom their jobs? In fact, traders were so unhappy at the looming threat to their livelihood that Leo said he received death threats. He had to hire a security officer to accompany him to the office.

But then Leo came up with a brilliant stroke. "I knew how I could win," he said. The new electronic system would only be used with *new* markets; it would not compete with any current markets in which members were trading.

"I was once a trader," Leo said. "I knew the mentality." He knew that as long as traders could keep what they were doing—trading in pork bellies, for instance—they wouldn't care if electronic trading was introduced in new markets.

In addition, he said they would give traders an "iron-clad guarantee" that electronic trading would not directly compete with regular trading hours. In fact, they called the system Post-Market Trade, or PMT, because this name drove his point home that electronic trading would take place *after* regular trading hours on the floor of the CME.

The normal hours of trading were from 7:20 a.m. to 3:15 p.m., and Globex currency trading would run from 2:30 p.m. to 6 a.m. So, there would only be forty-five minutes of overlap. When I visited Leo's office, he showed me his hand-drawn sketch, showing that there would be virtually no overlap with open-outcry trading on the floor. That rough sketch, which helped to sell the idea, is now framed and hanging on his office wall.

"To give the plan gravitas," Leo wrote in *Man of the Futures*, "we agreed to officially approach Reuters Holding PLC, the most prominent communications enterprise of the time," to work on building the electronic system.[16]

"I remember one guy on the Reuters board saying to me, 'Mr. Melamed, are you trying to tell us that those hard-bitten traders are ever going to be willing to trade electronically?' I lied and said yes."

Finally, as a sweetener to the proposed electronic trading system, Leo said they added a profit incentive to the plan. One of the exploratory committee members pointed out that electronic trading was going to generate a profit, so why don't they share some with the traders?

"I bought the idea instantly." Floor traders would receive 70 percent of the income from electronic trading, with 20 percent to the clearinghouse members and 10 percent to the CME.

"This was the icing on the cake," he said.[17]

With the exploratory committee's unanimous support, Leo approached the CME board in August of 1987. After extensive discussion, the electronic trading proposal received unanimous approval. Next, on September 2, 1987, they unveiled the proposal to the CME membership, with a referendum on October 7, 1987.

The members approved electronic trading, and what once seemed impossible became a reality. Then Reuters went to work.

Meanwhile, Leo also approached the Chicago Board of Trade

(CBOT), offering them a 50-50 partnership with the CME. As he put it, "I thought that once the Board of Trade came on board, then everybody would come on board, and my idea would blossom."

Initially, the CBOT resisted, and their board chairman likened electronic trading to the H-bomb of futures. "He said it's going to blow futures out of the water," Leo recalled.

However, Leo persisted, and negotiating teams from the CME, CBOT, and Reuters met weekly for a year, hammering out a joint venture agreement approved on October 27, 1990. The Globex Corporation was formed, with Melamed as its chairman. (By this time, the PMT name had been replaced by the Globex name.)

Finally, on June 25, 1992, Globex went live, becoming the world's first *international* electronic trading system. There were a few other electronic trading systems in other countries, such as Japan. But Leo pointed out that those systems were local area networks. "They didn't quite go all the way. Ours was international."

Leo made the ceremonial first trade on the new Globex system. But soon, things began to stall. According to Leo, the CME board "voted that the Globex Corporation could not do anything without its approval. That was a total veto of our authority." Moreover, the CBOT came to Melamed and insisted that their board should also get the same veto power as the CME.

"That was the end of Globex as far as I was concerned," he said. "So, I resigned because this clearly took away the right of Globex to advance. And we were still in the formative stages of Globex."

After Leo resigned, bickering erupted between the CME and CBOT, and the project went dormant. "Globex stopped growing, and our business started to erode, going down by as much as 50 percent."

On April 15, 1994, the CBOT officially ended its association with Globex, citing "irreconcilable differences" with the CME. It was like a divorce, with the CME retaining custody of Globex. It turned out to be a game-changer in the history of the two exchanges. For almost 100 years, the CME had operated in the shadow of the larger CBOT, but it would eventually become dominant by retaining possession of Globex.

None of this was evident in 1994 when the CBOT pulled from the deal. Globex was still stagnating. Therefore, a petition began to circulate to bring Leo back to Globex, but he said, "I told the petitioners that I would not come back unless you elected to the board at least some people who believed in Globex." Most of the current board, controlled by brokers, did not support the electronic trading system, he said.

In 1997, all of that changed. Leo argued that if the CME didn't keep up with the times, it would lose valuable business to foreign exchanges, which were also starting to trade electronically. Members of the CME responded by overwhelmingly voting to remove 50 percent of the board members, sending a clear message of support for Globex.

Leo returned to the board as chairman emeritus and senior advisor, and "the first thing I did was emancipate Globex," he said. "The rule had been that you couldn't advance Globex without board approval, so nothing happened. That's the first thing I changed."

Globex had been unleashed.

In 1997, Globex continued to honor the agreement not to offer electronic trading during traditional hours, so it wouldn't compete with floor trading. But then came the E-mini futures contract—a smaller-sized version of the CME's popular contract based on the S&P 500 stock index. Because it was technically a new futures contract—not a product currently traded—Leo and his attorney argued it did not compete with pit trading and, therefore, could be traded electronically twenty-four hours a day.

The result was a revolt among open-outcry supporters because allowing the E-mini futures contract to trade twenty-four hours a day was the proverbial "camel's nose under the tent." There were threats of lawsuits and explosive meetings.

But when the dust settled, the E-mini futures contract began trading electronically twenty-four hours a day on September 9, 1997, and it was an instant success. On the first day of trading, most new contracts will typically see maybe 500 to 1,000 trades, he said. But the E-mini recorded 8,000 opening-day trades, setting a new record in the history of the futures markets.

The beauty of the electronic system was that space no longer limited trading. An electronic trading space is not constrained by the number of people you could jam inside a pit.

After the CBOT pulled out of the Globex joint venture, they attempted to create their own electronic system—Aurora. But their platform operated as a kind of primitive video game, with trading brokers represented by icons on the screen. It was like an open-outcry system that operated on a screen instead of the floor. The trading space was still limited by the little icons representing traders. In contrast, Globex uses computer algorithms to match trades electronically without icons making trades, so space limitations do not constrain the system.

Even as electronic trading emerged, the CBOT decided to dramatically expand its trading floor. On January 17, 1995, Chicago's Mayor Richard M. Daley led the groundbreaking ceremony. When the work was finished in 1997, they had added 60,000 square feet of trading space for a total of 115,150 square feet. The new CBOT trading floor also featured enormous price boards mounted on the walls like oversized stadium scoreboards 600 feet long. It had become the largest trading floor in the world. Leo said he told the CBOT chairman that "he was building the last trading floor on planet earth. He did not believe it."[18]

No matter how big the building, the CBOT's trading space was still bricks and mortar, while the CME's Globex trading space was bits and bytes and could handle much higher trading volume. Eventually, the inevitability of electronic trading would win out, and on July 12, 2007, the CME and CBOT merged to form the CME Group. One pit is still open, but the cavernous CBOT trading floor is virtually empty today.

Although Leo Melamed had his doubts about whether electronic trading would work, he quotes economist Lord John Maynard Keynes, who allegedly said, "When the facts change, I change my mind. What do you do, sir?" Whether Keynes uttered those words is not relevant. The fact is that Leo did change his mind when he saw the possibilities of electronic trading, and he became its greatest champion. He credits it all to imagination.

Leo said his early days on the run from Nazis and Communists helped to develop this imagination. He didn't have other children with whom to play, so he played alone.

"I didn't have any friends because we kept moving," he said, "and I had nowhere else to go but in my mind."

Before I leave this chapter, let me return to that influential 1999 paper, "Is Noise Just Sound?" One of the conference discussants for this paper was Stephen Figlewski, a top finance professor from New York University. Figlewski thought the article was innovative, but he raised an important issue. Sure, the information from noise patterns in the pits may be valuable to floor traders. But do they use this information more for their benefit rather than that of their customers?[19]

To understand this question, be aware that floor traders often trade for themselves, as well as for the customers who phone in their orders. This has always raised a potential conflict of interest. Do floor traders take advantage of being physically present in the pits for their own benefit, putting their customers at a disadvantage?

For example, floor traders operated with an order book (which later became a tablet) that told them what orders they needed to fill for their customers. What happens if floor traders see that they need to fill a large customer order that will drive prices down?

In that case, floor traders might sell their futures contracts *before* filling the customer order, ensuring they don't lose money. Similarly, if floor traders notice that one of their large customer orders will drive up prices, they might delay selling one of their contracts—waiting for the prices to peak.

This kind of manipulation is called "front-running," and it's tough to prove. As noted earlier in Chapter 3, an FBI sting operation conducted at the CBOT and CME in the late 1980s targeted traders who were doing just this—trading for their gain, ahead of the needs of their customers.

So, although floor traders may have benefited from the noise patterns in the pits, the benefit may have done more to help them than their customers. The information gleaned from noise may be valuable to individual traders but detrimental to the overall success of the market, Figlewski suggested.[20]

On the other hand, electronic trading removes the advantage that floor traders have over customers who are not physically present. It levels the field, as Terry Duffy pointed out. However, that doesn't mean electronic trading is without its own set of problems and ways of gaming the system.

Electronic trading often boils down to who can access information the quickest—a data drag race, you might say. The goal is speed, and I know a thing or two about that as a racing aficionado. I also understand first-hand what it means to outrun your angels.

Chapter 18
Outrunning Your Angels

I leaned back in the passenger seat of my good friend Rick Vaughan's 1965 Plymouth Belvedere convertible, which we affectionately called the "Belvie." This model had small sculptured "chicken wings" sticking out at the rear. It sounds strange today, but the car was a beauty, and it could really move because it had a big, souped-up engine.

Rick had been dating my younger sister Jan for several years and would later become my brother-in-law. He was as much a speed freak as any Irwin, even before he officially became family. We had just spent the evening of July 3, 1978, joyriding in the Belvie, performing "donuts," in which you spin the car in circles as fast as you can. When Rick turned into an alley running through the heart of the little town of Yale, Iowa, he put his foot to the floor.

As we raced toward the back of a popular tavern, a giant pile of garbage in the alley came into view, a mountain of plastic bags filled with beer cans, food, and other trash from the July 4th weekend. Rick aimed his car at it like a kamikaze pilot. Being in a convertible should have given us pause, but we didn't care. We roared into the midst of the waste.

WHOOOOOOMP!

The mountain exploded. Trash bags burst open, hurling rotten food, beer cans, and other garbage to all sides. Food splattered onto the tavern wall to our right, and a bunch of it rained down, landing everywhere in the car. That junk must have spread out over a 25-yard radius.

It was like something out of a bad 1970s chase movie.

Surely, somebody must have witnessed our insane stunt, but we never got in trouble and never got a ticket. To this day, I don't understand how that was possible. Rick gunned the engine and smoked the tires to free us from that mess, which may have been the straw that literally broke the camel's back. The engine threw a rod as we roared out of town, and that was the end of the Belvie.

By now, it should be clear that my friends and I pulled some crazy stunts in our younger days. But as nuts as we were growing up, I don't think any of us equaled what my cousin Eric Hanson did in my parents' car a few months after the garbage explosion in the Belvie.

Eric was the oldest son of my mom's only brother (from whom I get my middle name, "Hal"). Even though he was five years younger, we were more like brothers. Eric's parents split when he was in elementary school, and his mom moved back to Iowa from California, so he was a frequent visitor to the farm, spending most of his summers with us. Unfortunately, during junior high, he began to get in serious trouble, so after he finished eighth grade, my parents became his legal guardians, and he lived with us permanently.

In September of 1978, when I was a junior at Iowa State, I returned home one weekend to help with the harvest. Eric had turned sixteen in June and received his driver's license, so he asked my mom if he could borrow her car—a beautiful two-door blue Mercury Cougar with a white Landau roof (all the rage back in the '70s).

"That car could regularly do in excess of 120 miles per hour, and it often did," Eric said when I sat down to review the details of what happened on that infamous night.[1]

Eric and his best friend, Ronnie Nielson, were both on the Yale-Jamaica-Bagley (YJB) football team but were injured that night. Eric wasn't too broken up about having to sit out because they were playing a powerhouse team from Coon Rapids, Iowa, which featured a 175-pound state champion wrestler at middle linebacker. What's more, the YJB football team was in the process of setting a state record for the longest losing streak in Class D Iowa football history. During Eric's four years at YJB, they never won a single game. Not one.

Although Eric and Ronnie were sidelined by injuries, they had to make an appearance. But by halftime, it became apparent it was going to be a blowout (not in YJB's favor), so they left. After the game, they started for a party at an old, deserted farmstead not far from a bridge going over railroad tracks—a place called "Squatters." It was way off the beaten path, even by our very rural standards—the perfect place for beer parties ("keggers"). So, they picked up Ronnie's girlfriend, Carol, and a case of beer before racing off for Squatters. In 1978 in rural Iowa, sixteen-year-olds could buy beer out the back door of the local tavern. It was indeed a different time.

The bridge near Squatters was unique because the railroad tracks ran below ground level. The wooden bridge ran north to south, with sharply angled sections on each end and a flat portion in the middle so it could clear the trains running beneath. The steep north and south sides of the bridge each looked "like a barn roof," Eric said. The road itself was gravel and usually filled with ruts.

"As we're heading toward the bridge, that Mercury Cougar was really fast and had a smooth ride," he recalled. "It was awful easy to get going a lot faster than you thought."

The bridge quickly came into view as they were barreling down the gravel road that night. Because Eric had never been to Squatters before, he looked at Ronnie and asked, "How fast can you go over this bridge safely?"

"I think about 15 miles per hour."

Eric looked down at his speedometer. They were going at least 60 miles per hour.

"I immediately pressed down on the brake pedal, but it was a little late for that," he said.

The Mercury Cougar shot up the steep north side of the bridge and went airborne. All four tires left the ground as the car flew over the middle, flat section of the bridge before it crashed, nose first, on the opposite steep side.

"It was a pretty good *Dukes of Hazzard* moment," Eric said, referring to the popular TV show at the time, featuring the most politically incorrect car in television history.

The show's heroes nicknamed their car General Lee, which featured an enormous Confederate flag on the roof. In the opening credits, their car races up and over a huge pile of dirt, going airborne in slow motion before landing on all four wheels.

Note that I said, "landing on all four wheels." Eric admitted their landing wasn't a perfect *Dukes of Hazzard* moment because they did *not* come down on all four wheels.

"When those guys jump, the car stays flat," he said. "But ours went more like a ballistic arc."

When the nose of their car smashed against the end of the bridge and into the road, it plowed up huge swirls of dirt and gravel. "She dug dirt just like a road grader, shoveling dirt over the bumper and grill and up under the hood so hard that the rocks flowed out from under the hood and over the windshield."

Fortunately, they wore seatbelts, or that crash might have killed them. When it dawned on everyone that they had survived, Carol and Ronnie burst out laughing, but Eric didn't find it humorous in the least. His first thought: *My Uncle Jim is going to kill me!*

According to Eric, "I remember looking over at Ronnie and shouting, 'Oh no, we wrecked it! We wrecked my Aunt Pauline's car!'"

Ronnie stared back at him and said, "What's this 'we' stuff?"

After the crash-landing, the car was miraculously still running, but every gauge on the dashboard lit up and flashed. Steam billowed from the engine, so they stopped to pop the hood and noticed that the entire engine cavity was clogged with soil, grass, and gravel. They also saw that the power steering belt was torn away, as were the fan belt and radiator hoses. That explained the steam.

When you have a hot engine, Eric said you have two options. You either get the fan going or drive the car as fast as possible to blow air across the engine to keep it cool. They chose the "drive fast" option and took off for Bagley after asking someone else to drive Carol home from the party.

When they reached Bagley, Eric pulled the car to the side of Main Street to pop the hood and get a better look. As they bent over the engine, one of my dad's good friends, Doc Gubser, and his son stopped to see if they could offer any help. Eric waved them on, saying he could handle it, but things got even more interesting when the county sheriff pulled alongside them.

"We hadn't had enough time to drink much beer, so we weren't drunk," Eric said, but the odor of spilled beer must have been strong and pervasive. "The sheriff could tell I was scared to death, and I think he had a pretty good idea that we were in big trouble with Uncle Jim."

So, the sheriff escorted them as Eric drove the mangled Mercury the short distance to our house at the other end of Main Street. My parents were already asleep in preparation for farmers' usual early wake-up time—5:30 a.m. It was close to 11 p.m. as I readied for bed when I noticed flashing lights in the window.

When I peeked through my window and noticed a police car in front of our house, I immediately thought, *Eric. What has he done now?*

After getting dressed, I ventured into the cool night to investigate and saw the mangled front bumper and the right front tire leaning inward. Something serious had happened.

I confirmed with the sheriff that, yes, Eric did live here, and this was my parent's car. Then the officer left him in my hands. No report. No paperwork. This was the 1970s.

Like Eric, I knew that my dad would blow a gasket and my mom would be sick when they discovered what had happened to their beautiful car. My mom loved this car, which was barely over a year old. I could not believe they slept through the flashing lights and the panicked conversation not far from their bedroom window. They were a pair of heavy sleepers.

After the sheriff left, I asked, "What happened?"

Eric immediately became very emotional. "Ronnie and I were

driving down a gravel road leading from the football stadium at Coon Rapids, and I hit a big washout!"

Every good lie contains a grain of truth. The Coon Rapids football field had a new gravel road leading away from it, and it had rained hard recently. So, hitting a washout was plausible. But when I looked at that car, I could only think: *That must be one monster washout to do this kind of damage.*

Our farm shop was only a few blocks away, so I managed to get the car started and pulled it into the shop, where I could put some lights on it and assess the damage. When I popped open the hood, I could not believe my eyes.

I wish I had a camera phone to capture what I saw that night. The engine compartment was packed with mud, gravel, and grass. All the hoses had popped off the radiator, and the fan belt came loose. Worst of all, the I-beam suspension for the right front wheel was severely bent, which explained why the tire leaned inward.

This was not the work of a washout. I turned to Eric and demanded he tell me the truth, and he proceeded to unravel a tale that made my hair stand on end. When he told me how they had gone airborne and then crashed nose-first into the ground, I realized it was a miracle that the car didn't do an end-over-end flip—the kind of deadly accident I had seen many times at sprint car races.

I explained to Eric that if we didn't do something about this, my dad would make mincemeat out of him. Since Eric tended to get in trouble and was a relatively new member of the family, I figured we needed to salvage the situation if we could. So, we went to work on the car, beginning shortly before midnight. We started by clearing out all the mud and grass. I had Eric and Ronnie lug away bucket after bucket of soil, gravel, and grass and dump it in our adjacent cornfield, where no one would find the evidence.

Our shop had all the equipment needed for repairs because we constantly fixed farm machinery. I had watched my dad and his hired men make many a repair, so I had an idea of what needed to be done. But in all honesty, I was not all that great with repairing stuff (better at breaking it), but desperate times require desperate measures. We pushed the bumper back in place so you could open and close the hood with greater ease. Then we jacked up the car, and I used an acetylene torch to heat the I-beam, softening the metal; that way, Eric and Ronnie could bend it back in shape using a large steel pipe as a lever.

We were racing the sun, but we finished our work early in the morning, just before my mom and dad awoke. Then I took Eric by the collar and said, "My dad is going to grill you on this! You've got to stick to the story that the damage was caused by a huge washout in Coon Rapids."

The funny thing is that when my dad got up and ran into us in the kitchen, we were fully dressed, so he assumed we were up and ready to go to work. He was impressed, unaware we had not been to bed!

I told my dad there was a problem with the Cougar, and I took him to survey the damage, recounting the story of the washout. But my dad held his anger in reserve until he could talk to Eric alone later in the morning when my cousin was running the grain auger out at Grandma Lurene's place.

"It was a real strong conversation," Eric recalled. "My Uncle Jim didn't buy my story at all. He looked me in the eye and said, 'You're not going to tell me you bent the front end in a washout. That I-beam is at least 1 inch out of shape. You bent the frame! I don't know what you boys were doing last night, and I don't want to know. But we're going to trade this vehicle, and we're not going to talk about it again.'"

When Eric told me about the conversation later in the day, I could not believe it! I guess my dad had more pressing farm things on his mind. Eric was extremely lucky.

Come Monday morning, my folks traded in that once beautiful car, and it was never seen again.

"I was adopted, but to this day, I say that Uncle Jim and Aunt Pauline must've really loved me," Eric said. "If they hadn't, they would have sent me back to where I came from."

Eric said he stuck to the washout story for over forty years—until late 2020 when somebody posted a photo of the Squatters party bridge on the Facebook page for YJB alums. One of the alums spotted the post and asked Eric online about his *Dukes of Hazzard* moment on the bridge.

The moment my mom read that Facebook post, she called me, asking, "All right, Scott, what's this about a *Dukes of Hazzard* moment? What *really* happened with my Mercury Cougar? I want to know."

At long last, I unloaded the entire story we'd hidden for over forty years. My mom rarely gets angry, but I could sense that she was upset, even though the event happened over forty years ago. As Eric put it, "I knew the statute of irritation" hadn't elapsed, so he was hoping Aunt Pauline had not seen the Facebook post.

Then my mom hit me with a line I'll never forget.

"Scott," she said, "you boys came close to outrunning your angels in high school."

Outrunning your angels. That's the perfect description of my life racing cars and pulling death-defying stunts on snowmobiles and motorcycles. Several times now, I've said that I must've kept my guardian angel very busy with all my accidents. But as my mom wisely pointed out, we were so wild that my buddies and I came very close to outrunning our guardian angels on multiple occasions.

Speed is exhilarating when you're talking about fast cars. But it's also exciting when it comes to fast trading. In the futures market, the increased speed of electronic trading has led to an explosion in the growth of the markets. It has also led to greater market efficiency, and economists love efficiency. But as with most things, some bad comes with the good. The market can move so fast that it threatens to outrun its angels.

When Leo Melamed was trying to sell the Chicago Mercantile Exchange (CME) on the Globex trading system, he said electronic trading would not compete with open-outcry trading in the pits. Despite his assurances, it was inevitable that the two systems would clash.[2] Someday, electronic trading would be done during pit trading hours, which is exactly what happened.

Not only did this spell the doom of pit trading, but it brought unforeseen issues about the speed of access to certain information, such as the all-important crop reports from the U.S. Department of

Agriculture (USDA). With the move to electronic trading, crop reports were eventually released into the midst of live trading. This meant that the fastest one to access that information would have a tremendous advantage in the market. Because algorithms, not people, run electronic trading, every millisecond counts. If the computer wizards at one firm can access crop report information faster than someone else, it can make all the difference in millions of dollars' worth of trades.

Think of it as electronic drag racing. Instead of cars roaring down Iowa country roads, we have computer programs racing to obtain USDA crop report information milliseconds faster than competitors. With apologies to Michael Lewis, it's a Flash-Boys world now.

Even before trading was ever done electronically at breakneck speed, there were attempts to gain access to crop information ahead of others. But these early attempts were sporadic, very complicated, and quite illegal. For instance, there was a breach in the USDA security for cotton production reports in 1905.

A trader paid off one of the USDA statisticians to give him information about the cotton report before it would be officially released to the public. If the cotton report was bullish, the USDA statistician would make sure the window shades were in a certain position. If the report was bearish, the window shades would be in a different position. To this day, whenever crop reports release, the window shades in the south wing of the USDA building are sealed shut.[3]

Because of the incredible value of the information in crop reports, they are guarded like nuclear secrets. In October of 1999, I had a chance to experience the lockdown process in the section of the USDA South Building in Washington, D.C., where they assembled the reports.

It was only through a family connection that I was able to penetrate this inner sanctum. My older sister was married to Duane "Pickle" Allen, and Duane's older brother, Rich Allen, was the head honcho for the agency responsible for the crop reports. Rich and Duane grew up in Yale, Iowa, one of the little towns that made up our school system. This was a very good connection indeed.

The USDA South Building has a system of metal doors that prevent anyone inside the lockup area from signaling to people outside. Armed guards stand at the doors, allowing no one in or out once lockdown begins roughly six hours ahead of a crop report's release.

USDA officials also use jamming devices to prevent anyone inside from communicating with people outside. In 1999, when I experienced lockdown, the Internet was hardwired, so they disconnected the system before releasing the report. Then, at the exact moment of release, officials would turn on the network connections for journalists from major publications, allowing them to communicate about the report. Remember, they took these precautions even when the crop report was being released *outside trading hours*, when no one could gain an advantage in trading on the information because the futures markets were closed. Today, the reports are released into live trading.

To understand how momentous this change really was, we need to review the steps leading up to it.

In 1981, when I lost my grad school loan by trading, the futures markets opened at 9:30 a.m. Central Time and closed at 1:30 p.m. The USDA's crop reports were released at 2 p.m. Central Time *after* the markets closed for the day.

This schedule meant that no traders would have an advantage over any others. Everyone would be in the same boat. They would have nearly an entire day to process the crop report information and then wait to trade on it the next morning. It was a level playing field in terms of the time available to analyze the information in the crop report and place trades based on it.

With the coming of electronic trading, the scenario depicted in the movie *Trading Places* became a possibility. In the movie, the villainous Duke brothers (no relation to the *Dukes of Hazzard*) obtain a copy of the crop report for oranges well before it was to be announced, giving them a considerable advantage over other traders. However, the movie's heroes, played by Dan Aykroyd and Eddie Murphy, stage an elaborate ploy in which they steal the oranges crop report and replace it with a forgery containing misleading information. Everything comes to a climax when the oranges crop report is announced in the midst of trading. The Duke brothers, trading on false information, are wiped out, while Aykroyd and Murphy's characters get rich by trading on accurate information.[4]

There was only one little problem with this plotline. The movie came out in 1983, and at that time, crop reports were not released during live trading. Therefore, gaining early access to a crop report, as Aykroyd and Murphy did, would really be no advantage. You still had to wait to trade on the information—and by that time, the report had already been released well before trading began. The screenwriters wrote around their plot hole by overlooking reality and having the crop report released in real-time.

That was 1983. Today, the *Trading Places* scenario has become a reality. It happened in 2013 when the USDA decided to release their reports at 11 a.m. Central Time, smack in the middle of trading.

The reason for this change had to do with a series of moves made by various futures markets around the world, such as what happened in the 1990s in Japan. To this day, the United States sets the world price for corn, so the U.S. corn crop report is vital to traders worldwide, including Japan.

In the early '90s, the Chicago Board of Trade (CBOT) began to pick up intelligence that the Japanese corn futures market was siphoning some of their futures market trading volume. The reason? Because of differences in time, the Japanese futures trading session overlapped with the release of the USDA crop report at 2 p.m. Central Time. Therefore, Japanese traders had an advantage over U.S. traders. They could trade on the crop information *immediately*, while U.S. traders had to wait for their markets to open the next day.

A former graduate student of mine, Phil Colling, was working for the USDA at this time and researched the issue, spelling out what was happening. As a result, the CBOT convinced the USDA to change the release time for crop reports. Instead of releasing the crop report at 2 p.m. Central Time, it would now be released in the morning, at 7:30 a.m. Central Time, when trading in Japan was closed—and just two hours before trading in the United States was set to begin. With this change, U.S. traders at the CBOT again had the advantage over traders on the Japanese futures exchange.[5]

During the years of pit trading, it was never easy to change trading hours. You'd be asking hundreds, if not thousands, of traders to move their work schedules, which wouldn't be easy. But with the advent of electronic trading, it suddenly became much easier for exchanges to alter their trading times, and that's exactly what happened in 2012.

The Intercontinental Commodity Exchange in Atlanta, known as ICE, announced a new corn futures contract, and their trading would be open during the time in the morning when the USDA released the crop report. Again, this would give their traders an advantage by being able to act on the crop report information immediately.

When the CME Group caught wind of it, they made a preemptive move and announced they were going to extend overnight electronic trading through the release of USDA reports. (Electronic trading previously had stopped at 7:15 a.m. Central Time.) This resulted in a continuous electronic trading session that stretched from 5 p.m. through 2 p.m. Central Time the next day. It was not quite 24/7 trading, but it was close. Of course, the real purpose was to make sure CME traders (remember that CME had merged with the CBOT by this time) would be able to act immediately on the release of the crop report. The writing was on the wall. The USDA realized they couldn't develop a fixed release time for the crop report that would be outside trading hours everywhere. Whenever they shifted the time of the crop report's release, some exchange somewhere would respond by changing their trading hours.

Therefore, in January 2013, the USDA finally concluded it would solve this problem by no longer even trying to release the crop reports outside of trading hours. The USDA would release them at 11 a.m. Central Time, in the thick of trading.

The *Trading Places* scenario had come to pass.

Once the USDA crop reports were released into live trading, everything changed. You had an enormous advantage if you could get to that information even a few milliseconds earlier than the competition. That's where the cyber-speed freaks entered the picture, trying to tweak their system to gain access to the information as fast as possible.

When the USDA first decided to release crop reports into live trading, my colleague Darrel Good and I noticed a curious thing. For up to fifteen minutes, we couldn't get access to the USDA servers due to congestion. I was suspicious. I wondered whether some firms with super-smart programmers were spamming the USDA servers to prevent others from getting to the information, allowing them to access it ahead of the competition. To this day, I can't say definitively whether the delay in access was due to spammers or just the expected congestion as everyone tried to access the USDA server simultaneously. But it looked fishy.

The USDA tackled this problem by increasing its server capacity. But I'm not sure the USDA has enough money to build a server capacity that would eliminate the advantage of high-speed traders who may be spamming the rest of us. I think a better, more straightforward, and elegant solution would be to tweet the crop report's "headline numbers." Twitter is too big to be spammed, so everyone could instantaneously get the headline numbers, and it would offer free access.

There might be five or six headline numbers for a big crop, such as U.S. corn yields per acre. Everyone gets instantaneous access if the USDA sends these headline numbers out in simultaneous tweets. I proposed this change in a *farmdoc daily* article in early 2020, and much to my surprise, I received a lot of blowback from the USDA.[6]

When the USDA switched to the real-time release of crop reports, they didn't foresee all the problems that could arise as they tried not to outrun their angels. The section of the USDA in charge of these huge, important crop reports is called the National Agricultural Statistics Service (NASS), and they're a bunch of statisticians (very good ones too). I think they had a hard time wrapping their minds around what might happen when releasing reports into live trading.

For example, a professional colleague, Mike Adjemian, and I published one of the first papers on the market impact of the change to real-time release of USDA crop reports. We were surprised to find that grain futures markets became significantly more volatile with the move to real-time release. While the heightened volatility lasted only a few minutes, this illustrated the unforeseen consequences that resulted from this momentous change.[7]

The USDA took steps to tighten security. From the outset, I advocated that media no longer be allowed in lock-up during the real-time release of crop reports. It had been a long-standing policy at the USDA and other federal agencies to give the media early access to important reports in lock-up, giving reporters time to write news stories. Although it was against the law to release the information early, any media leaks would not be very damaging during off-trading hours.

With the move to real-time release, the incentives were over-whelming for the media to give favored customers quicker access to the information. As long as media members have early access to the data, it's virtually impossible to prevent leaks with today's network technology. In 2018, USDA chief economist Rob Johansson said they were consistently finding a sudden surge in trading orders two seconds before the official release time of the crop reports. This was the end of the media in crop report lockdowns, which caused a furor. I still think it was the right thing to do.[8]

Currently, electronic trading is done through what is called a "continuous auction." An algorithm automatically and continuously matches buyers with sellers, matching the best bid to buy a futures contract (the highest bid) with the best offer to sell (the lowest offer). The person whose electrons get there first with the best bid or offer gets to make the trade—either as a buyer or seller. It's all about speed.

One way to solve the problem is through a "batch auction" system. With a batch auction system, it isn't the first bid to get there that wins the race and makes the trade. Instead, I propose that five to ten minutes before the crop report releases, the bids and offers would not be finalized. For a half hour (or maybe even a shorter duration), during which the crop report is released, traders can continue to enter bids and make offers. Still, they would not be matched immediately, so actual transactions do not take place until the end of the half hour.

This system would allow everyone time to view the crop report and still have a chance to adjust their bids and offers based on the USDA information. This batch auction would remove the speed advantage of certain trading firms. The only catch is that it might take federal regulations to get all the exchanges to make this change. Without regulations, why would any exchange observe a half-hour period when trades are not matched? Their competition might not observe the restriction. For the system to work, all the exchanges would have to do it.[9]

Without a doubt, the speed introduced by electronic trading was the most significant change to futures markets since their inception in the 1860s. But speed isn't the only innovation.

Exchanges are constantly on the prowl for new futures contracts to trade. In the beginning, futures contracts in the United States were available only for agricultural commodities, such as wheat, corn, and soybeans. But after World War II, things began to change with the advent of futures markets for livestock, currencies, and crude oil. Most new futures contracts don't make it, for lack of interest or opposition, as exchanges learned when they tried to start a futures market for movie box-office receipts (see Chapter 10). In the next chapter, we'll probe the biggest futures market of all—the one for crude oil. How it arose was pure serendipity.

Chapter 19
Twister!

The sky was pitch black in the southwest, plunging day into night. It was March 16, 1965, and my dad was at the wheat elevator in Medford, Oklahoma, where he was the general manager. As the sky darkened, my dad and another fellow decided to scout out the storm, so they took a lift to the "headhouse"—a square box perched on the top of the elevator, used whenever you needed to do work on the grain augers and grain-handling system.

The headhouse had a small, square, open window from which my dad and his buddy peered at the gathering storm. From the highest point in Medford, they spotted it on the horizon—a monster tornado heading straight for the city.

Scrambling back to the lift and taking it to ground level, my dad phoned my mom to warn her. We lived in a small ranch house in Medford, a city of about 1,000 people. I was six and was playing in the yard with my younger sister, Jan, and older sister, Cindy, when the sky began to turn black, and the wind started to whip.

To this day, Jan remembers seeing the pastor of a local church hurrying through the neighborhood, urging people to seek shelter. This was before radar warnings, tornado sirens, and up-to-the-minute weather updates on TV and radio. All we had were our eyes and the local pastor, acting as a meteorological Paul Revere.

After my dad's call, my mom hustled us into the one-car attached garage and had us crouch next to the deep freeze. My parents had tied a rope around the freezer, and she either looped the rope around our waists or had us hold on for dear life. I can't remember, but it must be an old Okie trick because if you re-watch the classic disaster flick *Twister*, you'll see Bill Paxton and Helen Hunt performing a similar stunt in the final climactic farm scene. They tied themselves to a thick pipe as the killer tornado made a direct hit where they sought shelter. When the twister roared overhead, they peeked into the heart of the funnel just before it lifted them feet-first into the air.[1]

Some of the scenes from *Twister* were filmed in Grant County, Oklahoma, where Medford is the county seat. Wakita, the town completely wiped out in the film, is located only sixteen miles away from Medford. When schools consolidated, the Wakita students started attending in Medford. That's how close we lived to that little town, now famous from the movie.

According to a twenty-year film retrospective in the *Tulsa World*, Wakita is "the home of the memorabilia-laden Twister Museum, which has been in operation since a few months before the movie was released in May of 1996." The *Tulsa World* story said Wakita was chosen for the movie because of a storm that occurred two years before filming, bombarding the town with hail the size of grapefruit.

The article explained that several buildings were never repaired, and that "worked in Wakita's favor when the 'Twister' people were scouting Oklahoma locations. They needed debris and lots of it to simulate tornado damage. Wakita had ready-to-destroy structures that could be transformed into debris."[2]

All of this is to say that my small city of Medford was located very close to the bullseye of Tornado Alley in the U.S. Since 1950, Grant County has had a total of 71 confirmed twister touchdowns—roughly one per year.[3] It's mind-blowing.

On that March day in 1965, the tornado bearing down on Medford was 300 yards wide—about the length of three football fields. As we later learned, it started near Nash, Oklahoma, southwest of Medford, and it cut a diagonal line going northeast—straight for Medford.

Being six years old at the time, I can remember only one thing. My sisters and I hunkered down by the deep freeze while my mom valiantly fought the winds, trying to close the garage door. Since the door was on a hinge, not rollers, my mom—a small woman—could barely pull it down.

She ran the real risk of being sucked out of the garage. She can't recall the winds lifting her off her feet, but she does remember tearing up her hands from gripping the garage door handle so tightly.

My older sister, Cindy, just had tubes put in her ears, so she was sensitive to changes in air pressure. Jan recalls Cindy screaming bloody murder because of the pain.

Recently, I found information online about that tornado, including a map showing the 82.7-mile track that the twister cut across Oklahoma and into Kansas. When I look at the map, I'm amazed at how it threaded the needle between seven towns—Nash, Jefferson, Medford, Deer Creek, Braman, Geuda Springs, and Winfield.

The path between Jefferson and Medford was especially narrow, with the colossal twister skirting our city by only a mile or two at most. Because no towns took a direct hit, there were no fatalities and only seven injuries. But we were sure close enough to experience the scary effects of a near-miss from a tornado![4]

It could have been much worse because this tornado was classified as an F4 twister—the second most powerful tornado on the Fujita scale. The National Weather Service classifies an F4 as a "devastating tornado" with wind speeds of 207 to 260 miles per hour. The official damage description is hair-raising and highlights just how fortunate we were that Medford did not take a direct hit from the monster tornado: "Well-constructed houses leveled; structures with weak foundations blown off some distance; cars thrown and large missiles generated."[5] If the twister had hit Medford directly, I'm not at all sure being tied to a freezer would have saved our lives.

After the storm had passed, my dad drove us around the country-side, surveying the damage to farms. During the storm, my mom never saw any flying cows, as famously featured in *Twister*, but she remembers seeing all kinds of dead cattle lying in the fields in the aftermath, with some speared by two-by-fours.

I have only one memory of the aftermath, but it's vivid. Oil spouted from the Oklahoma soil, six to eight feet into the air. The massive steel oil pumps, common on the Oklahoma landscape, had been completely ripped away by the tornado, leaving crude oil spurting into the air. If you want to see the kind of oil pump I'm talking about, check out *Twister*. The very first image in that movie is of an oil pump working away.

This was the first and only tornado I have ever experienced, and it was a doozy. To this day, it's the most powerful twister to hit Grant County, Oklahoma. It was also my first encounter with crude oil, but it certainly would not be my last, even though I had no idea how or why on that March day in 1965.

In my professional work, my first real encounter with crude oil was the controversy that erupted around speculation during the crude oil price spike of 2007-08. The Masters Hypothesis and all that jazz. However, this controversy did not require me to dig into the under-lying economics of crude oil and fuel markets. That changed around 2010 when I became fascinated with biofuel markets and policies. Ironically enough, I am probably at least as well known today for my work on the economics of biofuels, such as ethanol and biodiesel, as I am for my work on commodity futures markets.

To understand biofuels economics, you must understand the overall economics of these markets. Gasoline and diesel are cocktails of different fuel components; ethanol is one component for gasoline, and biodiesel is one for diesel. So, the economics of biofuels markets are inextricably tied to the economics of gasoline and diesel markets. And since gasoline and diesel are made from crude oil, everything starts there.

Over the past couple of chapters, I have been exploring the impact of electronic trading—the greatest change in futures markets since their inception in the 1800s. But change isn't just about speeding up the process of trading. It's also about creating new futures markets for different commodities, and crude oil is one of the best examples of how new futures contracts often arise from serendipities and near-disasters.

Crude oil is the largest commodity futures market in the world, but it didn't emerge until relatively late in the game. In a surprising twist, the origin of the crude oil futures market was linked to Maine potatoes, which nearly took down the old New York Mercantile Exchange (NYMEX).

In May of 1976, Jack Simplot, the biggest spud grower in the United States, defaulted on his futures contracts for Maine potatoes. By now, you know that all futures contracts must be settled on the last day of trading. For Simplot, who was on the short side—the sell side—that meant he had one of two options: deliver the potatoes or offset his short side with long contracts. But there was a catch. Because of growing problems that year, there weren't enough potatoes to deliver. What's more, if he offset his short contracts with long contracts—by *buying* potato futures—he would have lost big in the market.

The price for potatoes had gone through the roof, which meant he would have been buying at exorbitant rates. So, Simplot simply said he wasn't going to do either. He wouldn't deliver potatoes, and he wouldn't purchase long contracts. Instead, he would default on his short contracts in the futures market.

Although the Maine potato market was small, the decision to default was unprecedented, and it shook the futures world to the core. A futures exchange guarantees all contracts, so the NYMEX was left to absorb the costs of Simplot's contracts—and this nearly destroyed the exchange.

"The regulators were furious," wrote Emily Lambert in her book, *The Futures*. "They fined Simplot $50,000, but they put the screws on the exchange. The regulators essentially shut down potato trading and said that New York's exchange couldn't launch any new contracts."[6]

As members jumped ship, the NYMEX floundered. But in stepped

Michel Marks, who became chairman of the struggling exchange in 1978 at the young age of 28.

"I loved the opportunity, but I felt intimidated too," Marks recalled in an online interview in 2009. "I had no idea how to run a board meeting, and most of the people on the board were strangers, twice my age."[7]

Although NYMEX wasn't allowed by its regulator, the CFTC, to issue any new commodity contracts as punishment, it could modify existing contracts. As Marks said, "The exchange had a history of trading just about everything, but not very successfully." Among the commodities they had once traded were heating oil and residual fuel oil contracts. Therefore, the NYMEX staff rewrote the futures contracts for these commodities, hoping to find a winner, but it didn't seem to be working initially. Then came the Iranian revolution in 1979, when radicals took fifty-two hostages at the U.S. embassy in Tehran. "That's when oil prices exploded, and heating oil went up to 90 cents overnight," Marks said.[8]

Suddenly, the heating oil futures contract became a hit, paving the way for NYMEX's futures contract on West Texas Intermediate (WTI) crude oil in 1983. Today, crude oil is the most widely traded commodity futures contract in the world by a substantial margin, and it all started at a struggling exchange when its potato futures went down the tubes, and they had to find something to replace it.

Serendipity. That's how many of the most successful futures markets get off the ground. When troubles strike, people like Marks get creative. If necessity is the mother of invention, then desperation is the *father* of invention.

Today, the all-important benchmark price for much of the crude oil traded around the world is the futures price for the WTI crude oil contract at the CME Group, which acquired NYMEX in 2008. WTI crude also happened to be at the heart of what I think was the single craziest day in the history of commodity futures markets. On April 20, 2020, soon after the global Covid-19 pandemic began, WTI crude oil prices went negative. Not zero. They went below zero, eventually bottoming out at the unfathomable level of $-37.63 per barrel.

In other words, sellers were paying people to take their oil. It would be as if you walked into Walmart, and the clerks paid you to stroll out of the store with a new TV. Negative prices had never happened in futures trading, let alone in the largest commodity market of them all.

My colleague Craig Pirrong, an expert in energy markets, said two major factors were behind this unprecedented price freefall. The first was obvious—the pandemic. The demand for automotive and airline fuel dropped precipitously. The best metric reflecting this change, he said, is that the utilization of oil refineries dropped from 90 to about 50 percent. It was a freefall of unimaginable magnitude in a matter of weeks. When demand goes down, the economic response is to store oil. But with demand plunging, storage essentially became full.[9]

The last time oil storage had neared capacity was in 2009, amid the financial crisis. After that close call, oil storage capacity was doubled between 2009 and 2020. But even with this expansion, storage capacity was quickly reached during the 2020 pandemic.

During the pandemic, dairy producers faced a similar dilemma. With the restaurant and school closures, many dairy producers had nowhere to go with their milk. Prices naturally plummeted so much that it wasn't worth selling the milk. They couldn't indefinitely store their milk, so dairy farmers poured it out on the ground instead of selling it at a negative price. Essentially, they sold their milk for a price of zero because they had a way to dump it for minimal cost. But this was not the only time something like this had happened in commodity futures markets.

Craig said that in 1955, "when the price of onions was less than the cost of the bag to deliver them in, people were throwing onions in the Chicago River, which probably improved the water quality at that time."[10]

When oil storage is full, oil producers don't have the option of pouring their excess on the ground. Since environmental regulators would frown on that, oil producers were stuck. The only option was to pay people to take the crude oil and store it in costly places—like docked tankers and other temporary storage facilities. With their usual humor, traders talked of "filling up all the swimming pools in Cushing, Oklahoma, with crude oil." Cushing is the delivery location for the WTI crude oil futures contract.

The second factor behind negative prices, Craig said, is that a large number of positions still remained to be liquidated on the last two days of trading in the May 2020 WTI crude oil futures contract. This means there were a lot of longs (buyers of futures contracts), and when the April 20 settlement day arrived, they had two options. Option one: They could deliver oil to the delivery point in Cushing, Oklahoma. But this was not possible because oil storage in Cushing was already maxed out. Option two: They could offset their long contracts (buy) with short contracts (sell). But who wants to sell oil contracts when the prices are negative? It would have caused the vast majority of remaining traders to lose a ton of money. Prices officially went negative at 1:08 p.m. Central Time on April 20. From then on, those selling would be paying the buyers to take the futures contracts off their hands.

A number of traders found themselves in this predicament. According to Craig, roughly 200,000 contracts were still open going into the final two days of WTI crude oil trading before the April 20 settlement deadline.

"This is about 100 percent more than you would usually see on the last two days of trading," he said.[11]

He explained that certain investors in China had entered into a contract with a Chinese bank, which promised to pay its customers based on the oil price on the last day of trading. The bank mechanically maintained this position and found itself with a lot of futures contracts that needed to be liquidated on the last day of trading. But with prices plummeting, they were in a position to be squeezed in a major league way.

In all this, the most controversial player was a small trading group based north of London called Vega Capital London Ltd. This group consisted of nine traders working from their homes in Essex, a county northeast of London. Hence, they became known as "The Essex Boys." The group leader, Paul Commins was better known as "Cuddles," a former trader in London's International Petroleum Exchange (IPE) pits. The IPE was so rough it made the Chicago trading pits look downright peaceful.[12]

"Chicago was pretty raucous, but the IPE was off the charts" when it came to aggressiveness, Craig said.[13] As an example, he pointed to an all-out brawl in February 2005, when Greenpeace protestors barged onto the IPE trading floor, protesting oil in the name of fighting climate change. The thirty-five protestors tried to disrupt trading by blaring foghorns, alarms, and whistles. They would've been safer if they had walked into a biker bar and thrown drinks in people's faces.

The oil traders "were in a frenzy. They just went wild," one protestor was quoted saying in *The Guardian*. "They were trying so hard to hit us they were falling over each other." Other traders pulled down a metal bookcase on the protestors.[14]

"One trader pushed me against a wall, and as I turned back, a very tall trader punched me full in the face," said a protestor in the *Evening Standard*. "There was a guy unconscious on the floor, so we dragged him out. But initially, he was still getting kicked by the traders."[15]

Craig said the protestors couldn't have timed their protest worse because the IPE's working-class traders had recently learned that electronic trading would replace their jobs and weren't in the mood for Greenpeace.

When the IPE closed its pits in April 2005, some traders, including Cuddles, set up small firms to keep trading electronically. On April 20, 2020, the day crude oil went negative, Cuddles' Vega team bought thousands of TAS "trade-at-settlement" contracts. As the name implies, when you buy a TAS contract, you agree to pay the commodity's price at the day's end—the settlement price. By the end of trading on April 20, crude oil prices had gone negative at roughly $-37 per barrel. So, the Vega team was paid to buy crude oil.

At the end of trading, the Vega team walked away with $660 million to be split among them. Not bad for one day's work.[16]

"However, they're going to be spending a lot of quality time with their lawyers," Craig said. "Between legal fees and potential fines and/or civil judgments, I'm sure that a large fraction of that money—if not all of it—will go away."[17]

The CFTC is investigating the Vega team, a process that can take many years to untangle. A *Bloomberg Businessweek* article on December 9, 2020, laid out the concerns about possible price manipulation by the Essex Boys. Just as trading was winding down on April 20, the Vega Group hit the market with sell orders. The idea, called "banging the close," is to hit the market with enough sell orders that prices drop to artificial lows. That way, when they buy back at settlement, the price will be far lower than it might have been under normal economic conditions.

In this gambit, traders gain on the short (sell) positions used to pressure prices down, and then these positions are offset with the long (buy) TAS position bought earlier. They're out of the market at the settlement for the day, and a tidy profit is pocketed.

"Where traders have gotten into trouble in the past is when they've been caught trying to deliberately push the closing price, rather than simply benefitting from where it ends up," said the *Bloomberg Businessweek* article.[18]

Were Cuddles and his Vega Group guilty of doing just that? If this case follows the pattern of most such cases, it will take years of litigation to answer that question in court.

What happened on April 20 was an economic perfect storm. A tornado of the magnitude I experienced back in March of 1965 takes an incredible confluence of meteorological conditions. That's why it remains the most powerful tornado to strike Grant County, Oklahoma. Likewise, what happened with crude oil required a rare confluence of economic conditions fueled by a once-in-a-century pandemic.

After closing at $-37 per barrel, prices quickly rebounded, returning to the positive column the following day. Could it happen again? It's possible, especially if another pandemic hits us. It's also possible that Grant County could get walloped by another twister of 1965 proportions.

Despite the oddities of 2020, crude oil remains one of the greatest success stories in commodity futures trading. Every year, exchanges around the world try to strike it rich with new types of commodity contracts, and as in any competitive field, the vast majority of them crash and burn.

In the next chapter, we'll look at other futures market success stories and new trends as we continue to gaze into the future of futures.

Chapter 20
Out of the Box

I have a history of receiving strange packages at work. First is the one from the Destroying Angel, who challenged me to disprove his bizarre conspiracy theory behind the non-convergence in grain futures prices in 2007-08. Then came Rinny the Gopher.

This time it was a large box, shipped to my University of Illinois office. Setting the package on the table beside the window, I carefully peeled back the tape to peer inside. I was both surprised and amused to find a puppet staring back at me—a gopher puppet, to be precise.

As I reached in and lifted the puppet, I noticed the gopher was wearing a name tag for the upcoming biofuels conference sponsored by the Oil Price Information Service (OPIS). According to the tag, the puppet's name was Rinny. Stranger yet, someone filled the box with empty liquor bottles. I noticed a note attached to the puppet, declaring: "Sorry, but I drank my breakfast, lunch, and dinner before I got here."

While I did not expect Rinny the Gopher to suddenly show up at my office unannounced, I was already familiar with his name. Rinny the Gopher is the pseudonym of one of my most fascinating Twitter followers. Rinny lists his location as Houston, one of the planet's biggest oil and gas trading centers. Based on his tweets, I figure that

Rinny is an energy trader, for he is a sharp observer and knows his way around the fuel markets.

Traders typically remain anonymous on Twitter because their companies would not look too kindly on them if they voiced online opinions about fuel markets, possibly revealing valuable information. Hence the name: "Rinny the Gopher." But unlike other anonymous writers on Twitter, this guy didn't settle on a simple pseudonym. He created an entire character—an eccentric, liquor-swigging, alter-ego gopher.

Scattered among his many observations about energy markets (and life), this Houston trader posts photos of the gopher puppet hanging out at various bars. When this trader attends a conference, he often posts a picture of Rinny at the hotel bar with a drink set in front of him. One image showed the gopher wearing sunglasses and nursing a drink, with the caption saying, "You can't drink all day if you don't start in the morning."

Although this gopher may be in dire need of an intervention for his drinking, we have a strong rapport regarding energy markets and seem to agree on far more things than we disagree. I frequently retweet Rinny's hilarious messages, and he does the same for mine, although my humor does not hold a candle to him.

One day, I received a message from Rinny, asking if he could hitch a ride with me to the upcoming OPIS biofuels conference in Chicago, where I was scheduled to be the keynote speaker. I assumed he was joking—until a few days later when Rinny the Gopher showed up at my office in a box.

Rinny gets his name from RINs—Renewable Identification Numbers, which are credits used to comply with biofuel mandates under the U.S. Renewable Fuels Standard (RFS). The mandates were first passed in 2005 with a second version passed in 2007. RINs are a burgeoning commodity, assuming they can even be considered a commodity.

The RFS mandates that a certain number of gallons of biofuels be produced annually and blended into gasoline and diesel. The number is scaled upward each year. Today, the RFS mandate requires roughly

20 billion gallons to be produced and blended with gasoline and diesel. (In reality, the number of gallons required by the RFS varies year-by-year, depending on how much gasoline and diesel we use, but 20 billion gallons is close to the mark.)

Corn Belt politicians love the RFS because the two major biofuels, ethanol and biodiesel, are made from agricultural products. Ethanol is made from corn, and biodiesel is produced mainly from soybean oil. What industry wouldn't welcome the federal government requiring companies to buy its product? As a result of RFS mandates, ethanol plants suddenly began to sprout up throughout the heartland after 2005, and the price of corn spiked.

As a "freshwater" economist, I am philosophically opposed to mandating things to the market. It's a blunt policy instrument, and it can distort the market. Once something like this is established, it's challenging to eliminate or phase out. As Ronald Reagan famously said, "Nothing lasts longer than a temporary government program."

Because the RFS requires that a certain number of gallons of biofuels be blended into gasoline every year, the EPA must track it. Therefore, the agency assigns a RIN number to every single gallon of ethanol or biodiesel produced in the United States. When a refiner blends ethanol with gasoline, it reports to the EPA the RIN for every gallon of ethanol used. It does the same with biodiesel and the lesser-known biofuels.

After the Environmental Protection Agency first set up the RIN program, it made the numbers tradeable in a cash market. There is a logic to this system. Let's say I am gasoline Refiner A and blended more gallons of ethanol than I was obligated. But let's also assume that Refiner B didn't blend enough ethanol to meet the requirements. In this case, Refiner B can pay Refiner A for some of their surplus RINs, enabling them to meet government regulations. They trade RIN credits, which are almost exclusively traded in a cash market.

There have been a couple of attempts to start futures contracts on RINs, but they never really got off the ground. Still, trading in RINs is a good example of the out-of-the-box thinking that gives rise to new futures markets.

Exchanges are constantly on the lookout for new ideas and commodities to trade in the futures market, as the rise of the crude oil futures contract demonstrated in the 1970s after Maine potatoes nearly sunk the New York Mercantile Exchange (see Chapter 19).

A similar thing happened at the Chicago Mercantile Exchange (CME) when it hit hard times after the onion futures market was banned by Congress (see Chapter 10). In the wake of World War II, the CME had the most active market for trading onion futures. But when onion futures were banned in 1958, the CME had to get creative, or they might've had to close their doors. Therefore, in the early 1960s, they started trading pork belly futures, followed by live cattle and hog futures. Moving into livestock futures saved the CME, and these contracts became the exchange's specialty; what's more, this move set it apart from the larger Chicago Board of Trade (CBOT), which handled major grain contracts, such as corn, soybeans, and wheat.

The person best-known for thinking outside the box has been the CME Group's Leo Melamed, whom we met in Chapter 17. Not only was Leo the father of Globex, the mammoth electronic trading system, but some have also called him the father of financial futures markets. A few academics had talked about trading financial futures in the early 1960s, but Leo had the persistence and the vision to make it happen, beginning with currency futures.[1]

Leo's first lesson in currency trading goes back to when he was seven years old and living in Wilno, Lithuania. He remembers going to a bakery, where his father took out a złoty, a Polish unit of currency, and a litas, a Lithuanian currency. Young Leo was familiar with a złoty but not a litas.

"How much is a litas worth?" his father asked.

Leo shrugged. "I don't know. The same as a złoty?"

"Let's find out." His father turned to the baker behind the counter. "How much is the loaf of bread?"

"One litas," the baker said.

"Okay, we'll take it." Leo's father proceeded to hand him one złoty, instead of one litas.

"No, no, no," said the baker. "It's one litas, but *two* złotys."

After he paid and they took their bread and exited, Leo's father said, "You see? The only way you can find out what these currencies are really worth is through the marketplace."[2]

The irony is that Leo's father was a socialist, yet he had given his son his first lesson in currency value and the power of the marketplace. With this lesson tucked away in his memory bank, Leo would go on to pioneer a way to trade various global currencies in a futures market. The timing for such a market in the 1970s was just right.

After World War II, the world's financial system was in shambles, so the Bretton Woods system was created to coordinate currency exchange rates among countries. However, it was an inflexible system, in which all currencies were fixed in relation to each other and to gold. For instance, if the British pound was valued two to one with the U.S. dollar, you were guaranteed to exchange one dollar for two British pounds if you traveled from the United States to Britain.

According to the Bretton Woods system, these exchange rates were fixed, and they sometimes wouldn't change for several years. But the system was wracked by problems because of diverging interest rates and inflation in different countries.

"It was obvious to me that the Bretton Woods system was old and archaic," Leo said.

The system became untenable when President Nixon removed the dollar from the gold standard in 1971, and currency values began to float—no longer set at fixed rates. A cash market formed around currency trading, as foreign exchange rates changed by the minute.[3]

To someone like Leo Melamed, currency trading in the cash market looked a lot like the trading of any other commodity, such as hogs or corn. You just replace hog trading with the trading of different currencies. But with currency trading in a cash market, there also came risk. And where there's risk, there is a need for a futures market to enable traders to hedge their investments.

Once again, necessity was the mother of invention.

You can see why Leo thought the time was ripe for a futures market in currency trading. But it took some work to convince the

CME board of directors that a financial futures market was feasible. Leo, elected to the CME board in 1967, describes himself as a rabble-rouser who had a way of ruffling the feathers of veterans on the board.

"I was thirty-five years old, and they were 135 years old," he told me.[4]

Leo became chairman of the CME board two years later, in 1969, but initially, he was afraid to put forth his idea of currency futures contracts.

In the 1960s, "futures represented the lowest form of finance," Leo said. People in finance thought, "This is where the gambling dens exist and so forth. Finance was far too pure and important in the world to be considered as an item for futures markets."

Leo said he lived with the idea of financial futures markets for a year "before I would dare say a thing to anybody because I feared it was a laughable idea. Laughable!"

Sure enough, he said that when he presented the idea of financial futures contracts to the CME board of directors, "maybe eight of them laughed." He recalled, "They said that if financial futures were important and possible, don't you think New York would have done it? That's the capital of finance. How could you come up with such a ridiculous idea?

"I'm a lawyer, not an economist, and they were thinking this guy is going to lead us down the wrong path," he added. "So, I decided I needed some sort of verification from somebody who counts."[5]

That "someone who counts" was Milton Friedman, the legendary economist who would go on to win the Nobel Prize in Economics in 1976. "You couldn't get anybody more credible than him," Leo said.

When Leo was in law school, he would sometimes sneak into Friedman's classes at the University of Chicago, even though he wasn't a student there. After Leo became chairman of the CME board, he decided to run his idea of financial futures by Friedman, "who was just down the street at the university." Leo said the two of them met at the Waldorf Astoria on Walton Street, and he began his pitch by saying, "Don't laugh at me."

"I'm not laughing at anybody," Friedman responded. Leo said he didn't know it at the time, but Milton Friedman never laughed at new ideas, even when they came from a young guy like him. So, Leo told him that he was thinking of launching a futures contract for foreign currencies at the CME.

"Milton said, 'Oh my gosh, what a wonderful idea!' And I said, 'Wait a minute. Did you hear me? This is not an agriculture futures contract.' And he said, 'So what? It's a terrific idea.'"

According to Leo, "I thought I was going to faint." He then asked Friedman if he would put his endorsement of the idea in writing. Without the famed economist's opinion in writing, he was afraid people wouldn't believe it.

Despite working at the CME, Leo said he always admired the CBOT because it was the first of the major exchanges and operated the big grain markets. "But they were limited," he said. "They were all agriculture, and they rejected the idea of a currency futures market." Using a baseball metaphor, he said the currency markets "were the first base we conquered before the CBOT even had a runner."[6]

Under Leo's leadership, the CME created the International Monetary Market (IMM), the world's first financial futures exchange. It opened on May 16, 1972, trading currencies such as the Swiss franc, Japanese yen, British pound, and German deutschmark.[7] When financial futures got off the ground in 1972, "I knew the idea was so big that Congress wouldn't let us alone. I was positive of that," Leo told me. Although he says, "I'm a small government kind of guy," he knew that it would take federal supervision for financial futures to be allowed to thrive. That explains why Leo surprisingly pressed for passage of the Commodity Futures Trading Commission Act. When he got wind that President Gerald Ford was going to veto the act, he went to the president to make his case for the legislation.

"The president said to me, 'Mr. Melamed, I've read all about you. You're a free-market guy like I am. What do you want with another federal agency?'"

He told President Ford about his idea of transposing the futures markets from agriculture to finance. "'This is a very big idea if it works,' I said. 'Do you think you guys will really leave me alone without a federal agency?' He laughed and said, 'You've got my vote.'"

So, the Commodity Futures Trading Commission (CFTC) was born in 1974, replacing the Commodity Exchange Authority (established in 1936) as the watchdog for commodity futures markets. According to Leo, "My whole idea for financials was to diversify, diversify." That way, if the worst happened in one futures market, there might be strength in another one.[8]

Today, the CME Group continues to scout for new opportunities and new futures markets. For example, the CME Group already has a big stake in another up-and-coming financial commodity, which has been popping up regularly in headlines across the world—cryptocurrency.

Cryptocurrency, in the simplest terms, is digital currency. The "crypto" in the name comes from "cryptography," the art of writing or breaking codes because codes are the key to protecting this digital currency. One of my former graduate students, Peter Koziara, has had enormous success trading the most popular cryptocurrency, bitcoin. There are no physical dollar bills or coins you can jangle in your pocket. It's all online. Digital dollars. You can transfer bitcoins to different people or companies without a go-between, such as a bank.

"Many retailers do not take bitcoin," Peter said, "but that's been changing. Just recently, PayPal has joined the cryptocurrency network."[9]

As history has shown, currencies can be almost anything. In some ancient societies, seashells were the currency of choice. In World War II prisoner of war camps, POWs used cigarettes as a common currency valuing everything relative to a smoke. Cryptocurrencies are just the latest iteration in this development, generating a lot of buzz. But will it be widely accepted? In 2021, the electric car company Tesla began accepting bitcoin, but CEO Elon Musk soon backtracked.

Although people had been toying with digital currencies since the 1980s, the big breakthrough came in 2009, when Satoshi Nakamoto created bitcoins. No one knows who the ever-mysterious Nakamoto really is—or even if he is an individual. Some believe Satoshi Nakamoto is a team of experts.[10]

My former student, Peter, didn't jump into cryptocurrency trading until later in the game. Raised in Niles, Illinois, he followed a meandering route that began at Arizona State University in 2003; there, he picked up two bachelor's degrees—one in computer science and the other in finance. When he took an internship with Ronin Capital and wound up in Chicago, he witnessed, for the first time, the craziness of the trading floors there. Like me (and Terry Duffy and Leo Melamed), he was blown away by what he saw on the trading floor of the Chicago Board Options Exchange, or CBOE.

"I was transported to another world," he said.

Peter interned as an IT guy. "If a trader's tablet broke in the pit, we had to fix it," he said. "We had to do all of the network infrastructure work for the company, hauling equipment from the CBOE and the CBOT to the federal building at LaSalle and Jackson." During downtimes, waiting for work orders, he had front-row seats to the biggest show in town—the trading pits. On his second day of work, he witnessed a fight in the pit.

"It was wild seeing all these guys shouting left and right," he recalled. "I didn't know what was going on. I was thinking, 'Okay, they're buying and selling, but I don't know what.'"

After completing two bachelor's degrees in 2007, Peter landed a job with the TransMarket Group under the auspices of a famous trader, Ray Cahnman. He became a bond trader, working mostly with Eurodollars—one slice of the financial futures pioneered by Leo Melamed. While working for TransMarket, Peter showed increasing interest in physical commodities such as oil and grains. So, he decided to go deeper into the grain markets, which brought him to the University of Illinois. I supervised him as he completed his master's in agricultural economics in 2012. Then he worked for various commodity trading companies, taking him from Kansas to Connecticut to San Antonio.

"I didn't get into cryptocurrencies until 2017," he said. "It was a crazy year for crypto."

2017 was also a lucrative year for the various cryptocurrencies, such as bitcoin, because "the arbitrage opportunities were immense," he said. One form of "arbitrage" is when traders buy a commodity at one exchange and then turn around and sell it at another exchange for a higher price, gaining a tidy profit.

"You could go back and forth between two exchanges, and you could pick up $20,000 to $30,000 in one evening with cryptocurrencies," he said. "It was unbelievable."

Peter began to wonder why he was working so hard in ag markets, trying to pick up a half penny per bushel of grain when he could make up to 15 or 20 percent in one day trading bitcoin. After his successful run in bitcoin, Peter left his day job in March of 2018, and he took one year off, driving up to Alaska to celebrate his gains. Today, he lives on a farm near a small village in Poland, where he has built a website, GrainStats.com. (His parents emigrated from Poland in the 1970s before the fall of the Soviet bloc.)

Because the cryptocurrency market is much more efficient today, the arbitrage opportunities are no longer as lucrative, he said. But bitcoin value skyrocketed in early 2021, and it remains a volatile commodity. In November 2021, the value of a single bitcoin reached an all-time high of $69,000 before plunging dramatically in 2022 to under $20,000.[11]

Volatility makes cryptocurrency a big risk. Digital currency traders also face the threat of losing their money through hackers—or by losing their "private key." People store their bitcoins in digital wallets and gain access to them with their private key—a code. Lose that code, and you lose a lot of money.

The same is true for those who store their cryptocurrency on physical hardware, such as a hard drive. Take the infamous case of James Howells, a 35-year-old IT engineer from Newport, Wales. He had been storing 7,500 bitcoins on a hard drive—close to $300 million worth of bitcoins based on 2021 prices. The problem is that he had two identical hard drives, according to a CNBC report in January 2021. While cleaning his home in 2013, he accidentally threw out the wrong one.

His $300 million worth of bitcoins inadvertently wound up as buried treasure in a landfill.

Howells has been pleading with the Newport City Council, begging for permission to search the landfill for his lost treasure. Still, the council refuses his request, "citing environmental and funding concerns," said the CNBC report.

In 2020, Howells even offered to donate 25 percent of his treasure trove to a Covid Relief Fund, but the city council still said no. Somewhere, buried under mounds of disposable nappies and other refuse is several hundred million dollars' worth of bitcoins.[12]

As I said, futures markets often begin as cash markets, which is what happened with cryptocurrencies. The CBOE offered the first bitcoin futures contract on December 10, 2017, but the CME Group quickly followed by providing its first bitcoin futures contract only eight days later. The CME Group had the better platform, which forced the CBOE to discontinue its contract in 2019. The bitcoin futures market is just the latest evolution of the currency futures markets unleashed by Leo Melamed in 1972.

Each bitcoin futures contract with the CME Group is five bitcoins —and with a single bitcoin being valued over $42,000 (before the freefall), that made bitcoin futures a difficult stretch for your average investor. Therefore, in 2021, the CME Group began offering micro bitcoin futures contracts, which are the equivalent of $1/10^{th}$ of one bitcoin, much more accessible than five bitcoins with the standard contract.[13]

In addition to cryptocurrencies, another new out-of-the-box arena for futures markets has been environmental and natural resource credits, such as carbon or water credits. For example, the CME Group started offering futures contracts for water in California in the fall of 2020. To find out how this new futures market works, I sat down with Fred Seamon, the CME Group's agricultural markets executive director (who we met earlier in Chapters 4 and 16), and Dominic Sutton-Vermeulen, an economist at the CME Group. As Seamon explained, much of farming depends on water management. In the eastern United States, it's all about managing too much water, while in the West, it's all about managing too little water.[14]

Because water is such a precious commodity in the West, entities like a municipality or dairy farm claim rights for almost every drop from the Colorado River and other sources. In California, if you even want to collect rainwater from your roof, you must have a permit, or you can be fined, Sutton-Vermeulen said.

The United States uses roughly 322 billion gallons of water every day, and 9 percent of it is used in California—the most of any state. But water there is scarce, as the persistent droughts and forest fires underscore.

With water in short supply, farming is a risky business in Western states such as California. And where there is risk, there is a need for futures markets, which enable users to manage their risk. That was the reasoning behind the emergence of the world's first futures contract in water, beginning in October 2020.

Two years prior, in 2018, Nasdaq and Veles Water partnered with West Water to create the Nasdaq Veles California Water Index, or the NQH2O Index, which tracks the value of water rights in five categories in California. The first and most active category is surface water, while the other four are groundwater basins in the state. The index is priced according to U.S. dollars per acre foot of water—the equivalent of an acre of water at a depth of one foot, or 325,851 gallons.

When the CME Group announced the first-ever futures contract for water, there was the usual attack on speculators. Some critics said, "You can't put a value on water as you do with other traded commodities."[15]

This completely ignores that water rights were already traded in a cash market well before the futures market arrived, and cash markets put a value on water. The futures market makes it possible for farmers and municipalities to hedge their risk, just as in any other futures market.

Trading water futures is not highly active compared to other contracts. However, the CME Group still backs this market because it wants to have a stake in the natural resource and climate arena, which brings me back to where we started this chapter—Renewable Identification Numbers, or RINs.

RINs are a type of natural resource credit and have an active, thriving, large cash market—even more active than water rights, so they are ripe for someday being traded in a futures market. But RINs bring a note of caution, which applies to the entire realm of environmental and natural resource credits. These credits are often subject to the whims and ever-changing winds of politics, which can have a tremendous impact on their value in the market. When the government applies a heavy hand in the market, it can dramatically alter the futures price of these commodities, as happened with the RIN cash market.

Initially, the cost to purchase RINs in the cash market was quite low, under five cents per gallon of blended ethanol. But in January 2013, the numbers suddenly made a stratospheric climb, eventually peaking at $1.45 per gallon in July 2013. When this issue hit the front pages, the politicians in Washington, D.C., decided it was because of evil speculators trading RINs. Wall Street investment banks were hoarding the RIN credits, it was argued, causing their price to soar. Sound familiar? Congress launched investigations, and the RIN brouhaha landed on the front page of *The Wall Street Journal*.

Without going into the gory details, Darrel Good and I discovered the sudden jump in price had to do with a conflict between the RFS and E10 blend rules. The E10 blend rules stipulate that no more than 10 percent of a gallon of gasoline can be ethanol, while the RFS currently mandates that oil refiners blend roughly 15 billion gallons of ethanol in gasoline every year. (The ethanol mandate of 15 billion gallons is part of the overall mandate of about 20 billion gallons.)

Houston, we have a problem. Even if refiners put 10 percent ethanol into *every single gallon of gasoline* produced in the country, they still couldn't meet the RFS ethanol mandate of 15 billion gallons of biofuels. The way around this problem has been for oil refiners to purchase extra RIN credits for *biodiesel*. Because biodiesel reduces greenhouse gas more effectively than ethanol, biodiesel RINs earn more credits than ethanol RINs. But this creates a problem of another sort. We found that when refiners do this, the price of ethanol RIN credits rises to the level of the far more expensive biodiesel credits.

In 2012, when the RFS mandate was still lower than the E10 blend law, ethanol RIN credits traded for a few cents, while biodiesel RIN credits traded for close to a dollar. When the RFS mandate rose above 13 billion gallons of ethanol in 2013, which was the level of the E10 blend wall at the time, ethanol RIN credits went through the roof, rising to the level of the biodiesel RIN credits.[16]

After Darrel and I first floated this theory in July 2013, we encountered much resistance, but within a couple of years, most economists came to accept it. We found it more than a little ironic that some of the strongest early support for our RIN pricing ideas came from none other than Rinny the Gopher.

Understanding the pricing of RINs was easy compared to tracking the political battle over the RFS itself. The skyrocketing RIN prices of 2013 launched the political equivalent of trench warfare in Washington, D.C., over the RFS mandates, with literally no end in sight.

On one side sits the ag and biofuels groups, led by Senator Charles "Chuck" Grassley of Iowa, where ethanol is as American as baseball and apple pie. On the other side are the crude oil refiners and related petroleum companies concentrated in Texas. These companies see the RFS as having foisted expensive biofuels on American drivers, thereby taking away market share. They swear to do whatever it takes to kill the RFS.

I relate all this as a cautionary tale, as futures exchanges consider trading politically charged "commodities," such as environmental credits. Markets have difficulty pricing political and regulatory uncertainty, which could be the death knell for new futures markets on these kinds of instruments. I am not saying that futures exchanges should avoid trying to innovate in this space, only that starting a new futures contract is hard enough without having political and regulatory uncertainty piled on top.

It is important to realize just how large the risks can be in new markets. This was demonstrated in spectacular fashion by the epic meltdown of FTX in late 2022. FTX was one of the biggest cryptocurrency exchanges on the planet, and in just a few days may have lost as much as $10 billion of customer money. It turns out that the exchange loaned a chunk of the money to a subsidiary hedge fund that likely had massive trading losses. It will take years to sort out what may be one of the biggest financial scandals in history.[17] The losses are so large that other cryptocurrency exchanges may be eventually pulled under as well.

Ironically, one of the few people not taken in by the charismatic CEO of FTX, Sam Bankman-Fried, was Terry Duffy. During a meeting with Bankman-Fried in March 2022, Terry bluntly told him, "You know what? You're a fraud. You're an absolute fraud."[18] It is not easy to pull the wool over the eyes of an old futures trader.

Whether it's financial futures, cryptocurrency, or water rights, these "out of the box" contracts demonstrate that futures markets have come a long way from being strictly confined to ag markets. In the same way, I have come a long way from strictly focusing on ag commodities in my career. As mentioned earlier, I might be better known today for my work on biofuels and the RFS than for ag futures markets. My research, wielded by both sides of the RFS debate, even wound up in front of President Trump during the heated controversy over the RFS.

But one thing hasn't changed. In the autumn of my life, I still find myself stumbling and bumbling into dangerous situations. As I approached my sixtieth birthday, I was shocked to find myself grappling with huge animals in the night and trying my best not to get crushed.

It is an ideal metaphor for what this book is all about.

Chapter 21
The Running of the Cows

On a small country road in Iowa, an ominous sound carried on the breeze in the pitch dark—a chorus of mooing like the eerie sound of disembodied livestock.

The cows were coming.

The cows had escaped their pasture, and we had to track them down and herd them back to their enclosure, about a half mile away.

When we got word of the bovine breakout, my nephew, Reilly Vaughan, and I jumped into my SUV with my 15-year-old daughter, Stacey. We raced into the night, crossing hilly terrain—at least hilly for west central Iowa. Reilly's friend, Corey Grow, called to tell us where to position our vehicle at a crossroads, and we followed orders. Then waited.

As the huge, charcoal-black Angus cattle shambled into the beams of my red Highlander, we watched in awe. While Corey gave us the impression there were only a few on the loose, a seemingly endless stream of black cattle emerged out of the darkness. The actual number turned out to be closer to thirty cows! I also noticed that some had calves with them, which made them all the more dangerous. Like mothers everywhere, cows are especially protective of their babies, and we are talking about large animals, roughly 1,500 pounds. They had a lot of weight to throw at us.

As I watched the cows stream toward us, I wondered how in the world things like this kept happening to me. I was just about to turn sixty years old for crying out loud.

When Stacey and I drove to Iowa for the baptism of Reilly's new baby boy, I never expected that the weekend would include a night of wrangling cows. It was about 10:15 p.m. on a Saturday near the end of July 2018 when Reilly received the call from Corey, asking for help to corral his cattle. Corey's parents, Darwin and Pam Grow, were long-time family friends, so it seemed the right thing to do.

"C'mon, Uncle Scott! It'll be fun!" Reilly had exclaimed before we jumped into my Highlander.

Now, as the cattle lumbered toward my SUV, I was beginning to wonder about his idea of fun.

Holding my breath, I emerged from the vehicle I had positioned at an intersection like a police barricade. The cows halted and mooed in distress, bellowing as they often did when lost or confused. With the Highlander blocking their way, the first few had no choice but to turn onto another country road and head east toward their pasture. True to form as herd animals, when one or two turns, the rest follow.

"Yah! Yah! Move along, little doggies!" I shouted, running along the edge of the stream of cattle, waving my arms. I felt like I had wandered into the movie *City Slickers*, where urban-dweller Billy Crystal finds himself in the unlikely position of herding cattle back to a ranch.

Reilly and I gave each other high fives because the cows all made the turn and were now sauntering east down the gravel road. This was easier than I thought, and I savored the satisfaction of a job well done.

The feeling didn't last long.

As Reilly and I were about to clamber back into my SUV, something strange caught our eye. The cows suddenly took an unexpected turn.

"What in the world...?" Reilly said.

We took off, leaping back into the SUV, gravel spitting from all four tires. We caught up with the herd in short order and were horrified to see that all thirty or so cows had turned right and entered the Dodge Township Cemetery. Not only was it complete chaos, but watching the herd meander between headstones under the moonlight was one of the spookiest things I had ever experienced.

Looking over my shoulder, the glow of Stacey's phone made me wonder what she was telling her friends on Snapchat. It was a scary place to be alone in the middle of nowhere. Neither Reilly nor I had flashlights, but there was enough moonlight to make out the surreal scene—cows running every which way among the headstones. We could make out flashes of coal-black shapes and hear their movements in the silent graveyard. Thankfully, Corey and his friend, Jeff, who had the good sense to bring along a flashlight, had arrived to help.

"There's one over there!" one of us would shout as the bouncing beam caught a black-Angus beast straying amidst the headstones.

To make matters worse, I knew many people, including a class-mate, buried in the cemetery. It seemed sacrilegious running after cows in a cemetery as the animals scattered haphazardly among the gravesites, but we had no choice.

We continued for what seemed an eternity and a half until Jeff told us to be quiet. As we paused, we sensed something out there—some-thing moving in our direction.

That's when we heard it—a communal bellow rose from across a fence that ran alongside the cemetery. More cows moved through the eight-foot-tall corn plants on the other side of the fence. This explained why the cows we were chasing turned into the cemetery. They sensed their fellow bovines on the other side of the fence.

While we still couldn't see the cows in the corn, we could hear the SNAP, SNAP, SNAP of crackling stalks as they approached—like unseen creatures from a Stephen King novel. Their mooing increased, becoming louder as they slowly emerged from the rows of corn. While the animals nosed their way closer to the fence to reunite with the cows in the cemetery, we realized there would be a price to pay for the trampled crop. We were no longer talking about thirty cows because if you counted the cattle on the other side of the fence, there had to be closer to eighty. And if you included the calves, the number was over a hundred.

On the cornfield side of the fence, Corey and Jeff successfully herded the cows back into the pasture, which was adjacent to the east side of the cemetery. But on the other side of the fence, Reilly and I encountered a big problem. There was no gate to lead the cows from the cemetery into the pasture. Of course, this should not have surprised us. Why would there be a gate from a cemetery to a cow pasture? Our only option was to herd them back to the road along the northern edge of the graveyard, returning them on a much longer, roundabout way to the pasture.

Along the path to the road was an enormous evergreen tree with a canopy that had to be thirty feet in diameter. Since cows don't have great eyesight, especially in the dark, the poor cattle bumbled into the evergreen tree, one after another, and in their panic, they tried to turn completely around. Once again—chaos.

We eventually maneuvered them around the tree, and I breathed a sigh of relief when they were back on the country road, taking the long way to the pasture. Finally, our troubles were over.

No such luck.

Several cows rushed into a fifteen-foot-deep ravine along this stretch of the country road, which bordered their pasture home. Jeff and Reilly looked at me, and I threw up my hands and said, "This is where I get off."

No way was I going into a ditch in the pitch dark with 1,500-pound animals. In a confined space like a ditch, panicking animals were especially dangerous. So, I left the job of going into the ravine to the young guys, who were half my age with one-tenth my cautiousness.

After much struggle, Reilly and Jeff eventually drove the cattle back onto the road from the ravine, and we managed to return them to the pasture well past midnight. All of this made for a memorable prelude to my sixtieth birthday one week later.

This night is a fitting metaphor for my adventures in the commodity world. I've become used to witnessing the herd mentality in action, which is most evident among politicians and regulators whenever prices don't behave. The political herd will panic like cows lost in the dark, looking for villains to blame. You can count on it, as regular as the seasons on a farm.

Another regularity has been my tendency to get myself into some sort of fix, whether it's nearly getting killed by rotary hoes, motorcycles, and snowmobiles or nearly being trampled by steers and cattle.

History also repeats itself when it comes to my risky ventures in the commodity markets. After my debacle in graduate school, I stayed away from trading in the futures market for many years. However, I ventured back in 2011 and had some decent success. Then, history repeated itself in 2019, when I predicted a bull market, just as I had done thirty-eight years earlier in 1981. I lost big in 1981 and again in 2019, although this time I didn't violate the commandment, "Risk not thy whole wad."

The growing season in 2019 was absolutely insane, as the U.S. Corn Belt saw the wettest spring in sixty years—perhaps the wettest in the last century. Because of the soaking wet fields, farmers were delayed getting into the field to plant. In Illinois, farmers usually have half of their corn crop planted by May 1, and about 80 to 90 percent of the corn crop should be in the ground by May 15. In 2019, farmers still hadn't reached the halfway planting mark in early *June*.

Planting that late is expected to impact yields negatively, so I was among those economists advising farmers to go with something in their crop insurance plan called Prevented Plant. Farmers could take some of their land out of corn production and let it go fallow, and they would still get a partial insurance payment through Prevented Plant. The other two options would be to switch the land from corn to soybeans (which you plant later) or plant corn and take your chances on yields.

A colleague of mine at the University of Illinois, Gary Schnitkey, analyzed these three options and said the Prevented Plant program was probably the best choice economically for most corn producers.[1] I agreed with his analysis and highlighted it on social media. Normally, Illinois farmers plant about 12 million acres of corn every year, but I was expecting that the number would be reduced by at least three to four million acres as land went fallow in the Prevented Plant program. Fewer acres of corn would mean a lower supply, and a lower supply means higher prices. So, naturally, I was expecting prices to skyrocket —a bull market.

Boy was I wrong.

As it turned out, I was correct about Prevented Plant being the best option for most corn farmers. What I didn't expect is that most farmers would ignore the advice and take risks by planting corn. In the end, only 1.1 million acres were taken out of production in Illinois through the Prevented Plant program. Prices did not go through the roof, and I lost in the futures market.

It all came to a head with—you guessed it—the August 2019 crop report from the U.S. Department of Agriculture (USDA).

Once again, I found myself anxiously awaiting the release of the August report, but this time I was in front of a computer screen instead of a ticker machine. But the shock was much the same. The USDA production estimate was much bigger than what I expected— and it was also much bigger than what the market expected. In fact, the gap between what the USDA reported for the size of the corn crop and what market analysts expected was the largest of the last 55 years, even larger than on that fateful day in August 1981.

In terms of prices, it was déjà vu all over again—although in '81 my error was all about yields, but in '19, it was about acreage. In 1981, I predicted low yields, leading to high prices, but I was way off. In 2019, I predicted low acreage, which would lead to high prices, and again, I was wrong.

I have several theories about why farmers didn't turn to Prevented Plant as I thought they would. But whatever the reason, I had belly-flopped in the futures market, highlighting the ever-present risks inherent in these markets. I wasn't working with a lot of money, so I was fine.

I have had some successes in the markets that are worth noting. For example, corn and soybean prices began surging in August 2020, powered by heavy Chinese buying, and continued through the spring of 2021. However, signs began to indicate that the run-up might have been overdone, and I started making forward sales of our expected 2021 corn and soybean production for our farms back in Iowa.

On my mom's 86th birthday, May 7, 2021, I received a text from Reilly that the price of corn for harvest delivery at our local elevator topped $6 per bushel. I thought, what the heck, we have to sell some corn to mark the occasion. With such an extremely high price—"out of the field" by historical standards, we not only sold corn at some of the highest prices of my mom's long life, but we also hit the single highest daily price of the entire rally in corn prices before harvest of the 2021 crop. It was one of the best birthday presents I have ever given my mom. My dad would have taken great pride in hitting the top of the market this way.

So, what have I learned in my lifelong quest to understand the commodity futures markets?

First, I discovered it is not easy to beat the futures market, which is how it ought to be for a market that is performing well. My view on beating the market is captured perfectly by Philip Tetlock and Dan Gardner in their best-selling book *Superforecasting: The Art and Science of Prediction*. Tetlock calls himself an "optimistic skeptic" on whether predictions of future events can be made with any degree of accuracy.

On one end of the spectrum are what he calls the "debunkers," who say everything is random and a chimpanzee throwing darts can do as well as the most expert analyst. On the other end are the true believers who swallow all the stories that experts tell as gospel. An optimistic skeptic believes it is possible to consistently beat the market over time, but only for an elite subset of analysts and traders. The big question is figuring out if you belong in that elite subset.[2]

My position as an optimistic skeptic also fits perfectly with a common-sense view about the efficiency of commodity futures markets. If the markets were so efficient that no one could make money, then the markets would collapse. Who would spend vast amounts of money collecting information, developing forecasting models, and figuring out how to trade if it was all for naught before you even started? If no one has any incentive to do this, then the great engine of economic efficiency sputters to a stop. It is a strange paradox that the efficiency of commodity futures markets depends on enough people believing it is *not* perfectly efficient to keep them collecting information and trading on it.[3]

Second, I learned that even for the elite subset of traders who survive and make money, the futures market is a spectacularly high-risk environment. In market-speak, traders blow up with disturbing regularity. True speculators are fashioned more in the mold of your Evel Knievels, Jack Hunters, and the drivers who strap themselves into sprint cars at the Knoxville Raceway in Iowa.

Speaking of which...

Today, I still retain a love and fascination for fast cars, although I don't get to Knoxville or other raceways as often as I would like. So, as I end this book, let's return to the racetrack on one hot day in early August 2004, when I decided to treat my hot-rod-loving dad to the gift of a lifetime. We paid a few hundred bucks for my dad to ride along for four laps in a sprint car. Dave Blaney, a well-known sprint car driver, had created a ride-along program. He modified a sprint car to accommodate a passenger behind the driver and charged people for rides at a dirt track in Oskaloosa, Iowa, about an hour from Knoxville.

Remember, my dad was a guy who loved to drive his pickup trucks over eighty miles per hour along the country roads near our farm in Bagley. So, he was thrilled at the chance to ride in one of these sprint cars. Because it was a hot August day, my mom and I decided to seek shade while my dad went off to sign the waivers and suit up for his four-lap thrill ride. There had to be about twenty people signed up, but if you count all the friends and family members, there must have been over a hundred.

My dad came hustling back to us with a gleam in his eyes. He was excited, but not only because of the pending ride. "You aren't going to believe who I just ran into in line!" he exclaimed. "Jack Hunter!"

What were the odds? I hadn't seen my boyhood best friend and daredevil extraordinaire for several years, and he chose this day to show up for a ride-along in a sprint car? It seemed almost poetic. So, there they were: the two true daredevils, my dad and Jack Hunter, standing side by side in racing suits with helmets tucked beneath their arms.

Jack worked for a time as a UPS driver. They have tight rules, so I don't think he pushed his work truck to speeds that could qualify for a race at Knoxville. Later, back problems forced early retirement, and he wound up driving cars around the country for an outfit that sells vehicles on the internet. If somebody needs a car delivered cross country, Jack is your man.

"Irwin, you should've seen this Lincoln Continental I was driving!" he told me years later, describing one of the cars he got to deliver. "It had a sport engine in it. And it's the middle of the night, about 2 a.m., and I'm on the turnpike east of Cleveland, along Lake Eerie. The road is really flat, so I just had to see how fast this car would go."

"How fast did you go?" I asked.

"I buried it at 140 miles per hour," he said with his patented Jack Hunter grin.

As I said, some things never change. Jack must've been in his late fifties when he "buried it at 140 miles per hour." Definitely lively for a man knocking on the door of Medicare.

As for my dad, he was seventy years old in 2004 when he got his ride-along in a sprint car. They buckled him in like an astronaut strapped into a Mercury rocket. With these crazy cars, a slight tap of the brakes will slam you to the right. And when they round a corner, they go into a "drift," which is the same thing Jack and I did with our go-karts as kids. To maintain speed as you roar around those dirt corners, it's crucial that the sprint car's back end kicks out while you turn in the opposite direction. Check out the Pixar movie Cars, where Lightning McQueen learns how to do this. It's a difficult and sometimes dangerous maneuver.

As I recall, the sprint car had mechanical problems after only one lap of the ride-along, so we got some of our money back. But during that short drive, my dad was in motorway heaven. He had done what he had always dreamed—ridden in a sprint car for one mad dash around the track. It was over quickly, but alas, so is life. Some of us get many laps in life, while others only get a handful, but it's a thrill just the same.

My dad would get seventy-five laps in his life. Signs of Alzheimer's began to show up in 2007, and in 2008 we had to take away his driver's license. It was like pulling out his heart. One year later, in 2009, he passed away at age seventy-five.

There's no way to avoid it. Life is all about risk, whether sitting in a sprint car, getting chased by an angry steer, crashing a snowmobile, or going long or short in the futures market. There's no way to avoid it. Farmers know this more than most people, for their livelihood depends on the whims of the weather and the markets.

NASCAR racing legend Cale Yarborough once said, "Driving a race car is like dancing with a chainsaw."

This can also be said about the futures market—and more importantly, about life. Sometimes, you're dancing with a chainsaw—or trying to survive a collision that sends you tumbling end-over-end.

The best you can do is to don your crash helmet, strap yourself in, and then sit back and enjoy the ride, hoping and praying you have some talented guardian angels at your side, taking you into the future.

Endnotes

1. My Near-Death Experience

1. *Bayard News*, "Scott Irwin Injured When Hit by Pickup." Guthrie County, Iowa. Thursday, October 26, 1967. It took some doing, but I was able to dig out this newspaper article about my accident (thank you Carol at the Bayard library!). The article indicated that the truck was owned by a Coca-Cola distributor. That is strange because my entire life I have been told it was a blue Pepsi delivery truck. Unfortunately, all the eyewitnesses to the accident have long since died. I checked with several family members and friends who were around that day and are still living. To a person, they all say it was a blue Pepsi truck. So, I conclude that the newspaper article was either in error or the company cited in the article distributed both Coke and Pepsi products. One more thing. The article headline indicates the vehicle that hit me was a "pickup." Today that would clearly mean a pickup truck like a Ford F-150. I have always been told that the truck that hit me was not what we would today call a "pickup," but, instead, something closer to a beer delivery truck. This is much larger than a pickup truck, and the larger size is more consistent with how far I traveled in the air after being hit. Finally, I hope this discussion helps the reader understand how hard I worked to make sure the stories included in the book are re-told as accurately as possible with respect to the historical details.
2. For those interested in more information about my professional life, please visit my website at https://scotthirwin.com/. You can find a complete bibliography and curriculum vitae at the site ("Learn About Me"), along with links to current publications and a variety of other materials.
3. https://www.fia.org/resources/etd-volume-december-2021 (accessed July 21, 2022).
4. https://www.eia.gov/outlooks/steo/archives/may22.pdf (accessed July 21, 2022).

2. Daredevils

1. *Trading Places*, directed by John Landis, starring Eddie Murphy and Dan Aykroyd, 1983.
2. Banner, Stuart. "The Origin of the New York Stock Exchange, 1791–1860." *Journal of Legal Studies* 27(1998):113–140.
3. Hieronymus, Thomas H. *Economics of Futures Trading for Commercial and Personal Profit.* Second Edition, Commodity Research Bureau, 1977, p. 74. Reprinted by Ceres Books: https://www.amazon.com/Economics-Futures-Trading-Commercial-Personal-ebook/dp/B09QX57QGW (accessed July 22, 2022).
4. Lambert, Emily. *The Futures: The Rise of the Speculator and the Origins of the World's Biggest Markets.* Basic Books, 2011, p. 5.

5. McDermott, John. "A Eulogy for the Pit Trader." *MEL Magazine*, March 1, 2016.
6. Interview with Craig Pirrong, March 8, 2021.
7. Lambert, Emily. *The Futures: The Rise of the Speculator and the Origins of the World's Biggest Markets*. Basic Books, 2011, p. 8.
8. Worstall, Tim. "Commodity Speculation Kills People: So Says the World Development Movement." *Forbes*, September 14, 2011.
9. Hieronymus, Thomas H. *Economics of Futures Trading for Commercial and Personal Profit*. Second Edition, Commodity Research Bureau, 1977, pp. 322-324. Reprinted by Ceres Books: https://www.amazon.com/Economics-Futures-Trading-Commercial-Personal-ebook/dp/B09QX57QGW (accessed July 22, 2022).

3. Pit Bulls

1. Hieronymus, Thomas H. *Economics of Futures Trading for Commercial and Personal Profit*. Second Edition, Commodity Research Bureau, 1977, pp. 3-4. Reprinted by Ceres Books: https://www.amazon.com/Economics-Futures-Trading-Commercial-Personal-ebook/dp/B09QX57QGW (accessed July 22, 2022).
2. Janzen, Joseph P., and Michael K. Adjemian. "Estimating the Location of World Wheat Price Discovery." *American Journal of Agricultural Economics* 99(2017):1188-1207.
3. Interview with Terry Duffy, March 3, 2020.
4. *Ferris Bueller's Day Off*, directed by John Hughes, starring Matthew Broderick, Alan Ruck, and Mia Sara, 1986.
5. For additional information, see "Futures & Options 101: Hand Signals," StoneX Financial Inc., Daniels Trading Division, https://www.danielstrading.com/education/futures-options-101/hand-signals (accessed July 25, 2022), and "Futures & Options 101: Expiration Months," StoneX Financial Inc., Daniels Trading Division, https://www.danielstrading.com/education/futures-options-101/expiration-months (accessed July 25, 2022).
6. *Chicago Tribune*. "How FBI Worked Trader Sting." January 20, 1989.
7. Meyer, Gregory. "Trading: What Happened When the Pit Stopped." *Financial Times*, July 6, 2016.

4. Elvis and Evel in Iowa

1. "Evel Knievel: The Man: The Life of Evel Knievel." https://evelknievel.com/pages/the-man (accessed July 25, 2022).
2. "Evel Puzzle: What Popped Chute?" *The Desert News*, September 9, 1974.
3. Interview with Fred Seamon, March 3, 2020.
4. Working, Holbrook. "Hedging Reconsidered." *Journal of Farm Economics* 35(1953):544-561.
5. *Talladega Nights: The Legend of Ricky Bobby*, directed by Adam McKay, starring Will Ferrell and John C. Reilly, 2006.

5. My Spectacular Speculation Crackup

1. Irwin, Scott, and Darrel Good. "Opening Up the Black Box: More on the USDA Corn Yield Forecasting Methodology." *farmdoc daily* (6):162, Department of Agricultural and Consumer Economics, University of Illinois at Urbana-Champaign, August 26, 2016.
2. It turns out that the corn futures market did not end up going lock limit down on Friday as I feared and many predicted. At the low point for the day, the December 1981 corn futures contract was down a nickel. If I hadn't gotten out of the market, this would have been a loss of $2,500 instead of the $5,000 I was expecting. But it was still $2,500 I did not have. Things would have been even worse if I had waited for the market to "bounce back." Over the next few weeks, prices sunk well below $3 per bushel, which would have really wiped me out.
3. Irwin, Scott. "The Golden Number for Illinois Agriculture." May 10, 2022. https://scotthirwin.com/2022/05/10/the-golden-number-for-illinois-agriculture/ (accessed July 25, 2022).

6. The Engine of Efficiency

1. Malkiel, Burton G. *A Random Walk Down Wall Street*. W.W. Norton and Company, 1973.
2. Bogle, John C. "The Index Mutual Fund: 40 Years of Growth, Change, and Challenge." *Financial Analysts Journal* 72(2016):9-13.
3. Working, Holbrook. "A Random-Difference Series for Use in the Analysis of Time Series." *Journal of the American Statistical Association* 29(1934):11-24.
4. Cootner, Paul (Editor). *The Random Character of Stock Market Prices*. MIT Press, 1964.
5. Fama, Eugene F. "Efficient Capital Markets: A Review of Theory and Empirical Work." *Journal of Finance* 25(1970):383-417.
6. Bachelier, Louis. "Chapter 2: Theory of Speculation." In *The Random Character of Stock Market Prices*, Paul Cootner (Editor), MIT Press, 1964.
7. Working, Holbrook. "The Theory of Price of Storage." *American Economic Review* 39(1949):1254-1262.
8. Malkiel, Burton G. *A Random Walk Down Wall Street: The Time-Tested Strategy for Successful Investing*. W.W. Norton and Company, 2019.
9. Irwin, Scott H., Darrel L. Good, and Joao Martines-Filho. "The Performance of Market Advisory Services in Corn and Soybeans." *American Journal of Agricultural Economics* 88(2006):162-181.
   Cabrini, Silvina M., Scott H. Irwin, and Darrel L. Good. "Style and Performance of Agricultural Market Advisory Services." *American Journal of Agricultural Economics* 89(2007):607-623.
   Cabrini, Silvina M., Scott H. Irwin, and Darrel L. Good. "Should Farmers Follow the Recommendations of Market Advisory Services? A Hierarchical Bayesian Approach to Estimation of Expected Performance." *American Journal of Agricultural Economics* 92(2010):622-637.
10. Irwin, Scott, and Darrel Good. "Response to Meeting of October 10, 2001." Letter written on January 10, 2002.

7. Towing Icebergs

1. Kneeland, Douglas E. "An Alaskan Iceberg Upstages a Saudi Prince at Conference in Iowa." *The New York Times*, October 7, 1977.
2. Winter, Caroline. "Towing an Iceberg: One Captain's Plan to Bring Drinking Water to 4 Million People." *Bloomberg Businessweek*, June 5, 2019.
3. *Animal House*, directed by John Landis, starring John Belushi and Peter Riegert, 1978.
4. Thompson, Louis M. "Weather and Technology in the Production of Corn in the U.S. Corn Belt." *Agronomy Journal* 61(1969):453-456.

    Thompson, Louis M. "Weather and Technology in the Production of Soybeans in the Central U.S." *Agronomy Journal* 62(1970):232-236.

    Thompson, Louis M. "Weather Variability, Climatic Change, and Grain Production." *Science* 188(1975):535-541.
5. Tannura, Michael A. *Weather, Corn and Soybean Yields, and Technology in the U.S. Cornbelt*. M.S. Thesis, Department of Agricultural and Consumer Economics, University of Illinois at Urbana-Champaign, 2007.
6. Tannura, Mike, Scott Irwin, and Darrel Good. "Are Corn Trend Yields Increasing at a Faster Rate?" Marketing and Outlook Brief 2008-02, Department of Agricultural and Consumer Economics, University of Illinois at Urbana-Champaign, February 2008.
7. Edgerton, Michael D. "Increasing Crop Productivity to Meet Global Needs for Feed, Food, and Fuel." *Plant Physiology* 149(2009):7-13.
8. https://tstorm.net/yieldcast/ (accessed July 26, 2022).

8. Steer Crazy

1. https://www.aksarbenstockshow.com/ (accessed July 26, 2022).
2. Wiser, Mike. "Sievers Family Returned Pickles' Awards, Attorney Says." *Sioux City Journal*, May 2, 2014.
3. Napolitano, Jo. "National Briefing | Midwest: Illinois: Steer Fails Drug Test." *The New York Times*, August 14, 2003.
4. Lambert, Emily. *The Futures: The Rise of the Speculator and the Origins of the World's Biggest Markets*, Basic Books, 2011, pp. 10-11.
5. Lewis, Michael. *Flash Boys: A Wall Street Revolt*, W.W. Norton & Company, 2014.
6. Coppess, Jonathan. "A Brief Review of the Consequential Seventies." *farmdoc daily* (9):99, Department of Agricultural and Consumer Economics, University of Illinois at Urbana-Champaign, May 30, 2019.
7. Corlett, Oliver. "Nixon and the Shoyu Shokku." *Popula*, July 11, 2018.
8. Christopher, Ben. "How the Hunt Brothers Cornered the Silver Market and Then Lost it All." *Priceonomics*, August 4, 2016.

9. All That Glitters is Goldman

1. Beattie, Andrew, "The Evolution of Goldman Sachs." *Forbes*, May 21, 2010.
2. Abelson, Max, "The House That Goldman Built." *Observer*, December 9, 2009.
3. Greer, Robert J., Nic Johnson, and Mihir P. Worah. *Intelligent Commodity Indexing: A Practical Guide to Investing in Commodities*, McGraw Hill, 2012, p. 3.
4. Gorton, Gary, and K. Geert Rouwenhorst. "Facts and Fantasies about Commodity Futures." *Financial Analysts Journal* 62(2006):47-68.
5. Telser, Lester G. "The Supply of Speculative Services in Wheat, Corn, and Soybeans." *Food Research Institute Studies* 7(1967):131-176.
6. Moran, Nicole M., Scott H. Irwin, and Philip Garcia. "Who Wins and Who Loses? Trader Returns and Risk Premiums in Agricultural Futures Markets." *Applied Economic Perspectives and Policy* 42(2020):611-652.

   Irwin, Scott H., Dwight R. Sanders, Aaron Smith, and Scott Main. "Investing in Commodity Futures: Separating the Wheat from the Chaff." *Applied Economic Perspectives and Policy* 42(2020):583-610.
7. Aulerich, Nicole M., Scott H. Irwin, and Philip Garcia. "Returns to Individual Traders in Agricultural Futures Markets: Skill or Luck?" *Applied Economics* 45(2013):3650-3666.
8. Sanders, Dwight R., and Scott H. Irwin. "A Reappraisal of Investing in Commodity Futures Markets." *Applied Economic Perspectives and Policy* 34(2012):515–530.

10. The Onion Crying Game

1. Lambert, Emily. *The Futures: The Rise of the Speculator and the Origins of the World's Biggest Markets*, Basic Books, 2011, p. 41.
2. Lambert, Emily. *The Futures: The Rise of the Speculator and the Origins of the World's Biggest Markets*, Basic Books, 2011, pp. 42-43.
3. Lambert, Emily. *The Futures: The Rise of the Speculator and the Origins of the World's Biggest Markets*, Basic Books, 2011, p. 43.
4. Gray, Roger W. "Onions Revisited." *Journal of Farm Economics* 45(1963):273-276.
5. "The Onion Ringer," *The Wall Street Journal*, July 8, 2008.
6. Working, Holbrook. "Futures Markets Under Renewed Attack." *Food Research Institute Studies* 4(1963):13-24.
7. Gray, Roger. "Commentary: A Reexamination of Price Changes in the Commodity Futures Market," by Terrence F. Martell and Billy P. Helms. *Proceedings of the International Futures Trading Seminar*, Chicago Board of Trade, May 1978, pp. 153-154.
8. Gray, Roger. "Discussion: Grain Trading in the 1970s." *Proceedings of the History of Futures Seminar*, Chicago Board of Trade, September 1982, pp. 265-266.
9. Hieronymus, Thomas H. *Economics of Futures Trading for Commercial and Personal Profit.* Second Edition, Commodity Research Bureau, 1977. Reprinted by Ceres Books: https://www.amazon.com/Economics-Futures-Trading-Commercial-Personal-ebook/dp/B09QX57QGW (accessed July 22, 2022).
10. Salmon, Felix. "Onion Farmers, Hollywood Futures and the Law." *The New York Times*, May 10, 2010.

11. Salmon, Felix. "Onion Farmers, Hollywood Futures and the Law." *The New York Times*, May 10, 2010.
12. Salmon, Felix. "Onion Farmers, Hollywood Futures and the Law." *The New York Times*, May 10, 2010.

11. The Destroying Angel

1. Henriques, Diana B. "Odd Crop Prices Defy Economics." *The New York Times*, March 28, 2008.
2. Henriques, Diana B. "Odd Crop Prices Defy Economics." *The New York Times*, March 28, 2008.
3. Henriques, Diana B. "Odd Crop Prices Defy Economics." *The New York Times*, March 28, 2008.
4. Good, Darrel, Scott Irwin, and Philip Garcia. "The Performance of the Chicago Board of Trade Corn, Soybean, and Wheat Contracts after Changes in Speculative Limits in 2005." A Research Report to the Chicago Board of Trade, November 2006.
5. Email from the Destroying Angel, June 7, 2008.
6. Email from the Destroying Angel, June 13, 2008.
7. Email from the Destroying Angel, June 16, 2008.
8. The Destroying Angel, "The A. bisporigera Prize," July 16, 2008.
9. Email from Scott Irwin to the Destroying Angel, July 18, 2008.
10. Email from the Destroying Angel, July 19, 2008.
11. Email from Scott Irwin to the Destroying Angel, July 22, 2008.

12. Ferris Irwin's Week Off

1. *Ferris Bueller's Day Off*, directed by John Hughes, starring Matthew Broderick, Alan Ruck, and Mia Sara, 1986.
2. Interview with Craig Pirrong, March 8, 2021.
3. Interview with Craig Pirrong, March 8, 2021.
4. And yes, this is the same *New York Times* that published a hit piece on me just a few years later. Reminds me of that old Katy Perry song, "Hot N Cold."
5. Sanders, Dwight R., and Scott H. Irwin. "Futures Imperfect." *The New York Times*, July 20, 2008.
6. Sanders, Dwight R., and Scott H. Irwin. "Futures Imperfect." *The New York Times*, July 20, 2008.
7. Krugman, Paul. "Speculative Nonsense, Once Again." *The New York Times*, June 23, 2008.
8. Krugman, Paul. "Speculative Nonsense, Once Again." *The New York Times*, June 23, 2008.
9. Ruitenberg, Rudy. "Global Food Reserve Needed to Stabilize Prices, Researchers Say." *Bloomberg Businessweek*, March 28, 2010. The argument that higher food prices is uniformly bad for poor people around the world ignores the fact that many of the global poor are also farmers who *benefit* from higher prices. The reality of the net impact of higher food prices on poor people around the globe is complex and the subject of much debate and research.

10. United States Senate, Permanent Subcommittee on Investigations. "Excessive Speculation in the Wheat Market." Majority and Minority Staff Report, June 2009.
11. Irwin, Scott H., and Dwight. R. Sanders. "The Impact of 'Financialization' in Commodity Futures Markets." A Technical Report Prepared for the Organization on Economic Co-operation and Development (OECD), April 2010.
12. Irwin, Scott H., and Dwight R. Sanders. "The Impact of Index and Swap Funds in Commodity Futures Markets: Preliminary Results." *OECD Food, Agriculture and Fisheries Working Papers*, No. 27, OECD Publishing, June 2010.
13. Branson, Sir Richard, Michael Masters, and David Frenk. "Letter to the Editor." *The Economist*, July 29, 2010.
14. CFTC Energy and Environmental Markets Advisory Committee (EEMAC). "Report on EEMAC's 2015 Review and Consideration of the CFTC's Proposed Rule on Position Limits." February 25, 2016.

13. Bubble Boy

1. Dugan, Ianthe Jeanne. "Report Faults Speculators for Volatility in Oil Prices." *The Wall Street Journal*, September 10, 2008.
2. *The Wall Street Journal*. "See You Later, Speculator." September 15, 2008.
3. Yan, Lei, Scott H. Irwin, and Dwight R. Sanders. "Sunshine vs. Predatory Trading Effects in Commodity Futures Markets: New Evidence from Index Rebalancing." *Journal of Commodity Markets*, 26(2022), article 100195.
    Irwin, Scott H., Dwight R. Sanders, and Lei Yan. "The Order Flow Cost of Index Rolling in Commodity Futures Markets." *Applied Economic Perspectives and Policy*, available online June 8, 2022, https://doi.org/10.1002/aepp.13297 (accessed July 26, 2022).
4. *The Wall Street Journal*. "Political Speculators." June 24, 2008.
5. Masters, Michael W., and Adam K. White. *The Accidental Hunt Brothers: How Institutional Investors Are Driving Up Food and Energy Prices*. July 31, 2008.
6. Interview with Dwight Sanders, July 19, 2021.
7. Gilbert, Christopher L. "Speculative Influences on Commodity Futures Prices, 2006-2008." Working Paper, Department of Economics, University of Trento, December 2009.
8. Sanders, Dwight R., and Scott H. Irwin. "New Evidence on the Impact of Index Funds in U.S. Grain Futures Markets." *Canadian Journal of Agricultural Economics* 59(2011):519–532.
9. Singleton, Kenneth J. "Investor Flows and the 2008 Boom/Bust in Oil Prices." *Management Science* 60(2014):300-318.
10. Irwin, Scott H., and Dwight R. Sanders. "Testing the Masters Hypothesis in Commodity Futures Markets." *Energy Economics* 34(2012):256–269.

14. The Hatfields and the McCoys

1. *Bloomberg News*. "Who is the 'Big Shot' Behind Nickel's Bad Short?" March 12, 2022.

2. *Bloomberg News.* "Who is the 'Big Shot' Behind Nickel's Bad Short?" March 12, 2022.
3. *Bloomberg News.* "Who is the 'Big Shot' Behind Nickel's Bad Short?" March 12, 2022.
4. Interview with Craig Pirrong, March 8, 2021.
5. Pirrong, Craig. "25 Years ago Today Ferruzzi Created the Streetwise Professor." *The Streetwise Professor,* July 11, 2014.
6. Interview with Craig Pirrong, March 8, 2021.
7. Commodity Futures Trading Commission. "Staff Report on Commodity Swap Dealers & Index Traders with Commission Recommendations." September 2008.
8. Pirrong, Craig. "Igor Gensler Helps the Wicked Witch of the West Wing Create Son of Frankendodd." *The Streetwise Professor,* October 10, 2015.
9. Pirrong, Craig. "Gary Gensler, Naked and Exposed." *The Streetwise Professor,* August 8, 2012.
10. Pirrong, Craig. "Gary Gensler's Plan to Take Over the World." *The Streetwise Professor,* March 10, 2010.
11. Pirrong, Craig. "Igor Gensler Helps the Wicked Witch of the West Wing Create Son of Frankendodd." *The Streetwise Professor,* October 10, 2015.
12. Pirrong, Craig. "Cleaning Up After the Dodd, Frank, and Gensler Circus." *The Streetwise Professor,* September 8, 2014.
13. Irwin, Scott H., and Dwight R. Sanders. "Comments on the Commission's Notice of Proposed Rulemaking (NOPR) for Position Limits in Derivatives Issued on 13 January 2011." Letter written on March 28, 2011.
14. Morphy, James. "Court Vacates Position Limit Rules." *Harvard Law School Forum on Corporate Governance,* October 11, 2012.

15. All the Smears That are Fit to Print

1. Wiles, Mike. "Kinze Manufacturing's Long Road to 'Disruptive Innovation' in the Farm Equipment Industry." *Farm Equipment,* May 14, 2019.
2. Kocieniewski, David. "Academics Who Defend Wall St. Reap Reward." *The New York Times,* December 27, 2013.
3. Kocieniewski, David. "Academics Who Defend Wall St. Reap Reward." *The New York Times,* December 27, 2013.
4. Klein, Peter G. "Mendacious NYT Reporter Smears Economists on Speculation." *Mises Wire,* December 30, 2013.
5. Irwin, Scott H., and Dwight R. Sanders. "The Price Impact of Gresham Investment Management, LLC Positions in U.S. Futures Markets." Final Report, January 2013.
6. Salmon, Felix. "The Non-Scandal of Scott Irwin and Craig Pirrong." *Reuters,* December 29, 2013.
7. Hamilton, James. "A Lack of Ethics." *Econbrowser,* January 21, 2014.
8. Interview with Craig Pirrong, March 8, 2021.
9. Interview with Craig Pirrong, March 8, 2021.
10. Interview with Craig Pirrong, March 8, 2021.
11. See the following for Craig's perspective on his role in the position limit debates: "Position Limits: What a Long, Strange Trip It's Been." *The Streetwise Professor,* February 2, 2020.

16. The Market Finds a Way

1. Interview with Bob Wilson, July 12, 2021.
2. *Jurassic Park*, directed by Stephen Spielberg, starring Sam Neill, Laura Dern, and Jeff Goldblum, 1993.
3. Interview with Fred Seamon, April 6, 2022.
4. Irwin, Scott H., Philip Garcia, Darrel L. Good, and Eugene L. Kunda. "Poor Convergence Performance of CBOT Corn, Soybean and Wheat Futures Contracts: Causes and Solutions." Marketing and Outlook Research Report 2009-02, Department of Agricultural and Consumer Economics, University of Illinois at Urbana-Champaign, March 2009.
5. United States Senate, Permanent Subcommittee on Investigations. "Excessive Speculation in the Wheat Market." Majority and Minority Staff Report, June 2009.
6. Garcia, Philip, Scott H. Irwin, and Aaron Smith. "Futures Market Failure?" *American Journal of Agricultural Economics* 97(2015):40-64.
7. The storage rate explanation for non-convergence in our 2015 article (see endnote 6) received important and independent confirmation in a recent article: Goswami, Alankrita, Michael K. Adjemian, and Berna Karali. "The Impact of Futures Contract Storage Rate Policy on Convergence Expectations in Domestic Commodity Markets." *Food Policy* 111(2022), article 102301.
8. Interview with Glenn Hollander, November 20, 2018.
9. I wrote an article in 2020 that provides further details on this episode and the evolution of CBOT grain storage rates through time. This article also contains a nice graphical presentation of the market "making a way" when the futures storage rate is capped relative to the cash market price of storage. See Figure 14 in: Irwin, Scott H. "Trilogy for Troubleshooting Convergence: Manipulation, Structural Imbalance, and Storage Rates." *Journal of Commodity Markets*, 17(2020), article 100083.
10. Interview with Fred Seamon, April 6, 2022.
11. https://asmith.ucdavis.edu/data/convergence (accessed July 27, 2022).

17. Trading Spaces

1. Coval, Joshua D., and Tyler Shumway. "Is Sound Just Noise?" *Proceedings of the Spring Research Seminar*, Chicago Board of Trade, May 1999, pp. 1-34.
   Published version: Coval, Joshua D., and Tyler Shumway. "Is Sound Just Noise?" *Journal of Finance* 56(2001):1887-1910.
2. Wile, Rob. "It's the 30-Year Anniversary of the Greatest Wall Street Movie Ever Made: Here's the Story Behind It." *Business Insider*, June 27, 2013.
3. *Trading Places*, directed by John Landis, starring Eddie Murphy and Dan Aykroyd, 1983.
4. Coval, Joshua D., and Tyler Shumway. "Is Sound Just Noise?" *Proceedings of the Spring Research Seminar*, Chicago Board of Trade, May 1999, pp. 1-34.
5. Interview with Leo Melamed, March 3, 2020.
6. Melamed, Leo. *Escape to the Futures*. John Wiley & Sons, 1996, p. 13.
7. Melamed, Leo. *Escape to the Futures*. John Wiley & Sons, 1996, p. 14.
8. Interview with Leo Melamed, March 3, 2020.

9. Interview with Leo Melamed, March 3, 2020.
10. Interview with Leo Melamed, March 3, 2020.
11. Interview with Leo Melamed, March 3, 2020.
12. Interview with Leo Melamed, March 3, 2020.
13. Interview with Leo Melamed, March 3, 2020.
14. Interview with Leo Melamed, March 3, 2020.
15. Melamed, Leo. *Man of the Futures: The Story of Leo Melamed and the Birth of Modern Finance*. Harriman House, 2021, p. 205.
16. Melamed, Leo. *Man of the Futures: The Story of Leo Melamed and the Birth of Modern Finance*. Harriman House, 2021, p. 205.
17. Interview with Leo Melamed, April 6, 2022.
18. Interview with Leo Melamed, March 3, 2020.
19. Figlewski, Stephen. "Commentary: Is Sound Just Noise?" *Proceedings of the Spring Research Seminar*, Chicago Board of Trade, May 1999, pp. 35-39.
20. Figlewski, Stephen. "Commentary: Is Sound Just Noise?" *Proceedings of the Spring Research Seminar*, Chicago Board of Trade, May 1999, pp. 35-39.

18. Outrunning Your Angels

1. Interview with Eric Hanson, January 12, 2021.
2. Interview with Leo Melamed, April 6, 2022.
3. Allen, Rich. "Safeguarding America's Agricultural Statistics: A Century of Successful and Secure Procedures, 1905-2005." National Agricultural Statistics Service, U.S. Department of Agriculture, April 2007, pp. 1-3.
4. *Trading Places*, directed by John Landis, starring Eddie Murphy and Dan Aykroyd, 1983.
5. Colling, Phil L. "Do Japanese Soybean Futures Markets Respond to the USDA Crop Production Report?" *Proceedings of the NCR-134 Conference on Applied*, April 1993.
6. Irwin, Scott. "A Simple Proposal to Re-Level the Playing Field after the Release of USDA Crop Reports." *farmdoc daily* (10):12, Department of Agricultural and Consumer Economics, University of Illinois at Urbana-Champaign, January 23, 2020.
7. Adjemian, Michael K., and Scott H. Irwin. "USDA Announcements in Real-Time." *American Journal of Agricultural Economics* 100(2018):1151-1171.
8. https://www.usda.gov/media/press-releases/2018/07/10/usda-ensure-all-have-equal-access-crop-livestock-reports (accessed July 27, 2022).
9. Huang, Joshua, Teresa Serra, Philip Garcia, and Scott H. Irwin. "To Batch or Not to Batch? The Release of USDA Crop Reports." *Agricultural Economics* 53(2022):143-154.

19. Twister!

1. *Twister*, directed by Jan de Bont, starring Helen Hunt, Bill Paxton, and Cary Elwes, 1996.
2. Tramel, Jamie. "Revisiting Wakita 20 Years After 'Twister." *Tulsa World*, May 1, 2016.

3. https://www.weather.gov/oun/tornadodata-county-ok-grant (accessed July 27, 2022).

4. Narramore, Jen. "Nash, OK to Geuda Springs, KS Tornado Family – March 16, 1965." *Tornado Talk*, March 16, 2019.

5. See https://www.weather.gov/ffc/fujita, (accessed November 9, 2022).

6. Lambert, Emily. *The Futures: The Rise of the Speculator and the Origins of the World's Biggest Markets*, Basic Books, 2011, p. 155.

7. Bruce, Roderick. "Full Marks." *Risk.net*, July 6, 2009.

8. Bruce, Roderick. "Full Marks." *Risk.net*, July 6, 2009.

9. Interview with Craig Pirrong, March 8, 2021.

10. Interview with Craig Pirrong, March 8, 2021.

11. Interview with Craig Pirrong, March 8, 2021.

12. Vaughan, Liam, Kit Chellel, and Benjamin Bain. "The Essex Boys: How Nine Traders Hit a Gusher with Negative Oil." *Bloomberg Businessweek*, December 9, 2020.

13. Interview with Craig Pirrong, March 8, 2021.

14. Vidal, John, and Terry Macalister. "Kyoto Protests Disrupt Oil Trading." *The Guardian*, February 16, 2005.

15. Singh, Rob, and Catherine Bowen. "Mass Brawl on the Trading Floor." *Evening Standard*, February 15, 2005.

16. Vaughan, Liam, Kit Chellel, and Benjamin Bain. "The Essex Boys: How Nine Traders Hit a Gusher with Negative Oil." *Bloomberg Businessweek*, December 9, 2020.

17. Interview with Craig Pirrong, March 8, 2021.

18. Vaughan, Liam, Kit Chellel, and Benjamin Bain. "The Essex Boys: How Nine Traders Hit a Gusher with Negative Oil." *Bloomberg Businessweek*, December 9, 2020.

20. Out of the Box

1. Cootner, Paul H. "Common Elements in Futures Markets for Commodities and Bonds." *American Economic Review: Papers and Proceedings of the Seventy-Third Annual Meeting of the American Economic Association* 51(1961):173-181.

2. Interview with Leo Melamed, April 6, 2022.

3. Interview with Leo Melamed, April 6, 2022.

4. Interview with Leo Melamed, March 3, 2020.

5. Interview with Leo Melamed, April 6, 2022.

6. Interview with Leo Melamed, March 3, 2020.

7. Melamed, Leo. "Evolution of the International Monetary Market." *Cato Journal* 8(1988):393-404.

8. Interview with Leo Melamed, March 3, 2020. The quotations in this book do not tell the full story of the profound impact that Leo has had on global financial markets. Other experts eloquently make the case. For example, Milton Friedman, the Nobel Laureate in Economics, summarizes his contributions as follows: "He had the independence of mind and foresight to envisage the need for a public market in foreign currency futures, the imagination to invent a mechanism to make such a market feasible, and the courage and leadership ability to persuade his colleagues at the Chicago Mercantile Exchange to establish the International Monetary Market." (Source: Foreword of *Leo Melamed on the Markets*, 1993, John Wiley & Sons, Inc.)

Another Nobel Laureate in Economics, Merton Miller, stated it this way: "Melamed's idea ushered in the modern era of finance. It not only caused the transformation of futures markets from agriculture to their predominant place in finance today, it created what amounts to be a most efficient risk management tool, one indispensable in today's global and complex economic order." (Source: Selected Paper Number 63, "The Financial Futures Innovation," as noted by Merton H. Miller, in *Financial Innovation: The Last Twenty Years and the Next*, by Merton H. Miller, University of Chicago, Graduate School of Business)

Terry Duffy, CEO of the CME Group, adds, "As the founder of financial futures, Leo is a trailblazer, whose many contributions have changed financial markets. His far-reaching vision propelled the growth of futures to investors around the globe." (Source: Introduction of Leo Melamed at the Museum of American Finance 2022 Gala, honoring Leo Melamed with the Financial Innovation Award)

Chris Giancarlo, former Chair of the U.S. Commodity Futures Trading Commission (CFTC) notes that "Leo is...one of the central figures in American commerce and trade. In the world of derivatives, he has been a leader who shaped and guided our thinking. In electronic commerce, he actually took us into a new world." (Source: Keynote address before the Futures Industry Association, 2018 Annual Conference)

Finally, Leo was named as #6 in "Business's Top Ten of the Twentieth Century," from the chapter "Butter to Billions: Leo Melamed" in the book *Chicago and the American Century: The 100 Most Significant Chicagoans of the Twentieth Century*, by F. Richard Ciccone, (former) editor, Chicago Tribune, published by Contemporary Books, 1999.

9.   Interview with Peter Koziara, April 8, 2021.
10. Vigna, Paul. "Who is Bitcoin Creator Satoshi Nakamoto? What We Know—and Don't Know." *The Wall Street Journal*, December 7, 2021.
11. Nibley, Brian. "Bitcoin Price History: 2009-2022." *SoFi*, July 19, 2022.
12. Browne, Ryan. "Man Makes Last-Ditch Effort to Recover $280 Million in Bitcoin He Accidentally Threw Out." *CNBC*, January 15, 2021.
13. https://www.cmegroup.com/trading/micro-bitcoin-futures.html (accessed July 27, 2022).
14. Interview with Fred Seamon and Dominic Sutton-Vermeulen, January 19, 2021.
15. Office of the United Nations High Commissioner for Human Rights. "Water: Futures Market Invites Speculators, Challenges Basic Human Rights—UN Expert." December 11, 2020.
16. Irwin, Scott, and Darrel Good. "RINs Gone Wild?" *farmdoc daily*, Department of Agricultural and Consumer Economics, University of Illinois at Urbana-Champaign, July 19, 2013.
17. Huang, Vicky G., Alexander Osipovich, and Patricia Kowsmann. "FTX Tapped into Customer Accounts to Fund Risky Bets, Setting Up its Downfall." *The Wall Street Journal*, November 10, 2022.
18. Terry's statement was made during an episode of the CME Group podcast *On the Tape* from November 18, 2022. The full podcast can be found here: https://www.youtube.com/watch?v=V4SWraem1e0 (accessed November 28, 2022). His takedown of Bankman-Fried was notable not only for its bluntness, but also for its prophetic nature, coming months in advance of the FTX meltdown. It is well worth reading through the full text of the conversation:

"I had a meeting with Sam Bankman-Fried for the first time in March this past year. I never met the man. He asked to meet with me at a conference and I sat down with him. I said, 'What is your end goal?' He says, 'Well, I want to compete with you.' I said, 'Great, I'm all for competition. What do you want to do?' He says, 'Well, I want to compete with you in crypto.' I said, 'Why would you do that?' I said, 'I'll give you one better. How about if I give you my crypto franchises worth $30 million and we'll go from there?' He says, 'Well, what do you want?' I said, 'You know what I want. Let me be your risk manager. I'll clear it to make sure it's done properly.' He says, 'Well, you won't deploy my model.' I said, 'Your model is crap. Why would I deploy a model that's going to introduce risk to the system? Of course, I'm not going to deploy your model.' He turned me down flat out, turned me down, and that's it right away. I said to him, I said, 'You know what? You're a fraud. You're an absolute fraud. You're supposedly worth $26 billion, and you're an altruist.' I said, 'If you're an altruist at $26 billion, how come there's not a $10 billion donation going to somebody right at this moment in time? How about a $15 billion donation?' I said, 'You know what?' I said, 'My net worth doesn't start with any Bs. I'll give you three to one that I have more money than you.' I said, 'I'll tell you what, I'll give you a four to one I got more money in my right pocket than your net worth.' I said, 'You're a fraud, and I'm going to make sure that we get this out there.' And that was it."

21. The Running of the Cows

1. Schnitkey, Gary, Carl Zulauf, Krista Swanson, and Ryan Batts. "Prevented Planting Decision for Corn in the Midwest." *farmdoc daily* (9):88, Department of Agricultural and Consumer Economics, University of Illinois at Urbana-Champaign, May 14, 2019.
2. Tetlock, Philip E., and Dan Gardner. *Superforecasting: The Art and Science of Prediction.* Crown, 2015, pp. 1-23.
3. Paulos, John Allen. *A Mathematician Plays the Stock Market.* Basic Books. 2004, pp. 187-489.

Suggestions for Further Reading

Blass, Javier, and Jack Farchy. *The World for Sale: Money, Power, and the Traders Who Barter the Earth's Resources*. Oxford University Press, 2021.

Hieronymus, Thomas A. *Economics of Futures Trading for Commercial and Personal Profit*, Second Edition. Commodity Research Bureau, 1977.

Hull, John C. *Fundamentals of Futures and Options Markets*, Ninth Edition. Pearson, 2011.

Kingsman, Jonathan. *Commodity Conversations: An Introduction to Trading in Agricultural Commodities*. CreateSpace Independent Publishing Platform, 2017.

Kingsman, Jonathan. *Out of the Shadows: The New Merchants of Grain*. Independently published, 2019.

Lambert, Emily. *The Futures: The Rise of the Speculator and the Origins of the World's Biggest Markets*. Basic Books, 2011.

Lewis, Michael. *Flash Boys: A Wall Street Revolt.* W.W. Norton & Company, 2014.

Malkiel, Burton G. *A Random Walk Down Wall Street: The Best Investment Guide that Money Can Buy*, 50th Anniversary Edition, W.W. Norton and Company, 2023.

Morgan, Dan. *Merchants of Grain: The Power and Profits of the Five Giant Companies at the Center of the World's Food Supply.* Viking Press, 1979.

Schwager, Jack D. *Market Wizards: Interviews with Top Traders.* New York Institute of Finance, 1989.

Taleb, Nassim N. *Fooled by Randomness: The Hidden Role of Chance in Life and in the Markets.* Random House, 2005.

Tetlock, Philip E., and Dan Gardner. *Superforecasting: The Art and Science of Prediction.* Crown, 2015.

Tomek, William G., and Harry M. Kaiser. *Agricultural Product Prices*, Fifth Edition. Cornell University Press, 2014.

Williams, Jeffrey C., and Brian D. Wright. *Storage and Commodity Markets.* Cambridge University Press, 1991.

Author's Note: Scott Irwin

I am so appreciative that you took some of your precious time to read my book, *Back to the Futures*. Not only is this my first book, but it is also my personal story. This makes me even more grateful for your interest and attention. If you enjoyed reading *Back to the Futures*, I would greatly appreciate it if you would provide a review online. The review does not need to be lengthy. Just a few sentences can make a big impact.

When reading this book, you may have been struck by the thought that the crazy personal and professional stories simply could not all be true. Surely some embellishment was involved for the sake of enter-tainment. I can understand how you might think that. Several times during the editing process I caught myself thinking things like "Did all of that really happen?" or "Was that really me?"

I can say without hesitation that all the stories are true and that every attempt was made to reconstruct them as accurately as possible. Some idea of the process that we went through to write the book may be helpful in this regard. The process started with Doug interviewing me about all the crazy personal and professional stories that I could recall. The conversations mainly took place over about a three-year period. Doug recorded the conversations digitally and created a typewritten transcript for each interview. I would be remiss if I failed to point out how much fun we had during these interview sessions. There was much laughter, and if I'm honest, an incredulous look on Doug's face much of the time.

After the interviews were completed, Doug created an outline that wove the crazy stories with the topics about commodity futures markets that I wanted to cover in the book. If you can believe it, many stories were left on the cutting room floor at this stage because they did not fit the outline we developed. I don't know what it says about my life that I have an excess number of crazy stories! I only regret omitting one story. It involved fire extinguishers filled with water and college boys driving around looking for victims to soak. Maybe in my next book.

During the next phase of the process, Doug put together a first draft chapter-by-chapter. This started a two-year process of editing and revising, editing and revising...well, you get the picture. During this writing stage, I had numerous conversations with family and friends about the stories we decided to include in the book. Fortunately, everyone involved in the stories is still living except my dad. These conversations were extremely helpful in jogging my memory, filling in details, and even learning things I had never known about. This was a very important part of the process as some of the stories were more than forty years old.

Another benefit of the lengthy revision process was that it allowed me the time to think really hard about the details of the stories and make sure I had everything nailed down as well as possible. As a side-note, it is a rare thing to take so much time reflecting about one's youthful years. I am sure it has changed me in ways I don't fully appreciate.

After a full draft of the book was completed, I asked anyone quoted in the book to review the sections containing their quotes, including the crazy stories. This process resulted in only a few minor changes to some of the stories. Wherever possible, I also consulted external sources to confirm dates, places, and other details. These are documented in the extensive endnotes provided for each chapter in the book.

Hopefully, this explanation of the process used in writing the book will help convince you that the stories were reconstructed with great care. To the best of my abilities, I can say this is the way things really happened.

About the Author: Scott Irwin

Scott Irwin holds the Laurence J. Norton Chair of Agricultural Marketing in the Department of Agricultural and Consumer Economics at the University of Illinois at Urbana-Champaign. He earned a B.S. in agricultural business from Iowa State University and both an M.S. and a Ph.D. in agricultural economics from Purdue University.

Scott is a global leader in the field of agricultural economics. His research on commodity markets is widely cited by other academic researchers and is in high demand among farmers, market analysts, traders, and policymakers. He is regularly interviewed by leading media outlets such as *The Wall Street Journal, New York Times, Washington Post, Financial Times, Bloomberg, National Public Radio, Farm Journal*, and *Successful Farming*.

Scott has published hundreds of scholarly articles and is best known for his work on commodity speculation and biofuels. He has also written articles and op-eds for the *The New York Times, Washington Times*, and *Time* magazine. He is the most widely followed agricultural economist in the world on social media, with over 28,000 Twitter followers.

In addition to his research, Scott is a pioneer in developing agricultural extension programs that have helped hundreds of thousands of farmers in Illinois, the U.S., and throughout the world make more informed production, marketing, and financial decisions. His leadership and vision have been the driving force behind the award-winning *farmdoc* project at the University of Illinois since its inception in 1999. The articles on *farmdoc* have earned a place on the "must read" list of farmers, educators, journalists, traders, market analysts, and policymakers around the globe. This has earned *farmdoc* the title of "the Wall Street Journal of ag business."

During his career, Scott has taught a wide range of courses to hundreds of undergraduate and graduate students. This includes courses on Commodity Price Analysis, Commodity Futures and Options Markets, Introductory Statistics, Agricultural Finance, and Futures Market Research. He is regularly ranked as an outstanding teacher at the University of Illinois. In addition, he has served as academic advisor to more than forty M.S. and Ph.D. students.

Scott has received numerous awards during his career from the Agricultural and Applied Economics Association (AAEA), the leading professional association of agricultural economists in the world. He was named a Fellow in 2013, the highest honor bestowed by the Association. He has also received the Distinguished Group Extension Program Award (four times), the Quality of Research Discovery Award (two times), the Quality of Communication Award, and the Bruce Gardner Memorial Prize for Applied Policy Analysis.

Detailed information on Scott's professional activities can be found on his website: https://scotthirwin.com/. There are several convenient ways to stay up to date with Scott:

Email updates: https://scotthirwin.com/email-updates/
Twitter: https://twitter.com/ScottIrwinUI
LinkedIn: https://www.linkedin.com/in/scotthirwin/
Facebook: https://www.facebook.com/profile.php?id=100087183264151

About the Author: Doug Peterson

Doug Peterson is a Gold-Medallion-winning author of seventy nine books and has been a writer for the University of Illinois for over forty years.

Seven of his books are historical novels, with five of them based on real people. For instance, *The Disappearing Man* tells the true story of Henry "Box" Brown, a slave who mailed himself to freedom. In 1849, Brown escaped by shipping himself in a box from Richmond to Philadelphia. This book was chosen by Canton, Ohio, for its "One Book, One Community" celebration.

Doug has authored forty-two children's books for the popular VeggieTales series, and he was co-storywriter for the best-selling VeggieTales video, *Larry-Boy and the Rumor Weed*. He also co-wrote six fantasy comic books and is currently developing a series of American history comic books, illustrated by Marvel artists.

At the University of Illinois, Doug has written for numerous colleges and departments. He specializes in interviewing professors about their research and translating their work into stories that a lay person can understand—much the same as he did with Scott Irwin in *Back to the Futures*.

In addition to his novels, non-fiction, comic books, and children's books, Doug has written two stage plays on historical figures and many magazine features and short stories. His short story, "The Career of Horville Sash," was even made into a music video featuring Grammy-winner Jennifer Warnes. He also co-wrote "Roman Ruins," part of the best-selling How to Host a Murder mystery role-playing games.

You can find him online at www.bydougpeterson.com, or on Facebook under "Doug Peterson Author."

Acknowledgments: Scott Irwin

Writing this book has been a true labor of love over a five-year period. I owe a huge debt of gratitude to numerous people for making the book possible. There are so many people that have helped me along the way that I fear I will miss thanking someone important. I simply ask for forgiveness in advance for any omissions. Each and every contribution is deeply, deeply appreciated.

The book would not have been possible without the people who generously agreed to be interviewed. Some people submitted to several interviews. The interviews were incredibly interesting, and it was a treat to be in the room or on a zoom call with such amazing and fascinating people. Everyone was generous with their time, and it was fun to boot. The persons interviewed for the book include Terry Duffy, Eric Hanson, Peter Koziara, Leo Melamed, Craig Pirrong, Dwight Sanders, Fred Seamon, Dominic Sutton-Vermeulen, and Bob Wilson.

I know from my academic experience just how important reviewers are to developing a first-rate publication. The following people reviewed and commented on the complete manuscript or parts of it: Cindy Chancellor, Terry Duffy, Darrel Good, Kathy Gullang, David Hamilton, Kate Hamilton, Eric Hanson, Jeff Hemer, Jack Hunter, Pauline Irwin, Don Irwin, Kim Irwin, Matt Irwin, David Kendall, Kurt

Kenney, Peter Koziara, Leo Melamed, Nancy Peterson, Ric Peterson, Craig Pirrong, Joyce Purdy, Dwight Sanders, Fred Seamon, Aaron Smith, Mike Tannura, Sally Thompson, Jan Vaughan, Rick Vaughan, Reilly Vaughan, and Bob Wilson. My thanks to each and every one of them for taking the time to read and comment on the book. We made many changes to the writing based on feedback, and this undoubtedly improved the finished product considerably.

Several people were indispensable in the production and marketing of the book. The brilliant cover for the book was the handiwork of Kirk DouPonce of DogEared Design. The lovely interior design was provided by Catherine Posey of Hannah Linder Designs. Kim Hough of Okie Creative provided copyediting services and did much to improve the readability of the book. Joanne Sprott of Potomac Indexing created the outstanding index for the book, while Tessa Hall of Salt and Light Copywriting provided terrific copy for marketing materials. Vincent Davis III of Warrior Book Marketing was an invaluable guide to marketing books on Amazon and so much else.

Several other people deserve special mention for their contributions to the book. Anita Liskey and Samira Kanacevic of the CME Group opened doors at the CME and helped in several important ways, including tracking down old futures trading pictures. Nancy Appleyard was always helpful in setting up appointments and arranging our meetings with Leo Melamed. Phil Colling provided invaluable background on the effort to ban futures contracts on movie box office receipts.

My family deserves much of the credit for this book. Without their love, support, and encouragement, I would not have been able to push through to the end. Thank you, Kim, Matt, Kate, David, Stacey, and Jayvon, from the bottom of my heart. I was also incredibly blessed by the birth of my two granddaughters, Izzy and Rhema, during the writing of the book. My Mom, Pauline Irwin, deserves special mention as well. Not only did she help with the details for several of the crazy stories, but she did so with unfailingly good humor. Well, maybe except for what happened to her beloved Mercury Cougar.

Last, but certainly not least, I need to thank my partner in crime,

Doug Peterson. He was the first to encourage me to proceed with the project, and he saw potential for the book that I could not see. What an incredible stroke of good fortune to be able to work with such a pro in writing your first book. He has patiently worked through interviews, transcripts, outlines, and a seemingly endless string of drafts. Doug sat through more conversations about commodity futures markets than anyone should really be asked to endure. But as a side benefit, he may now know more about commodity futures than any other non-economist on the planet. The best part of the experience was the journey itself. One rarely gets to attempt a project like this with one of your best friends. The Bible teaches us that "…there is a friend who sticks closer than a brother" (Proverbs 18:24). A perfect description of my friend and co-author, Doug Peterson.

Other Books by Ceres

Don't miss this rare opportunity to learn about commodity futures markets from a legendary expert.

The classic must-have book on the commodity futures market

For decades, *Economics of Futures Trading* has been known as "the bible" of the commodity futures market. This updated edition provides the foundation for everything you need to know in commodity basics and the economics of futures trading.

Dr. Hieronymus' witty and engaging writing ushers you into the world of trading so you can attain success in these ever-growing markets. The underlying principles presented in this classic remain unchanged, and your understanding of all the complex concepts in futures trading will be enhanced, such as:

- Operation and performance of the commodity market
- Hedging and speculation
- Historical developments
- And much more

This remains the ultimate guide and go-to resource for anyone interested in the operation of commodity markets. Set yourself up for success as you navigate the complexity of the market by first gleaning from a gold mine of insight offered in this easy-to-digest classic.

See more about *Economics of Futures Trading* at: scotthirwin.com/books/economics-of-futures-trading/

Available at the Amazon Bookstore in both Kindle ebook format and paperback!

www.amazon.com/Economics-Futures-Trading-Commercial-Personal-ebook/dp/B09QX57QGW/

If you are a fan of this classic book, please remember to leave a review on Amazon. Thanks!

Index

Made in the USA
Monee, IL
26 September 2023

43399199R00203